Feminism and the Family

WITHDRAWN

Aldham

Liverpool J

To my late father and mother, Archibald Bayne and Agnes Gray, whose lives, in different ways, inspired this book

Feminism and the Family

Politics and Society in the UK and USA

Jennifer Somerville

Consultant Editor: Jo Campling

First published 2000 by
MACMILLAN PRESS LTD
Houndmills, Basingstoke, Hampshire RG21 6XS
and London
Companies and representatives throughout the world

ISBN 0–333–51701–6 hardcover
ISBN 0–333–51702–4 paperback

A catalogue record for this book is available from the British Library.

This book is printed on paper suitable for recycling and made from
fully managed and sustained forest sources.

10   9   8   7   6   5   4   3   2   1
09 08 07 06 05 04 03 02 01 00

Printed in China

Published in the United States of America by
ST. MARTIN'S PRESS, INC.,
Scholarly and Reference Division,
175 Fifth Avenue, New York, N.Y. 10010

ISBN 0–312–23366–3 (cloth)
ISBN 0–312–23367–1 (paper)

Contents

Acknowledgements

This book has had a long gestation period and many midwives. The first were Paul Hirst and Sami Zubaida of Birkbeck College, University of London, and Jeffrey Weeks of South Bank University, who encouraged me to develop my doctoral thesis for publication. Jo Campling inspired the specific focus for the study and has remained hopeful and patient ever since. My associates and colleagues at University of North London, John Thompson, Margaret O'Brien, Norman Ginsburg, Mohammad Nafissi and Jenny Collison, assisted in the delivery with much coaxing and coaching. Catherine Gray at the publishers finally applied the forceps.

On the way, the work was nurtured and energised by the many discussions with friends, colleagues and students about the various private tribulations and public controversies thrown up by the tumultuous changes in contemporary personal and family life.

I would like to thank them all.

Last but not least, I also have to acknowledge the generous encouragement and accommodation of my own family despite the time and attention (though not love) denied them as a result.

JENNIFER SOMERVILLE

Introduction

Why a book about feminism and the family? Well, for one thing in all the major western countries, and particularly in the UK and the USA, the family has become a *cause célèbre*, an issue which excites much media attention and which has become a prominent item on the public policy agenda. So great are the changes in the formation, size, duration and dissolution of families and households since the 1970s, that some international social science commentators believe they amount to a 'great disruption' in western society equivalent to that of the nineteenth-century industrial revolution (Fukuyama, 1999). This transformation is intimately associated with the changes in the role of women and hence with feminism. Inasmuch as the family continues to be widely held as a stabilising force in society integrating psychological needs, moral consciousness and social roles primarily through the socialisation of children, high levels of divorce, serial cohabitation and fatherless families are seen by many to be alarming signs of the social disintegration and de-moralisation of society as a whole. For some, feminism is the major cause in that it is thought to promote the interests of women before those of others, including children, a promotion which is seen to be incompatible with the health of families.

For another thing, as one of a generation of feminists now approaching, or having reached a personal half century, I am drawn to review the ideas, values and experiences of both feminism and family life and the relation between the two which we have lived. It is rather sobering and not a little humbling to recognise the intensely personal and sometimes painful episodes of one's life in the statistics of demographic trends and to see them traced in one form or another

1

in the contradictions and tensions that have plagued the coupling – feminism and the family – since the emergence of the modern feminist movement in the middle of the nineteenth-century. In one of the most thorough and insightful studies of this relationship, the American historian Carl N. Degler observes: 'The equality of women and the institution of the family have long been at odds with each other' (Degler, 1980, p. vi). That structural tension has been at the heart of the personal experience of feminists of my generation, and from the privilege of middle age, one might interestingly speculate on what lies in store for our 'I'm not a feminist but . . .' daughters (and sons) in their personal and familial relationships of the twenty-first century.

The co-incident political, public policy and personal pertinence of the family, therefore, requires an investigation of the popular assumption that the twentieth century saw the triumph of feminism and consequently the demise of the family.

One problem in doing so, is that reviews of family change commonly take 1971 as their starting point. This obscures the fact that the 1960s was an exceptional decade in that it reflects the marital and fertility patterns of those born in the immediate post-war baby boom. The 1940s cohort of women, regardless of social class and education, had a greater propensity to marry than previous generations and married at the earliest average age ever recorded since civil registration started in 1837; 60 per cent were married between the ages of 18 and 23, 80 per cent by 25 years of age (Kiernan, 1989; Elliott, 1991). It is this behaviour and the size of the cohort which then produced the second post-war baby boom of the 1960s. A distorting impression is given of current family formation because it is measured against a supposed norm created by this cohort's exceptional behaviour. Brass (1989) has shown that the apparent dramatic decline in marriage and births in the 1970s and 1980s is the effect of the cohorts of women born in the mid-1950s and 1960s who began marrying and giving birth later than those born in the 1940s. Since then the British fertility rates have made a significant recovery as the *tempo* effects (those of changes in the timing of marriages and births) begin to be reflected in the statistics. Brass concludes that since about 1972 the overall level of fertility has been pretty constant at close to the replacement 2.1. In other words, what has been interpreted by some as a rejection of marriage and 'the twilight of parenthood' was in fact a return to previous patterns of marriage and fertility.

A related problem is that much commentary is based on a statistical snap-shot of a moment in time, for example the composition of households on census day. Hence it appears that in 1996 the nuclear family of married couple and dependent children constituted only 23 per cent of all households in Britain and 25 per cent in the USA, a statistic headlined by defenders and critics of the traditional family. However, using a life-cycle approach, you would add to the British group the 29 per cent of households consisting of married couples with no children, who are either younger and, on the basis of attitude surveys, may reasonably be expected to have children in the future, or older couples whose children have left home. In addition, there is also the 6 per cent of households consisting of married couples with independent children. Added together, these facts produce a rather different picture, one which suggests a much greater resilience of marriage and continuity in family patterns, particularly if you take the perspective of children, the majority of which live with their married, never divorced/ separated parents (Clarke, 1996; US Census Bureau, 1999).

For example, despite the much publicised 'decline in marriage' about 95 per cent of people continue to wed at some time in their lives. On current trends about two-thirds of British marriages will endure until the death of a spouse. Readers will be familiar with the now commonplace view that the family is being undermined by a new phenomenon of 'irresponsible males' who are 'in flight from commitment'. Yet according to a British report (Burghes et al., 1997) 80 per cent of fathers are married, 85 per cent of them live with their first families, only a minority of fathers have children in more than one family, over 90 per cent of children are born to married men and over 80 per cent of fathers are in full-time employment. What is more, the decline in marriage rates may well be compensated by the increase of cohabitation. In 1979 fewer than one in thirty women between 18 and 49 were cohabiting, whereas in 1996 it was one in ten, with one in five women in the 20–24 age group (HMSO, 1997). In the United States there are five times more cohabitees than in 1970. Britain's largest social research commissioning organisation, the Economic and Social Research Council (ESRC), reports from its 1997 British Household Panel Study that cohabitation may be replacing the long engagement as a prelude to marriage, and hence is accounting for the later age of marriage.

Seventy-three per cent of people in private households in the UK in 1996 lived in families headed by a married couple. Of these, 41 per cent consisted of a married couple with dependent children; the remainder had either non-dependent children or none living with them. Of dependent children, 80 per cent lived with their married parents. For 71.8 per cent, these are their biological parents (HMSO, 1997). Though 59 per cent of all mothers were employed outside the home in 1996, 37 per cent worked part-time, with 17 per cent and 31 per cent of mothers with pre-school children working full-time and part-time respectively. In the USA about 67 per cent of married women with children were employed, with 60 per cent of those with young children in work. Again there are more mothers working part-time than full-time, though as in Britain this varies with the age of the youngest child and with ethnic and cultural differences in child-bearing and employment patterns (US Census Bureau, 1996).

Furthermore, the ESRC's British Household Panel reports that family concerns were rated as most important in people's lives, more than twice as important as the nearest category, employment. Most young people continue to expect to marry and have children at some time in their lives (Jowell *et al.*, 1995. Wilkinson and Mulgan, 1995). While 20 per cent of young women respondents of research undertaken by the UK Family Policy Studies Centre in 1990; stated categorically that they did not want children, this may be counterbalanced by the increase in births to women in their late 30s and early 40s reported by the Office of Population Censuses and Surveys in the same year. It appears that as women approach the biological limits to fertility, they may change their minds. Seventy-two per cent of Americans would advise a young person to marry, the majority believe that married people are happier than the unmarried, and of the western nations they are most likely to see marriage as an end in itself, rather than for the purposes of having children or of financial security (Jowell *et al.*, 1993). Support for marriage has come too from what might be considered an unexpected quarter, that is in the movement to extend equal marriage rights to gays and lesbians, with 80 per cent of homosexuals and one-third of the voters in favour in the American polls in 1996.

Another feature which underlines continuity in family life is the maintenance of extended kinship networks. For example, relatives, including partners, are the major providers of childcare for American and British working mothers, followed by fathers and other relatives (HMSO, 1996; Hofferth and Phillips, 1991; Gelles, 1995; US Census Bureau, 1999). Again the greatest proportion of care and support for the elderly, disabled and those with special needs is provided through kinfolk. While a much smaller number of families share households than was the case in the 1950s and 60s, familial ties are maintained through complex relationships of reciprocal duties and responsibilities between relatives, aided by the telephone and the motor car (Finch,

1989; Ungerson, 1990; Finch and Mason, 1993; Gelles, 1995; HMSO, 1997; US Census Bureau, 1999).

Marriage, children and familial relationships, therefore, appear to remain popular as an ideal, and the nuclear family remains a reality at some phase in most people's life cycle.

This is not to ignore, however, the considerable discontinuities with the past. I have already touched on some of these. The following data derive from British official statistical sources but they are also indicative of American and pan-European trends in population and lifestyle patterns, though of course there are regional differences both between and within country profiles.

Much greater control over fertility effectively separating sex from reproduction has been a major factor in radical changes in sexual behaviour and mores and consequently in traditional patterns of legitimated sexual union and family formation. This is not to reduce such changes to biotechnology: there have been many other social, economic and cultural transformations which have contributed. However, the development of effective contraceptive materials and techniques and their widespread availability, has facilitated, reinforced and accelerated other non-biological trends in a complex interaction of cause and effect.

One obvious example has been the normalisation of pre-marital sex (Scott, 1998). During the 1950s and 60s less than one-third of women had experienced sexual intercourse before marriage. It is now the behavioural norm for young people This is a contributing factor to the rise in cohabitation over the same period. In the age range 18–49 one in ten women in Britain in 1966 were cohabiting compared to one in thirty in 1979. While age is a differentiator, social class and education is not: all socio-economic groups show a similar incidence of cohabitation. In the USA, cohabiting households made up 4.8 per cent of all households in 1997, compared to 1.5 per cent in 1977 (Casper *et al.*, 1999).

In the majority of cases cohabitation is a prelude to marriage and is therefore one cause for the growing tendency to marry later; the average age for British men and women in 1996 was 28.2 and 26.2 and for Americans 27.1 and 24.8 respectively (US Census Bureau 1999). This has led to the later commencement of childrearing. Women in their early thirties are more likely to have a baby than those in their early twenties. It is interesting, however, that the decrease in the number of children per family predates the normalisation of cohabitation. This decreased from 2.0 in 1971 to 1.8 in

1981 but thereafter has remained the same (HMSO, 1997). In this respect the UK has not declined as much as its European partners, such as Italy, where there is a real concern about the prolonged effects of a below replacement birth rate. There is also a growing incidence of childlessness. While infertility accounts for approximately 5–7 per cent, though this may be increasing as a result of those delaying children until the late 30s and 40s, there is clearly a small but growing number of the voluntary childless.

Another reason given for the late first marriage rate is the growth of female educational achievement and career aspirations. More than half of all university graduates are women and they have made serious inroads in managerial, administrative and professional employment with the result that the career patterns and remuneration of women who do not take a break from work to rear children are becoming much closer to their male counterparts. The greatest departure from the past in terms of sheer numbers, however, is in the increase in employment of married women, particularly those with school-age children (Dex and Joshi 1999).

It would be a mistake, however, to interpret this as evidence of aspirations to greater gender equality though it may lead to that in practice. The dramatic growth in the number of working mothers has to be seen in the context of fundamental shifts in the global economy, intermittent periods of recession and increasing insecurity in labour markets. This has included the continued replacement of manufacturing jobs with those in the service sector and the impact of the new information and communication technologies on the organisation of labour processes, the knowledges and skills required and the size of labour forces. This has resulted in the USA and the UK in the loss of full-time jobs, the increase in part-time, flexible labour contracts and the downsizing and flattening of organisations affecting managerial and professional employment traditionally little affected by fluctuations in the economic cycle. These trends have not only reduced 'male' jobs and created 'female' jobs, but have created a climate in which it is either necessary for both partners to work to maintain the living standards to which people aspire, or in which anxieties about employment insecurity induce the belief that this is the case (Walby, 1997; Blau and Ehrenberg, 1998; Creighton, 1999; Dex and Joshi, 1999; O'Connor *et al.*, 1999). The phenomenon of the 'dual worker' family is now general and normalised, though the 'dual carer' family has not yet emerged.

Research indicates that women continue to do the majority of caring and domestic tasks even when they are employed, though the type of occupation and educational background affects the lifestyle and relationships within the family (Gelles, 1995; HMSO, 1997). In families of manual workers, the value placed on the male as the chief 'breadwinner' still prevails, even where there is experience of un- and under-employment. Hence, traditional gender roles in relation to housework, childcare and control over household finances and deci-sion-making within the family continue (Kiernan, 1992: British Social Attitudes, 9th Report; Vogler and Pahl, 1994; Mintel Report, 1994) Creighton, 1999. In dual career families a greater shift has occurred, though there is often alternative paid help with housework and child-care. The age of the New Man has not yet arrived though there are some new-ish ones around.

Another aspect of the changes in sexual morality is the increase in births outside marriage, from 6 per cent in 1961, about 12 per cent in 1981 to around 35 per cent in 1996 in the UK. The percentage of all births occuring to unmarried women in America in 1997 was 32 per cent, declining by 2 per cent per year since 1994. (National Center for Health Statistics 1999) In 1961 these births were largely to unmarried teenagers; in 1996 they mostly appear to be the result of the increase in relatively stable relationships outside marriage. Thus four-fifths were registered by both parents, with the majority of these sharing the same address. There are clear signs of an increased acceptability of having children without formal marriage and this is reflected in legislative change. For example, the 1987 Family Reform Act in Britain removed the remaining differences in the legal rights of children born within and outside wedlock and the term 'illegitimate' may no longer be used in legal documents. Nevertheless Britain has the highest rate of teenage pregnancy in Europe at 58.7 per 1,000 girls aged 15–19, topped only by America where one in 10 women of this age were mothers. However, much less known is the fact that the teenage birthrate in the US has dropped in all states, on average by 16 per cent over six years prior to 1997 (National Center for Health Statistics 1999).

Probably the most dramatic discontinuity with the past, recent and otherwise, is the rate of divorce. This is often confused with 'broken families'. As family historians have properly reminded us, the num-bers of multiple marriages, children living with step-parents, step-siblings and relatives other than their parents or in public care, were just as great in the distant past and at the height of Victorian values as they were at the end of the twentieth century. However, the cause in these instances was death, not divorce. The multi-generational intact family, which has become the idealised family form against which the

contemporary family is measured, seems to have belonged to a relatively brief period between the 1930s and 1960s when economic
growth and the improvement of general living conditions, public
health and education combined to decrease mortality and morbidity-
rates, in particular of maternal and infantile deaths. However, it has to
be conceded that there is the world of difference between the break-up
of families as a result of involuntary death and as a consequence of the
voluntary choice of married partners. As we shall see in Chapter 1,
divorce was simply not an option in western societies for most of this
period for any but the most socially elite, institutionally privileged and
profoundly wealthy. The second half of the twentieth-century saw the
democratisation of divorce as a result of an accelerating revolution in
the law on, and the costs of, divorce.

In the period under discussion, divorces in Britain increased more
than threefold between 1969 and 1994, since when there has been a
levelling off and a recent decrease. Based on current rates, it is estimated that two in five marriages will end in divorce (HMSO, 1997).
However, these data may obscure continued family break-down
because cohabiting couples who separate are not included in divorce
statistics. Britain has the highest divorce rate in Europe at 3.1 per
thousand, followed by Denmark on 2.5, France on 1.9 and Spain,
where divorce was allowed only in 1981, having the lowest rate at 0.7.
The UK cannot compete with the USA, however, where the rate is
about 4.7, but where too a plateau appears to have been reached.

Seventy per cent of all divorces are filed by wives whose main
reason is the unreasonable behaviour of their husbands who by contrast cite adultery as the cause for the irretrievability of the marriage.
On average, marriages which end in divorce last around 10 years. The
lowest income groups have both the earliest marriage age and the
highest divorce rate. The material effects of divorce on men and
women are very different: the economic circumstances of men are
little affected while those of women are substantially worsened,
reflecting the differential position of men and women in the labour
market and in child custody practice. This drop in living standards
applies to women of almost all income groups because people tend to
marry within a limited social class and status group and because of
the economies of scale of living together, particularly in relation
to housing costs (Weitzman, 1985; Arendall, 1986; Millar, 1989;
Glendinning and Millar, 1992; HMSO, 1997).

Divorce has been the principal cause of another notable feature of
contemporary family life – the rise of lone parent families, from 7 per

cent in 1971, to 14 per cent in 1981 and 20 per cent in 1996. 90 per cent are headed by women. Britain again leads Europe in this respect but has not yet reached the USA proportions of 32 per cent of all families with dependent children. While one must not forget the wide diversity in the financial circumstances of lone parents, the single most distinctive characteristic of the majority relative to two-parent families is that they have low incomes (Bradshaw and Millar, 1991).

The combined effects in Britain and the USA of the generally low pay levels of women's work, the lack of affordable and decent child-care provision, irregular paternal maintenance and means-tested benefits results in a low labour participation rate of lone mothers compared to that of other working mothers and to lone mothers in Europe (Bradshaw, *et al.*, 1996). European countries have different approaches to family policy, but they do place a premium on children and provide support for them in one form or another which protects against their impoverishment when families break up. The culture of Britain and America is one in which the rearing of children is regarded as a private responsibility and state subsidies are tolerated only for a very low safety net. Hence in Britain almost 60 per cent of lone parent families live on incomes below the poverty line of half the average income, compared to just 24 per cent of couple families. Put another way, twice as many children in families with below half contemporary mean income are from lone parent families (43 per cent) than from two-parent families. About 44 per cent of this income comes from means-tested benefits. Maintenance payments are intermittent at best and inadequate on the whole, even with the policing work of the Child Support Agency. Since until recently they were deducted from benefit, they made little improvement to those mothers who need help most. It is, therefore, the burden on public expenditure of lone parent families as much as the effect on their 1.9 million children under five living in poverty or the moral concern about the decline of conventional family life that has made lone parents the object of so much public debate. The situation in the United States is complicated by the increasing ability of the states legislatures to vary welfare and benefit support.

The impoverishment of women after divorce contributes to another distinctive phenomenon of the current period, that is the increase in remarriage. For the reasons outlined above, remarriage is a better option for lone mothers for improving economic circumstances than is the labour market (Duncan and Hoffman, 1988; Ermisch, 1989). For men, the economic advantage of remarrying may lie in the fact that most divorced women retain the marital home as part of the divorce settlement. Whatever is the case, remarriage formed approximately 38 per cent of all marriages in 1996 and is the primary source of flows out of lone parentage. The median duration of lone parenthood is about five years for divorcees, three years for single mothers. The sad facts are that younger, more psychologically robust and educated women with greater experience of employment before divorce or single motherhood and with a smaller number of dependent children are more likely to remarry, leaving a small but growing core of the most economically and socially disadvantaged and psychologically vulnerable lone-parent families excluded by virtue of their poverty and social location from participation in the mainstream society. Remarriages result in what has been termed 'reconstituted' families with increasing numbers of children living with a step-parent and sometimes step-siblings.

Another change has been the rise in the number of people living on their own: 11 per cent in 1961, 23 per cent in 1981 and 29 per cent in 1996. While the largest proportion consists of the elderly, particularly women because of the shorter life expectancy of men, there has been a growth of younger people. Here, Britain may be catching up with Europe where this has been an established pattern for much longer because of the greater availability of private housing rental. Of particular significance is the increase from a very low base in the number of men living alone, at 12 per cent, three times more than in the 1960s. This is a function of both later first marriage and divorce, and disproportionately affects middle-class men (Mintel Report, 1994).

The last major discontinuity in relation to British family life, is the extent of ethnic variation in family forms and family relationships. Britain has always been a multi-racial, multi-ethnic society but the period after the Second World War and the collapse of the British Empire witnessed the arrival in substantial numbers of people from the New Commonwealth. As their children and grandchildren reach maturity, we can begin to see distinctive demographic patterns emerge. The most notable difference from the indigenous population is the relatively small proportion of elderly, because migration is predominantly undertaken by young adults, and as one might expect as a consequence, higher fertility rates.

The groups in the population which most approximate to the idealised British traditional family are those from the Indian subcontinent. Generations live together or close by in a vertically extended household structure often characterised by economic inter-dependence through family businesses. Almost all heads of house-holds are male and the traditional gender division of authority and responsibility within the household prevails. These groups, particu-larly Pakistani and Bangladeshi, have the highest fertility rates in the UK, though some of this may well be a temporary effect of an un-usually extended fertility rate as a result of resumed childbearing following the arrival of wives and children in Britain some time after their husbands (Diamond and Clarke, 1989). Chastity before and fidelity after marriage is rigorously enforced. Early marriage is the norm; there are very few extra-marital births and divorce is discour-aged. These groups have the lowest level of women in paid work outside the home, though many are engaged in low-paid, casualised 'home-working', often vulnerable to health and safety hazards. Family incomes are amongst the lowest in Britain. East African Asians, by contrast, exhibit patterns of family formation, size, structure, fertility and income similar to white middle-class professionals, though with considerably lower divorce rates and incidence of one-parent families. They are well qualified, with the education and occupational levels of the women higher than any other ethnic group of women, including whites.

The family traditions of the other major minority racial group in the UK, Afro-Caribbeans, provide for very different patterns. The most noticeable characteristic is the combined role of women as both major economic providers and housekeepers, making the mother figure central to the Afro-Caribbean family and community life in Britain. For example, more than one-third of Afro-Caribbean women, including the married and cohabiting, are registered heads of households, much greater than other groups. Also Afro-Caribbean mothers have higher full-time employment rates than other ethnic groups including whites. This dominant role is said to stem from a tradition in the Caribbean in which young males did not cohabit on a permanent basis with their sexual partner but established a 'visiting relationship' with the girl, continuing to live in the house of her mother. Hence a pattern of early childbearing, followed later though not always by cohabitation or marriage, is a feature of Afro-Caribbean culture, as is, as a consequence, half-siblingship and illegitimacy for some of the children within the family. Around 50 per cent of all Afro-Caribbean births are to single women and 25 per cent of all Afro-Caribbean women are single mothers. While Afro-Caribbean women have children at a younger age than do their white counterparts, their overall fertility rates are very similar. Wider family networks are very important to support this family structure and neighbourhood prox-imity is very common (Diamond and Clarke, 1989; Church and Summerfied, 1995).

Ethnic diversity has been a feature of American family life from the creation of the nation because it was literally formed by immigration. Precisely because of America's radical political origins, it offered immigrant groups the opportunity and security of belonging to a supra-national state – the federation – while retaining the freedom to maintain their cultural traditions and heritage. The concept of sub-sidiarity, central to the European Union debate, appears to have operated in practice in the USA not only at the level of the individual states but also, as far as the family is concerned, at local level where there is often a vibrant culture of language schools, cultural societies and familially connected networks of employment and charitable ventures in operation. While this keeps alive familial cultural trad-tions, it has not prevented a general assimilation to patterns of white gender and family norms. Afro-American families exhibit similar pat-terns to those in Britain – their high incidence of lone parents being a common obsession with the media though the birthrate to unmarried black women has declined by 18 per cent since 1991 (Dickerson 1995; Center for Health Statistics 1999;). The second largest minority group in the USA is Hispanics. Despite their reputation for 'machismo' or patriarchial domination, Hispanics exhibit high levels of female-headed families and, like blacks, rely on the extended family for financial, employment and other material support. The fastest growing racial-ethnic constitutency is the Asian American, largely from Pacific Rim countries. Of all minorities, these are the most strict observers of traditional gender differences and statuses, and family obligations, and the most resistant to the general demographic trends in gender relations and family structures, size and roles operating in the USA (Mindel *et al.*, 1988; O'Hare, 1993; Gelles, 1995).

The various socio-economic and cultural factors which have led to these changes in and diversification of family forms and relationships are discussed in Chapter 2 as are some of their economic and social effects. However, the evidence suggests that such changes must be seen in the context of a continuing commitment by the vast majority of the population to a framework of belief in the value of family life and to behaviour which seeks to approximate to that ideal. Clearly some, though by no means all, of the behavioural forms in which such beliefs are manifested are different from those of the past and do present a challenge for moral world views and public policy assumptions and administrative arrangements rooted in a different timeframe. However, there seems to be no grounds for denying to family life, that evolution in human conduct accommodated in other spheres. Equally, the fact that behavioural norms, conventions and patterns of interpersonal relationships change over time does not have to lead to complete moral relativism in operational terms. It is perfectly possible to develop reasonably robust criteria for judging what behaviour, institutional as well as individual, is anti-social, exploitative, irresponsible and destructive relative to our era, which can attract a fair measure of popular support. It is also possible to identify what contexts are most conducive to such behaviour and to devise public policy which can minimise both negative incentives and outcomes for individuals and for society more generally. However, to do so requires a commitment to open, inclusive, accessible public debate and an obligation on the part of participants to apply reason to both intellectual and emotional processes.

It may seem odd for two of the most highly educated, economically prosperous and developed liberal democracies in the world, but in fact public debate on the family in both Britain and America has been crippled by contending polarities of thought and reaction, and meanwhile the public policy needed to address the issues in a coherent and holistic way and to put in place a package of measures to tackle those problems amenable and appropriate to social intervention is in a state of paralysis. Existing public policy in the area of the family in both countries is a mess of incoherent, ambiguous, self-defeating contradiction. At its heart lies an unresolved ambivalence about the role of women and the role of government action, in particular the expenditure of public money in the personal sphere.

The ambivalence and the paralysis in part reflect the pragmatic attempts by successive governments to accommodate, balance and deflect the often vociferous demands of groups in the population who hold very clear and unambiguous, if conflicting, views on these issues and who have the potential to command support among sufficient blocks of voters to swing elections and unseat politicians at local, regional and national level.

This book explores the reasons why the family became such a contentious issue in the UK and America in the last decades of the twentieth-century and why it is inextricably associated with feminism in both countries. Similar fundamental shifts in demographic morphology, economic and employment structures and in cultural consciousness which lie behind changes in family life have occurred elsewhere, but nowhere have they resulted in the politicisation of the family on the scale of Britain and the United States.

There are of course many reasons for the closeness of the British and American experience. There is the historical connection, the similar individualist, liberal and pragmatic culture as compared with the more collectivist, corporatist and legalistic ethos of Europe, in addition to the common language, most important in facilitating social and cultural interchange. Additionally both countries have pursued broadly similar economic policies, particularly with the dominance of economic liberalism since the late 1970s. Historically their inherent antagonism to 'Big Government' has kept the economy at arm's length from the state, and consequently there has been little to counterbalance the tendency to invest in those sectors that offer short-term profits at the expense of longer-term investment in the industrial infrastructure, resulting in an economy with considerable segmentation and flexibility in labour markets and wage levels. They stand in contrast to countries like Sweden, Germany and France where a historically closer association between industry, the banks and governments, and a 'partnership' between the state, employers and employees, secured the manufacturing base necessary to succeed in international markets, a high wage economy, relatively stable levels of employment and the wealth to support their substantial family-based welfare provision, at least until the emergence of the 'South Asian Tigers'.

In the case of feminism and the family, two more specific factors have been at work. First, the feminism on both sides of the Atlantic has had a reciprocal influence since at least the mid nineteenth-century, both as intellectual endeavours and as political movements, and this is particularly the case in relation to attitudes towards the family. Of course definitions of feminism both within and outwith the movement have changed from generation to generation but those in Britain and America have tended to change in tandem. Particularly since the Second World War, they have been much more critical of familialism on the whole than European feminism. Secondly, the simultaneous emergence in both Britain and the USA of governments committed to radically deconstructing the liberal democratic political culture and its related policy goals and instruments, has implicated the family in politics in similar ways. In relation to both the family and feminism, therefore, it can be said that a 'special relationship' exists between the two nations. There are, however, differences between them that

account for divergences in issues, intensity of debate and policy outcomes, which are also explored.

The book traces the emergence of the definition of the family in the
late twentieth century as a social problem about which certain sections of the public in the USA and the UK have mobilised in pursuit
of government intervention to restore what they saw as essential
prerequisites for family and hence social stability. This 'pro-family'
movement has been seen by some as simply a part of a general anti-
feminist backlash (Faludi, 1992; French, 1992) in the face of the
success of feminism in improving women's position and in undermining patriarchal privilege and status. According to this view, the
issue of the family is merely an invention by right-wing, reactionary,
largely male mysogynists as a smokescreen for an attack on feminism.
This is a somewhat understandable viewpoint given the opportunistic
manipulation of the family issue by conservative politicians and
governments in both countries. However, the issue was not invented
by them and is much more complex than the backlash theory would
suggest. It does not adequately account for the fact that 'pro-family'
organisations have had a genuine grassroots basis in a mass
movement of women mobilised to challenge feminism's claim to
speak on their behalf; nor for the fact that the political affiliations of
grass-roots supporters did not fall neatly into the usual party political
oppositions but were cut across by regional, ethnic and above all
religious lines.

The problem with such polarisation and demonisation of the combatants in the 'war over the family' (Berger and Berger, 1984) is that it
deflects us from serious consideration of the issues and our own experience and understanding of the relationship between the family and
feminism. The exploration undertaken in Chapters 1 and 2 reveals
that many of the issues, contradictions and tensions were identified by
and posed the same dilemmas of principle and action for women in the
previous two centuries. On the one hand women appropriated for
themselves the great liberal principles of individualism, meritocracy
and democracy which have characterised, however unevenly, the development of western societies since the Enlightenment. On the other they
did so on the basis of the centrality of their role in the maintenance of the
major building block of society and cement of social relationships – the
family. The heart of women's dilemma lay in this paradox – that the
basis of the claim for greater autonomy and personal development
rested in an institution which operates on a value system antithetical
to those principles, that is on those of ascribed authority, involuntary

association, life-time membership and the subordination of the interests of individual members to those of the group.

The limitations of traditional, patriarchal family life led women to
pursue the means to reform it, but the means themselves provided
women with capacities and aspirations beyond the confines of that
life. Advancing their case on the basis of domesticity, on the differences between men and women, and the civilising influence of female
qualities, proved to be an effective strategy in gaining the support of
women generally and efficacious in winning sufficient support from
influential male personages and organisations to advance on an
impressive number of fronts from the reform of family law and the
extension of education and civil liberties to women, to the widening of
access to employment and the professions. Nevertheless, the equality
issue, the question of the rights to equal participation in society on the
basis of an in principle equality with men was present from the late
eighteenth century at least, but was one that caused intermittent
friction and factionalisation within the movement for women's
advancement and certainly did not attract women outside the movement to the cause.

The equality issue came to the fore with the post-war generation of
feminists in the very different culture of first world egalitarianism and
third world liberationism of the 1960s and 1970s, and has been
sustained in the prioritisation of individual choice and mobility in
the neo-liberalism of subsequent decades. The further freedoms
which the twentieth-century brought, particularly those in relation
to sexuality and reproduction, have increased the genuinely complex
nature of the issues. For many women, the increased expectations of
self-realisation through romantic love and companionate marriage
result in disappointment which they are less prepared for or willing
to accommodate than previous generations and are more able to
survive without, as a consequence of smaller families, greater job
opportunities, a less than generous but nevertheless basic welfare
supplement and liberal attitudes to sexual relations outside marriage.
At the same time, employment for most is not a liberating experience
providing an alternative avenue for self-realisation and autonomy, but
merely a practical necessity. The physical and psychological association of women with children remains an obstacle to obtaining work
that provides the same remuneration, function, meaning and source
of self-esteem as it does for men of the same social group. Therefore
social esteem, emotional gratification and material support continues
to derive primarily from their roles as mothers. The dilemma for

women nowadays is less the conflict of interest between their own needs and those of their husbands/partners, than in relation to those of their children. Their continuing attachment to the family and suspicion of feminism may be seen in these terms.

There is increased pressure on men and a willingness in some to take on more responsibility for domestic and childcare arrangements, but this has not been accommodated by the reform of the conventional framework of employment, fiscal and social policies which continue to be linked to the deep-seated though increasingly outdated assumptions of the male breadwinner (Creighton, 1999; Dex and Joshi, 1999). The public costs, however, of providing a policy framework which would reconcile the rights of women as citizens with the welfare of families would be prohibitive, but so too are the public and private costs of the current situation. The financial costs of family and economic instability constitute a major problem; however, the emotional costs may be much greater and of longer-term significance.

For these reasons, the family, and hence the role of women and hence feminism stand at the centre of an economic, social, ideological and moral maze. The long revolution is not yet complete and stands in danger of being overtaken by the very diversity and fragmentation of contemporary experience to which the successes of feminism itself have contributed. Feminism as an ideology and a politics does not appear to offer young women today the key to the conundrum, though the fundamental feminist values, beliefs and self-perceptions appear to almost unconsciously inhabit the marrow of their bones in a way it did not for their mothers or grandmothers. These may well provide the guide for their personal resolution and render their aspirations and their desire for intimacy in familial-type relationships less at odds with each other than for their forebears.

1

Historical Precedents

It is important, as a corrective in the current heightened climate of debate, to point out that the intensity and range of institutional investment in the 'family question' and hence the 'woman question' is not a unique feature of the late twentieth-century. Since at least the Middle Ages the family has been the object of intermittent political attention precisely because it was an essential element in the ownership and control of economic property, in the distribution of the powers of governance, and in the social regulation of the population. While each of these has substantially changed in character, they continue to provide the context for public policy and flashpoints for public concern in contemporary society.

Aristocratic patriarchy, conceptions of family and the position of women

The hierarchical principles of the aristocratic regime, which all European states originally shared until the end of the eighteenth-century, were embodied in the delegation of the patriarchal authority of the monarch to the heads of the greater and lesser families and from thence to a plexus of relationships organised around village communities, trades, professions and urban corporations. The head of the family, which included dependants who were not blood-related such as household servants, bondsmen, serfs, apprentices and certain categories of tenants, was accountable for the behaviour of its members. In return for the discharge of his duties to keep public order and pay the various forms of feudal dues, the head of the family had almost unlimited discretionary powers over all who owed him allegiance, backed by the support of the law and the authorities. Thus, he had the right to levy rent and taxes, to allocate functions and control labour, to determine the education, career and domicile of his children and dependants, to arrange matrimonial alliances, and to impose punishments for error, non-conformity or disobedience, including the confinement or imprisonment by public authorities even of his own children. There were national and regional differences in family forms and familial relations (Laslett, 1971; Rabb and Rotberg, 1973; Shorter, 1975; Stone, 1977; Flandrin, 1979; Anderson (1980); Mitteraur and Sieder, 1982; Houlbrooke, 1984; Macfarlane, 1986; Davidoff and Hall, 1987; Coontz, 1988; Duby, 1994). Nevertheless, domestic patriarchy as a reflection of and a metaphor for state patriarchy was a consistent pattern.

Following medieval common law and custom, a woman's legal status became incorporated into that of her husband on marriage, a system known as *couverture.* This is reflected in the convention of most European countries, by which women lose their own family name and adopt that of their husbands. A wife could not hold property in her own name; whatever she had by inheritance or by her own enterprise or labour became his. She could not enter any legal contract. She had no legal rights over her own children and only at her husband's expressed wish could she be made their legal guardian at his death. If she left the marriage, she could take nothing with her, not her children, not even those possessions which were hers prior to the marriage or were personal gifts. Her husband could force her to return unless she was able to get a legal separation which was extremely costly and difficult to obtain. As always there are exceptions and note should be made of the English Royal variant of primogeniture which applies also to a small number of hereditary peerages, whereby a daughter if she is the eldest legitimate child may inherit. This exception gave the British Isles three long Golden Ages of peace and prosperity under the reigns of the Queens regnant, Elizabeth I, Victoria and Elizabeth II.

It was not until the seventeenth-century that marriage became formally indissoluble in Catholic Europe. In Protestant countries divorce was permissible but very difficult. It was based on the doctrine of matrimonial offence, the grounds for which were almost invariably stricter for female petitioners. For example, in England divorce required a petition to Parliament by a Private Act. While adultery was sufficient ground for male petitioners, wives had to provide additional grounds of aggravation such as repeated acts of violence. The costs were prohibitive, particularly for women, given their propertyless state in law. Thus, only four wives were ever granted Acts, all in the nineteenth-century (Hoggett and Pearl, 1991; Dewar, 1992; Fredman, 1997). Of course the internal distribution of resources within families of property in practice did not strictly reflect the law: families of property found ways to protect their fortunes from irresponsible sons-in-law, for example by transferring property to a trustee; not all wives suffered physical violence at the hands of their husbands; divorce was sometimes obtained by collusion between husband and wife. In addition among the labouring classes marriage was not that common, particularly after the Marriage Act of 1753 which required a formal ceremony in the Church of England, parental consent for those under 21 and the payment of a fee for the licence. Hence their unions and their relations were considerably removed from the legislative framework. Nevertheless, the situation in law endorsed potential tyranny in the home by continuing the feudal principle of patriarchal discretion.

The enlightenment, the 'social contract' and the 'sexual contract'

Ideologically, the ideas of the Enlightenment struck at the heart of aristocratic principles of political authority by challenging its conception of the origins of society and sovereignty. The notion of traditional or divinely ordained hierarchical order inherited through the blood via the father and sustained by reciprocal relations of responsibility and obedience was replaced by the idea of a 'social contract' associated most notably with the English political philosophers, Hobbes (1651) and Locke (1690) and in France with Rousseau (1762). The fundamental premise of classical social contract theory is that sovereignty rested on the natural equality of individuals, who surrender their rights to a separate overarching power enabling a disinterested and impartial resolution of disputes and conflicts and the protection from arbitrary infringement of their property and liberty by others. Hence the authority of the sovereign power depended on the consent of the people. It was also delimited by them to the sphere of public intercourse and public interest. The sphere of personal and private life was to lie outside of and protected from state interference. Hence, by constructing two separate spheres within civil society, the original contract provided protection for individual liberty in both public and private life by the rule of law which regulated the power and action of the sovereign power as much as that of the citizenry. With its humanist emphasis on the application of reason to human affairs, and its assertion of natural law, the equality and inalienability of rights, liberal political discourse undermined the juridical and cultural legitimacy and hegemony of the aristocratic regime.

In England, the largely middle-class Parliament's determination to challenge the divine right of the King, Charles I, to rule led to the English Civil War (1642–48) and, in his defeat and execution and the establishment of the short-lived Republic, to the undermining of the old aristocratic order, which the restoration of the monarchy in 1660 only partially tempered. The extent to which the ideas of the Enlightenment described above affected political thought in the English-speaking world in the century following can be seen in the words of the American Declaration of Independence (1774):

> We hold these truths to be self-evident; that all men are equal; that they are endowed by their Creator with certain alienable rights; that among these are life, liberty, and the pursuit of happiness; that to secure these rights, governments are instituted among men, deriving their just powers from the consent of the governed.

The ideas of the Enlightenment, as well as the failures, excesses and brutalities of the *ancien régime* in France, finally erupted in the Revolution of 1789 and led to the establishment of the Republic.

These progressive steps towards the protection of individual liberty enshrined in the civil liberties of the modern state, however, excluded women. As Carole Pateman (1988) has elaborated at length, the social contract is predicated on an assumption of a *sexual contract*, the marriage contract. This is the subject of an agreement in the private sphere. However, while women may be formally free to consent, given the inequalities between the parties and the terms of the contract, they contract into subordination. The legal identity of a woman and any property that acrues to her, becomes incorporated in that of her husband – hence he speaks for both in the public sphere. The two spheres are constructed as separate but they are linked, and it is the husband alone who traverses and unifies the two in his person. The individual of the discourse of liberalism, the individual of civil society, therefore, is in essence male because the only humans endowed with the attributes and capacities necessary to enter into the social contract, in particular the ownership of property in the person, are men. The only occasion when the idea of equal citizenship was carried to its logical conclusion was in the heyday of the French Revolution when its civil legislation, the *droit intermédiaire*, extended the principle of secular citizenship to private areas of law including familial relations. A law of 1792 overthrew the principle of domestic patriarchy by establishing marriage as a civil contract between equal partners, not a religious sacrament. The conditions of entering and leaving the contract were to be the same for both partners, establishing the legitimacy of divorce and the same grounds for husbands and wives. In the conservative reaction which followed the turmoil of the 'reign of terror', this revolution in family law was partially revoked in the *Code Napoléon* of 1804. While the obligatory civil marriage and divorce were retained in line with republican anti-clerical principles, the egalitarian basis of marital relationships was removed and replaced by the traditional incorporation of the wife's legal existence in that of her husband (Vogel, 1992).

In fact the philosophical and legal separation of the public and private spheres had the effects of further curtailing the liberties of women by reinforcing the effects of economic and technological changes. New centres of wealth, knowledge and power were created along with new forms of employment and new types of authority. These had already and increasingly required the separation of units of production from units of consumption. Given that these developments took place in the context of the historical link betweeen women, procreation and the care of children, they in effect limited women's ability to take the opportunities offered by the new commercial and industrial conditions which were the source of the new egalitarian philosophies and radical politics. Indeed, with the exception of women of the poor who became the most exploitable fodder for factories, mines, sweatshops and the most menial domestic labour, such power as women possessed from their participation in economic activity was reversed during the nineteenth-century.

The challenge from the new social constituency of the bourgeois and professional middle classes was not confined to the political authority of the upper classes but extended to their moral legitimacy. In an age of economic growth and state expansionism making greater demands on the social discipline of the population, the physical, mental and moral state of the lower orders was great cause for concern.

The increasingly prestigious medical profession was alarmed by the high rates of infant and child mortality and abandonment, as well as the poor health and physique of those who survived. The behaviour of the upper classes provided no model, leaving their own children to the questionable supervision of servants and proliferating large numbers of illegitimates (Ariès, 1960). The religious and municipal authorities were alarmed by the increasing costs of supporting the growing population of orphans and abandoned children, especially when so few survived to an age when they could be put to profitable work. Political authorities confronted the anxiety of the citizenry for the safety of their persons and property in the context of the expansion of the 'dangerous classes'. Employers and the military complained about the poor mental and physical quality of recruits and their apparent imperviousness to discipline and training. Both the upper and the lower classes were held to be the cause of what Donzelot (1980) calls 'a lack of social economy' which was seen to threaten the economic growth, welfare and security of the nation. The bourgeois and auxiliary classes responded to this situation in a series of reform movements which, while never united into a coherent, consistent reform programme, nevertheless taken together had the effect of transforming western society.

Anti-clericalism, religious non-conformism and the radical tradition

Despite the obstacles to communication and travel of the times there was a great cross-fertilisation and fermentation of radical ideas and political activity between the Old and the New World. A key factor, and one which acted as a conduit for the subversion of the established order, was the rejection of establishment religion or churches. In France the Revolutionaries' anti-clericalism led to the separation of the Church from the State. In England, opposition to the established Church of England was led by those Protestants who denied the right of the state to determine the manner of their worship. These Dissenters – Independents, Presbyterians, Baptists and Quakers – suffered various forms of persecution, leading to large-scale emigration to the New World from the sixteenth-century onwards. They took Parliament's side in the Civil War and after the Restoration were denied entry to civic life, the universities and the professions. Forced into trade, where they prospered by and large, their importance on a wider political canvass was that they were firmly non-hierarchical, believing in the equality of all believers before God. With their strong family, religious, intellectual and trade ties with North America over several generations, they were a conduit for the subversion of the old order there and supportive of the new. The Declaration of Independence reflected their beliefs as much as those of the Enlightenment.

Although originally Calvinistic, Nonconformists in England and their co-religionists in the United States were much influenced by the eighteenth-century evangelical movement associated in both countries with Methodists. This movement, which affected the Church of England as well, awakened the churches' interest and involvement in social and political issues in the nineteenth-century in both Britain and America. These included the anti-slavery movement, educational reform, temperance, prostitution, homes for the poor, 'ragged schools' and the care of orphaned children. Nonconformists were predominant in philanthropic movements which had as their goal the 'conservation of children', for in them lay the possibility of moulding the future, for example in the Sunday School movement. Religious influence on political organisations, including the trade unions, friendly societies and the Labour Party, dates from this period.

One might have expected that nonconformist zeal would address the extensive inequalities that existed between men and women. However, with the exception of the Unitarians whose views consolidated at the more radical end, non-conformist interest was limited to the promotion of the welfare and education of women in the dissenting tradition and a concern for their vulnerability to ill-treatment, violence and impecuniosity at the hands of brutal and irresponsible husbands and male relatives. For most, the concept of 'man' employed in the doctrine of the rights of man was interpreted literally. Women were equal souls before God, sharing a common humanity with men and hence in principle their equal.

Bourgeois patriarchy, the 'cult of domesticity' and 'the woman question'

It can be no accident that it was among these upright, socially conscious and public-spirited social groups that the cult of domesticity developed in the late eighteenth- and nineteenth centuries and, through their various philanthropic interventions, carried to the lower classes. Marriage, the rearing of children and the domestic unit were so important to the ethical foundations and material aspirations of the emerging bourgeois and middle classes that they became part of the rationale for improving the legal and social position of women.

Hannah More's scathing critique of the degenerative effects on middle class women of the adoption of the frivolous manners, and unproductive, parasitic life style of aristocratic ladies and her advocacy of a rigorous intellectual and moral education for girls, marriage based on friendship rather than sexual attraction and a life of useful activity, exemplify the themes of the reforming literature of the period. As Lasch (1997) has pointed out, there was much common moral ground between the anti-feminist reformer, More, and her contemporary, the feminist egalitarian, Mary Wollstonecraft. While they disagreed about the fundamental premises of sexual difference, they shared a similar view about what gained women dignity and respect. The promotion of the status of women in the name of motherhood provided justification for extending the 'maternal influence' to the service of society through women's participation in public affairs and even to employment in fields which were seen to be synergous with their domestic duties.

Nevertheless, it is not surprising that a political and moral environment characterised by men talking about equal rights and natural justice also produced the first glimmerings of a feminist rebellion against the perpetuation of patriarchal authority, embodied in the person, political activity and writings of the fiery and unconventional Mary Wollstonecraft.

Wollstonecraft's circle included the great names of intellectual dissent in the liberal and radical persuasions, such as Tom Paine, William Blake and William Godwin whom she later married. Much of the hostility and derision with which her *Vindication of the Rights of Women* (1792) was met, was a reaction to her scandalous personal life: her sortie in revolutionary Paris, her disastrous amorous attachment to an American adventurer she met there, her illegitimate child by him and her attempted suicide when she could no longer ignore his infidelity and indifference to her. However Wollenstonecraft's critics also correctly recognised it as the first truly feminist manifesto, in that its fundamental premise was that political and civil liberties are due to women *as of right*, based on the equal humanity in reason with men. It rejects the characterisation of the inequalities between men and women as a reflection of innate natural or divinely ordained differences and asserts that they are generated from a socially constructed system of political and cultural domination that amounts to no less than tyranny and servitude regardless of the social position and status of the individuals concerned.

Addressing herself exclusively to the middle classes as the only social group with the capacity or will to change society, Wollstonecraft finds her female contemporaries inferior beings to their male counterparts and is as scathing about their behaviour as any chauvinist detractor of the time:

> Pleasure is the business of a woman's life, according to the present modification of society; and while it continues to be so, little can be expected from such weak beings. Inheriting... the sovereignty of beauty they have, to maintain their power, resigned the natural rights which the exercise of reason might have precured them, and chosen rather to be short lived queens than labour to obtain the sober pleasures that arise from equality... Confined, then, in cages like the feathered race, they have nothing to do but to plume themselves, and stalk with mock majesty from perch to perch. It is true that they are provided with raiment, for which they neither toil nor spin; but health, liberty and virtue are given in exchange. (Wollstonecraft, 1972; 1985 edn, pp. 145–6)

However, there is no doubt that she believes that this 'degradation' is induced by the total dependence of women on men endorsed in law, the consequent overriding need for daughters of the propertied and professional classes to make a good match and hence an education for girls which Wollstonecraft regards as little better than a training for a 'Turkish seraglio'. Slaves themselves in the political and civil sense, women have learnt the art of 'serpentine wrigglings of cunning' by which to gain power and influence by illicit means. This they exert, according to Wollstonecraft, in the pursuit of narrow selfish interests and private gain, instead of public good, induced by the narrowness and pettiness of their domestic confinement, and in doing so feminise their husbands and lead them astray. And these arts they ensure will become second nature to their daughters.

Her solutions concentrate, therefore, on revolutionising the socialisation and education of girls such that they will develop the same critical powers of reason, experience the same physical freedom, outdoor activities and the contact with the real world outside the home, as boys. Indeed Wollstonecraft was an early advocate of a national system of co-education day schools with a common curriculum and activities for both sexes and, at elementary level, for all classes. Such an upbringing would provide women with the capacity to earn their own living, thus increasing their material and psychological independence from men and widening their range of interests and enjoyments. There could be no grounds for refusing these New Women the civil and political rights that in any case are their due on the basis of a common humanity.

Nevertheless, even the radical Wollstonecraft did not wish to subvert the institution of the family and marriage which she respected 'as the foundation of almost every social virtue' (Wollstonecraft, 1792;1985, p. 165). Rather she wished to rescue it from the unnatural distortions wrought upon it by the material excesses and lasciviousness of the age. In true Enlightenment thinking she believed that it is through changing the environment of the young that societal change can be brought about. And she did not shrink from seeing this as 'one of the grand duties annexed to the female character' (p. 265). As such the care of children should be performed by those with enlightened minds, measured judgment and the highest virtue, and this would not be achieved 'until the person of a woman is no longer preferred to her mind' (p. 315). In Wollstonecraft's logic, this would come about only when women shared the political and civil rights and responsibilities of men:

Make women rational creatures and free citizens and they will quickly become good wives and mothers. (p. 299)

Wollstonecraft died in childbirth in 1797 by which time fear of French Jacobinism and the outbreak of war with France had provoked a wave of political repression of radical activity in Britain and halted further progress toward parliamentary reform.

Most historians of feminism tend to assume that, apart from a few radical figures, feminist argument was suspended in embryo between Wollstonecraft's death and the beginning of an organised movement in the 1850s. Gleadle (1995) has demonstrated, to the contrary, the existence of a widespread nascent women's rights movement in the early decades of the nineteenth-century. This, she argues has its roots and milieu in what she calls 'radical unitarianism', an offshoot of the main body of the Unitarian mainstream, much less conservative and patriarchal. Centred round the unconventional Unitarian ministry of W.J. Fox at the famous South Place Chapel in London, this group attracted people from other denominations seeking a progressive movement informed by the simplicity and egalitarianism of the early Christianity. This wider progressive circle provided a supportive environment and a platform through its publications for feminist ideas. These carried forward both strands of Wollstonecraft's feminism – the principle which insists on gender equality in civil rights and that which seeks to strengthen women's status and capacity within the family. Gleadle argues that radical utilitarianism thus provided the intellectual origins for the later Victorian feminism.

The movement also had close links with that other strand of radical thought in the early nineteenth-century – communitarianism – which had by far the most libertarian views of relations between men and women.

Communitarianism and sexual radicalism

Followers of the French radicals, Saint-Simon and Fourier, communitarians or early socialists believed the progress of civilisation depended on basing social relations on co-operation and collective interest, and this included relations between men and women. They caused considerable stir in London in the 1830s and in the United States in the 1840s respectively with their demand that marriage and familial relations should be reconstructed on the basis of equality of rights including female suffrage. For them, marriage should have no basis in familial alliances of property and influence, but should be entirely the outcome of love choices of the individuals concerned. As such, divorce should enable individuals to leave marriages which had become loveless.

In Britain, Robert Owen, a mill owner-manager and social reformer, proposed communal alternatives to household labour, such as community nurseries, canteens, kitchens and laundries as part of his philosophy of mutual co-operation in which model working, educational and living environments provided by employers would be rewarded by a loyal, healthy, disciplined and skilled workforce. Owen is remembered for implementing these experiments in labour management in his New Lanark cotton mill villages in the second decade of the nineteenth century. Less well-known are his *Lectures on the Marriages of the Priesthood in the Old Immoral World* published in 1835 which contain not only arguments for the liberalisation of marriage and divorce but also for the abolition of the system of 'single family arrangements' with its narrow, selfish, individualised emotional and material bonds, and its replacement with the communalising of kinship obligations and duties across the community and the celebration of spontaneous sexuality for both sexes (Taylor, 1983).

There were some short-lived experiments in sexual and social egalitarianism in America, such as in the Oneida community, and strands of their radicalism survived in the anarchistic tendency of American socialism which re-emerged in the bohemian culture of New York's Greenwich Village at the turn of the century (Rendall, 1987).

However, sexual libertarianism was not adopted as general practice by the communitarian movement. While Owenism was the most proto-feminist of all the radical movements in Britain, its aim was closer to that of Wollstonecraft, that is to rid marriage and family life of those social and legal features which made it often a moral hypocrisy at best and a miserable prison at worst.

While communitarian ideas on workers' collective self-help led to the development of the successful co-operative movement in Britain, those about sexual equality were less popular in the growing working-class movements. These were often, through their leadership, linked to the more morally conservative Christian sects, particularly the Methodists. The discipline of the trade union and the discipline of the Chapel combined to produce a dearly prized respectability. Marks of that social and personal achievement were to be able to keep one's wife out of gruelling wage work by earning sufficiently and regularly, out of too many childbeds by self-restraint, and out of reach of the Poor House by temperance and thrift (Thompson, 1971; Lown, 1990). Hence the most dynamic movement of lower-middle and working class agitation in the first half of the nineteenth-century, Chartism, did not include a demand for female suffrage in its People's Charter (though the radical leader William Lovett had it in the original draft), and the substantial activities of Chartist women do not seem to have been organised around issues specific to their sex (Taylor, 1983).

Social purity, women's rights and social reform

The social reform movements of the nineteenth-century involved from the start large numbers of mainly middle-class women. While their motivation might have been religious conversion, they became preoccupied with the origins of the social evils they encountered. While they established charities and refuges for the disabled, the sick, the destitute, the insane, for women in childbirth, they also started campaigns against prostitution, drunkenness and other vices. It was through this work that they came to see that much immorality was the effect of the lack of regular legitimate employment, poverty, the overcrowded, insanitary conditions of slum living and the culture of hopelessness and brutality they induced. The brunt of this was starkly borne by women and children. Social purity work led women evangelists into social reform, providing a hands-on training in organisation and administration and in techniques of what is now known as pressure group politics.

In America this process began earlier – in the 1820s and 30s – and with more fervour. It was also more easily politicised, given the liberal principles of the American Constitution and the turbulent effect on American culture of the slavery issue and the Civil War. The experience of impotence to affect public policy in the face of obdurate male politicians led evangelical women into political activity much more readily than their British counterparts. For most the extent of their ambitions was sufficient formal freedom and power as women to be able to improve the material and moral lives of those less fortunate. The one issue of equality that did engage them was the 'double standard' of morality by which women were ostracised and criminalised for behaviour that was tolerated in men. However, this did not lead them to demand sexual liberation for women, but the control of sexual gratification in men. Sexual equality for these 'evangelical feminists' (Banks, 1981; Rendall, 1987) meant sexual purity for both sexes.

There were women, however, who were radicalised by their involvement in these movements of moral reform. In particular, engagement with the anti-slavery movement threw into stark relief the similarities of the legal position of slaves and women in relation to property, political and civil rights but, of particular sensitivity, the sexual ownership of women's bodies. It was Quaker women in America, like Lucretia Mott, the Grimke sisters and Susan Anthony, who articulated the similarities and extended demands for a greater public role for women to assertions of complete legal equality between the sexes. Much influenced by Wollstonecraft, they united the concerns of Christian morals and social reform with the equal rights perspective of the Enlightenment. With Elizabeth Cady Stanton they organised a convention at Seneca Falls in 1848 at which the participants signed a Declaration of Independence, a document that paraphrased the one that began the war against British colonial rule, to clearly include women as bearers of natural rights and legitimate claimants of the conditions of equality. If *The Vindication* is regarded as the first feminist tract, the Seneca Falls Convention must constitute the founding political event of the feminist movement.

The main thrust of their activities was economic independence for women. Most of their campaigns concentrated on lobbying state legislatures on questions of the rights of married women to their own property and earned income, equal rights in divorce, rights in relation to their children and protection from abuse. The other main objectives were the improvement of the education of girls and the expansion of the types of employment open to them.

There was substantial success partly because some of these campaigns coincided with the interests of those who might not otherwise support feminist causes. For example, there were various Married Women's Property Bills which were supported through a number of state legislatures during the mid-decades of the nineteenth-century because they were seen as a safeguard against feckless sons-in-law and against property leaving consolidated family stocks. In the case of education, the academies and colleges established for girls from the 1830s did raise the intellectual standards of female education but most did so from within the parameters of a philosophy of 'separate spheres' and a curriculum that focused on improving the quality of mothering and household managment. In addition, the growing demographic feature of 'surplus women', as a result of male internal migration, justified greater educational and employment opportunities where they did not challenge male preserves. However, in the United States there was always a strong public challenge from equal rights feminists to the moral conservatism of evangelical efforts to improve women's position.

Nevertheless, these reforms, whether based on equal rights principles or those of moral improvement, were not accompanied by the denigration of marriage or the family in general. On the whole they dealt with increasing the status of women within marriage, curtailing the opportunities for abuse by husbands and fathers, lessening the vulnerability of women when marriages failed and providing alternative means of support of women who did not marry.

From improvement to emancipation: Harriet Taylor and John Stuart Mill

In Britain, ideas about female emancipation appealed to middle-class intellectuals such as the Utilitarian reformers like Jeremy Bentham and John Stuart Mill and the more radical Unitarian sect of the nonconformists which played in England the equivalent role of the Quakers in the USA. Harriet Taylor, Mill's wife, came from a strong Unitarian background. Some of the differences in their philosophical heritages can be seen in their polemical essays in support of female emancipation which constitute the next major literary landmarks in feminist argument: Harriet Taylor Mill's *Enfranchisement of Women* in 1851 and her husband's *The Subjection of Women* in 1869.

Echoing Wollstonecraft, both writers situate the various issues of the day about women's position in a general theory of patriarchy which roots male domination of women in the laws which regulate marriage and family life: 'Now that negro slavery has been abolished...marriage is the only actual bondage known to our law. There remain no legal slaves, except the mistress of every house' (*The Subjection*, p. 147). Likewise they are highly critical of the cramping effects of contemporary family life. They are struck by the irony of the fact that 'the progress of civilisation and the turn of opinion against the rough amusements and convivial excesses which formerly occupied most men...have thrown the man very much upon home and its inmates' (ibid, pp. 175–6), yet the domestic culture of the home, in which women have been immersed from birth, trivialises social intercourse, stultifies the intellect and privatises interests to those that directly relate to the family and its immediate social circle. In these essays, then, the domestic idyll cultivated by the bourgeois middle classes is ridiculed as emasculating both men and women and undermining the quality and robustness of public life.

Both works reject the argument that the differences between men and women are reflections of their natural aptitudes. The only natural factor they will concede is the biological differences in physical strength which were relevant in primitive times, but which has been largely abandoned as a principle in ordering human relations, thus its persistence in the law organising relations between the sexes is an anachronism and an abuse of power. To the argument that women consent to and prefer the current sexual division of labour, they reply, like Wollstonecraft, that in women's current situation of total economic dependence on and legal subordination to men, it is not possible to ascribe their behaviour to preference, since they are not in a position to experience or exert free will. Indeed, J. S. Mill makes the fine point that if the current arrangements of marriage and motherhood are so natural and attractive to women, they should not need the force of law to ensure that women cannot do anything else.

The balance of argument in *The Subjection*, tips toward the utilitarian advantage of the benefits that female emancipation would bring to men in being loved and respected as an equal by an equal, to society in the increase in the pool of talents and in the increase of democratic sentiments consequent on its experience in family life, as well as the happiness gained by women themselves in achieving 'a life of rational freedom'. By contrast, the arguments and claims in *Enfranchisement* are more consistently based on the abstract principle of equality and natural justice:

> The real question is, whether it is right and expedient that one-half of the human race should pass through life in a state of forced subordination to the other half. (p. 23)

Enfranchisement is also more through-going in the logical consequences of female liberation. For example, marriage and motherhood should be no impediment to equal rights in employment and public office. Indeed Harriet is quite brutal about it:

> There is no inherent reason or necessity that all women voluntarily choose to devote their lives to one animal function and its consequences. Numbers of women are wives and mothers only because there is no other career open to them, no other occupation for their feelings or their activities. (p. 18)

And even for those who do choose maternity, she maintains there is no reason why 'they shall be either mothers or nothing else during the whole remainder of their lives' (p. 17).

While J. S. Mill is as genuinely committed to the principle of opening up all employment to women and amending their education to equip them to benefit from it, he is much more ambivalent about it in practice as far as married women are concerned. He does not think it 'a desirable custom that the wife should contribute by her labour to the income of the family' (*The Subjection*, p. 88). In his view the management of the household and childcare is an exhausting enough occupation. His point is that 'the power of earning' (the *capacity* for financial independence) 'is essential to the dignity of a woman' (*The Subjection*, p. 89) because it would enable her, if marriage was an equal contract, to make marriage and family a true choice of profession.

Despite these differences of emphasis, neither challenge conventional ideas about the division of household responsibilities nor about sexuality. Interestingly, both pieces stress the interconnectedness between the private and public spheres and the necessity of a continuity between private and public morality. Hence, marriage is 'the most fundamental of the social relations' and the 'moral regeneration of mankind' will begin only when it is placed 'under the rule of equal justice' (*The Subjection*, p. 177). Similarly, the family is central to a moral and political education appropriate to the modern age:

Citizenship, in free countries, is partly a school of society in equality; but citizenship fills only a small place in modern life, and does not come near the daily habits or inmost sentiments. The family, justly constituted, would be the real school of the virtues of freedom. (*The Subjection*, p. 81)

This tension between sexual equality, female emancipation and the family ideal is a persistent theme in the political debates and activities about the position of women in the latter part of the nineteenth-century.

Engels, the bourgeois family and the 'woman question'

Marxism produced leading champions of women's emancipation and the most radical attack on the bourgeois family form. Karl Marx himself wrote very little about women, marriage or the family. It was Frederick Engels who developed what has become regarded as the Marxist theory of the family in *The Origin of the Family, Private Property and the State* (1884;1970) in which he decries bourgeois marriage as 'crassest prostitution' and the epitome of the oppression endemic to capitalist society. In *The Origin*, he traces the development of the bourgeois family from the pre-history of the human race, drawing on Lewis Henry Morgan's ethnological account of the kinship systems of American Indians published in 1887 on which Marx had been working before his death.

Put briefly, Engels characterised the organisation of earliest groups as 'primitive communism' in which the economy is one of the 'appropriation of products in their natural state' (that is, hunting and gathering) possessed and distributed collectively by the 'tribe'. Reflecting this communality of ownership, sexual relations take the form of 'group marriage', that is, where there is no pairing or exclusivity, the only form of sexual prohibition being between the generations. In this situation, paternity is unknowable and so the identity of the group is defined by common descent through the female line. Engels believes that since the means of production and distribution are owned communally there are no grounds for antagonistic economic relations between groups. Only a natural division of labour exists based on age and sex:

The man fights in wars, goes hunting and fishing, procures the raw materials of food and the tools necessary for doing so. The woman looks after the house and the preparation of food and clothing, cooks, weaves, sews. (*The Origins*, p. 567)

This situation changed with the domestication of cattle, because this produced a surplus over and above subsistence in the men's sphere accumulated as wealth. Engels argues that with this expansion of production, more labour is required and this is obtained through the capture and enslavement of rival peoples. Slavery itself led to further expansion and further surpluses and with them the increased power of males over women. The critical point occurs, however, when wealth stimulates the desire in men to limit its distribution to their own biological children. This drove men to introduce monogamy and establish inheritance through the male line. Engels claims that there was little resistance to this from women since they had already shown a preference for the 'pairing family'. Nevertheless, 'the overthrow of mother-right was the world-historic defeat of the female sex' (p. 488).

Finally Engels argues that the development of private property and the mechanism for its accumulation through inheritance provided the conditions for the establishment of inherently antagonistic social classes, and a state to represent and reconcile their conflicting class interests. In the process women became economically, legally and politically subordinated to men. In Engels's view, since it was the exclusion of women from productive wealth that made them subordinate to men, it is only by regaining their place in the productive process that women will regain their independence. Paradoxically, it is the highest development of private property in modern, large-scale capitalist industry that provides the conditions for women's emancipation, because it increasingly displaces muscular power by that of machines.

The Origins has not been short of critics, within and outside Marxism. Empirically, anthropological evidence of the diverse functions of marriage and kinship and of a variety of forms of property-holding and transmission in pre-modern societies has thrown into doubt the particular selection of data that constitutes Engels's speculative history of the family (Aaby, 1977). Theoretically, much has been made of the contradiction between Engels's main postulate of economic determinism on the one hand and his assumptions of a natural division of labour and a biologically determined sexuality on the other, and various attempts have been made to rescue Engels from it (Delmar, 1976; Coward, 1983). Criticism has also focussed on Engels's attribution of a psychological impulse (the desire to transmit property exclusively to genetic offspring) and of juridical conceptions of rights and access to property to a population in which, according to the principles of historical materialism, the material conditions for that impulse – private property – have not yet been established (Brown, B. 1978; Brown, L. 1979).

It has also been pointed out that Engels's account provides the classic criterion for considering women as a social class distinct from men, in that the generation of surplus in the context of a 'natural' division of labour constructs a differential relationship of the sexes to the means of production. Yet Engels refuses this conclusion because it suggests that there may be forces of history as important as those of economic class. Instead he subsumes the economic differences between the sexes in the political domination of women by men in marriage, and arrives at the desired end – the monogamous family as the economic agent in primitive accumulation and the development of capitalism (Coward, 1983). It is a simple step from here to call for the abolition of the bourgeois family as an essential part of the revolutionary process by which the whole capitalist economic order is to be overthrown.

It would be a mistake, however, to think that by this Engels meant to call for the end of the family *per se*. It is the family as an economic institution that was to be abolished. In bourgeois societies men own women in marriage as a result of women's economic dependence thereby securing and perpetuating their property. In the proletarian family, however, these conditions no longer pertain: the male having lost his property is reduced to a wage labourer, and the women absorbed into production earn in their own right. Thus:

> The last remnants of male domination in the proletarian home have lost all foundation – except for some of that brutality towards women which became firmly rooted with the establishment of monogamy... When the man and woman cannot get along they prefer to part. (*The Origin*, pp. 499–500)

Elsewhere Engels is less sanguine about proletarian family life:

> Thus the social order makes family life almost impossible for the worker... The husband works the whole day through, perhaps the wife also and the elder children, all in different places; they meet night and morning only, all under perpetual temptation to drink; what family life is possible under such conditions? Yet the working-man cannot escape from the family, must live in the family, and the consequence is a perpetual succession of family troubles, domestic quarrels, most demoralising for parents and children alike. (Engels, 1892;1987, p. 154)

As Fletcher (1988) has remarked, such passages which abound in the work of both Marx and Engels, suggest not an opposition to the family but an outrage 'that decent family life for the labouring poor was made impossible' (p. 65).

Such apparent contradictions become clear when one asks what Engels believed the abolition of capitalism and the bourgeois family would bring about. Engels is quite unambiguous about this. Freed from the unnatural trammels of private property, sexual relations would be restored to their simple natural form – *individual sex love*. 'Since sex love is by its very nature exclusive . . . then marriage based on sex love is by its very nature monogamy' (Engels, 1884; 1970, p. 507). Engels has no doubt that in the post-revolutionary world where the means of production have become common property, and where housework and childcare have become a collective responsibility, sexual relations would be heterosexual and monogamous. Under such conditions, 'monogamy, instead of declining, finally becomes a reality' (ibid, p. 502). For Marx and Engels, then, there is nothing inherently oppressive in marriage or the family once it is entered into by free and equal agents on the basis of mutual love and affection and provided that it may be formally ended by the mutual desire of the couple involved.

Engels and Mill were among the most radical advocates of equality for women, yet neither of them consider the role of reproduction in the subordination of women. The falling birthrate in the nineteenth-century clearly indicates that birth restriction was widely practised in all social classes. Although abortion had been illegal since 1803, abortifacients were cheap and available and in general use among working women. Contraceptive techniques were less well known and devices like the condom, diaphragms, sponges and douches were expensive, making them used primarily by the upper classes. Nevertheless, neither Engels nor Mill, at least in their public writings, gave birth control a role in women's emancipation. In this, however, they were not out of step with other radicals and reformers of the day. As we shall see, contraception was a very controversial and divisive issue in the reform movement generally and among feminists.

If it is true to say that Marxism generally had little direct impact on British socialism in the nineteenth century, it is also the case that *The Origins* had little impact on either socialism or feminism. For much of the nineteenth-century working women were marginal to the labour movement, partly because of the casual and low-paid nature of their work and partly because the skilled craft trade unions tended to exclude them for fear of labour dilution. The development of a 'family wage' strategy and the moral conservatism of the labour leaders have already been noted. Hence there was little challenge to the conventional familial role of women in the discourses with which working-class women were familiar, and their political education was severely limited. When they did take action in pursuit of their interests it tended to be in relation to immediate local disputes or in support of the claims of their male fellow workers. It was not until 1874 that they got their own trade union, the Women's Protective and Provident League (later the Women's Trade Union League) founded by Emma Paterson, but this was actually initiated by middle-class feminists informed by the liberal philosophy of Mill rather than the historical materialism of Marx (Strachey, 1928;1978).

The fight for suffrage

These radical discourses on female emancipation informed the activities of a group of British middle-class women, mostly Unitarian, who had been involved in progressive causes such as the anti-slavery movement, penal reform and electoral and parliamentary reform. In 1856 they established a centre in Langham Place in London for campaigns specifically for women's rights in marriage and divorce, education and employment. This may be said to mark the beginning of an organised feminist movement in Britain. The British equivalent of the Seneca Falls group, the 'Ladies of Langham Place', included Barbara Leigh Smith (later Bodichon), Bessie Raynor Parkes, Emily Davies and Elizabeth Garrett Anderson, all of whom became famous women pioneers in bastions of male privilege. Their activities supported notable reforms, such as the Married Women's Property Acts of 1857 and 1882, the Divorce Act of 1857, the founding of Queen's College and Bedford College for Women, the establishment of women's colleges at Oxford and Cambridge, the controversial repeal of the Contagious Diseases Acts in 1886, and the raising of the age of consent in 1885.

The obstacles to reform, however, were formidable not least because of a predominantly unsympathetic male House of Parliament which caused the Langham feminists to turn their attention to the issue of female suffrage. They established the National Society for Women's Suffrage in 1867 and persuaded J. S. Mill to present a petition to Parliament. From then until the end of the century hardly a year passed without a Private Member's Bill in Parliament on the subject, without success.

There were both parliamentary and extra-parliamentary obstacles to female suffrage. First, it was confronted with very substantial anti-feminist sentiments among conservative men of both the Conservative and the Liberal parliamentary parties. Second, although the Liberal Party was associated with the support of progressive causes and certainly had more members sympathetic to feminist principles, it was nevertheless fearful that votes for women meant votes for the Tories if the franchise was tied to property. Third, there was also pressure on MPs from some powerful economic interest groups, like the brewers and manufacturers who feared that women would use their votes to pressure for social purity and protective labour legislation. Fourth, the cause did not have sufficient support among the general public, nor indeed among women themselves, to act as a spur to politicians.

Despite the apparent invulnerability of Westminister, there was a gradual erosion of male privilege in other political and public offices. The overwhelming female presence in welfare work resulted in the eligibility of those rate-payers among them to be elected to and vote in School Board elections after 1870 and as Poor Law Guardians after 1875. Legislation of 1869, 1888, 1894 and 1907 enabled women to vote in municipal, county, district and local elections and to stand as councillors. By the beginning of the new century, therefore, the public was more used to the idea and the reality of women in politics and this assisted suffragettes in building support among women for the cause of full female political emancipation.

Among middle-class women, there was overlapping membership of suffragette associations and welfare organisations in the growth of support for votes for women among the more traditional evangelical reformers. Typical here were leaders of the Charity Organisation Society, Octavia Hill and Helen Bosanquet, whose highly articulated mission for voluntary social work targeted female members of individual families as the mechanism through which the physical condition and moral discipline of citizens could be improved. However, this conservative view was tempered by the intimate knowledge they had of the unrelenting harshness of such women's lives, and led Bosanquet at least to consider that they of all women needed the vote (Lewis, 1991). The opposition and chauvinistic reaction these social reformers met in the pursuit of the interests of the needy also softened their initial hostility to the suffrage, and by the end of the century most had been recruited to the cause.

The alliances built up with working class women (Thane, 1991) were strengthened by the formation in 1893 of the Independent

Labour Party as the political wing of the labour movement. The ILP established a progressive alliance between a number of different elements, such as the non-conformist, evangelical, temperance, Unitarian, socialist and radical constituencies, that had sufficient affinity in their values and goals to submerge class divisions and, with the feminist sympathiser, Keir Hardie, as its leader, added its weight to the growing support for female suffrage.

However, the question now became whether the aim of the campaign would be limited franchise for women or universal suffrage, a question which led to parliamentary impasse and, in frustration, the emergence of militancy by some groups of the suffrage movement, led by the Women's Social and Political Union (WSPU) established by Emmeline Pankhurst in 1903. Breaking with both the Labour and Liberal Parties, the WSPU flirted with the Conservatives who brought in a Conciliation Bill for limited franchise. When this was defeated and the Speaker of the House refused to accept a Labour amendment to a new Franchise Bill to include women, the suffragette movement accelerated its campaign of direct action. This resulted in the violence for which it is most often noted in historical records and which did not cease until the outbreak of the First World War in 1914 when the suffragettes, caught up in the nationalistic fervour, suspended their activities.

When the issue appeared again at the end of the war there was no active suffragette movement but the visible contribution women had made in the war effort in jobs traditionally done by men – the media loved photographs of women driving trams, buses, trains, ambulances – had its impact on popular opinion and that in the House of Commons as to their right to the vote. It is worth noting in passing, however, that the same appreciation was not extended to the right to the jobs for which they had proved their capability. As Clarke (1996) comments wryly, 'Despite all the fuss, the war had not created vast new opportunities for women, just photo-opportunities' (p. 95). The women's vote piggy-backed on the Bill bringing in adult male suffrage and had the support of the Prime Minister, Lloyd George, and his coalition government. The compromise conceded the principle of female suffrage but restricted its application. The 1918 Act introduced the vote for women over 30 years of age who were local government electors or the latter's wives, or university graduates. It took another ten years for full adult suffrage to be achieved for women in the face of continued opposition from an alliance of those who feared they would impose a stringent puritanical regime on British public and private life (Banks, 1981).

In the United States, the issue that divided the country and those in favour of female suffrage was not property qualifications, but race. Liberal and radical male opinion was not prepared to risk the chance of achieving black male suffrage by hitching female suffrage to the campaign. The refusal by Susan Anthony and Elizabeth Cady Stanton to support the Fifteenth Amendment which prohibited disenfranchisement on the grounds of race but not sex, split the feminist leadership and led to the setting up of the women-only National Woman Suffrage Association in 1869 by Anthony and Stanton, followed by Lucy Stone's more cautious American Woman Suffrage Association.

Neither of these suffrage organisations had much success beyond municipal, district and local electoral reforms over the next twenty years and finally merged in 1890 to form the National American Woman Suffrage Association (NAWSA). During this period the suffrage cause lost much of its original radicalism through the closer alliance with the Women's Christian Temperance Union, the largest women's organisation in the USA led by the feminist purity campaigner, Frances Willard. It is likely that this strengthened its support among women. As in Britain two further key constituencies were recruited to the cause – working-class women and settlement workers.

American women workers faced the same hostility from the labour unions as their British counterparts, such that their political activity was largely of a supportive nature and the few attempts at their own labour organisation were short-lived. They eventually were reluctantly granted entry to the first national trade union movement, Knights of Labor, in 1881, and to its successor the American Federation of Labor which finally approved universal suffrage in 1890. The Women's Trade Union League was established in 1903 supported by middle-class women settlement workers. Their unproblematic adoption of a strategy of pursuing protective legislation stands in contrast to the British case. Even more indicative of the different environments of the two countries is the fact that they had to fight a Supreme Court wedded to the liberty of contract granted in the Constitution to have the need for special protection recognised! Their wholehearted support for a case based on the doctrine of physiological difference and maternal function was not only derived from a tactical calculation that in the context of exploitative and unregulated employers, protection was the most immediate and effective reform possible, but also from their unquestioning assumption of the primacy of the family and women's role in it. Votes for women, therefore, became associated

with the protection of the family and the promotion of the feminine
virtues into the male world of public affairs.

The suffrage movement in the United States had to work without
the support of a major electoral force like the British Labour Party
unifying the social and liberal democratic, labourist and radical
strands of the centre-left in the nation's politics. In America these
elements had developed much more independently. Their ideological
and strategic contradictions and antagonisms were reflected in splin-
tered organisational forms, and the effectiveness of the small
socialist strand, was limited as much by its anarchist tendency as by
its hostile environment. Add to this the complexities of operating in a
federal system and it is easy to see why the suffrage movement
had little option but to operate as a lobby, taking advantage where
it could of the vulnerabilities of the Republican and Democratic
parties.

New life was brought into the campaign by younger American
women such as Alice Paul and Lucy Burns, who had witnessed the
militancy of the British suffragettes. They founded the Congressional
Union in1913 and targeted Congress for its lobbying and demonstrations, much to the dismay of the NAWSA which pursued a policy of
state campaigns. The consequent rift led Paul and Burns to form the
Woman's Party in 1914. The gradual success of the suffrage campaign
in the states, the public visibility of the Woman's Party techniques of
agitation, finally turned the Democrats to adopting women's suffrage
in 1918. It took two years to finally defeat the opposition of southern
landowners, northern industrialists and sections of the labour movement, and get it through the House of Representatives and Senate and
be ratified by the necessary 36 states.

After the 'vote'

Historians often mark the achievement of the vote as the end of 'first
phase feminism'. In terms of an active self-conscious politically motivated movement with substantial support and able to cross-cut the
class divisions of the time, this is probably the case. However, the
movement to improve the position of women continued apace but in
different ways and by different means as the alliance that had been
sustained by the overriding goal of the vote dissolved into its constituent parts and pursued their own individual goals relatively
independently and on occasion in opposition to each other.

Those who came to the suffrage movement from charitable organisations and social work used their newly found political influence to gain support for legislative provision for mothers and children. In America in the 1920s, NAWSA, under its new name, the League of Women Voters, was an important force in the passing of the Maternity and Infant Protection Act in 1921, in strengthening funding for the Women's Bureau and the Children's Bureau set up by settlement workers, and together with the Women's Trade Union League and the Consumer League in promoting restrictions on female and child labour. They made natural allies for Roosevelt's 'New Deal' policies ushered in by the Depression of the 1930s.

Only the small radical Woman's Party continued to pursue issues of gender equality. In 1923 its members submitted to Senate an equal rights amendment to the Constitution, which was prevented from further progress largely by the opposition of an alliance of the Women's Trade Union League, the Consumer League and the League of Women Voters who argued that formal legal equality would undermine progress that had been made to improve the lives of working women by protective legislation and by health and social services and cash benefits focused on family welfare. The same groups continued to obstruct all further attempts to get the amendment out of the committee stage. It was not finally discharged from committee into Congress until 1971 with a new wave of feminist agitation. In the national mêlée that followed, the same arguments and the same divisions between women about definitions of what constitutes women's interests and who has the right to determine these, were once more exposed as hinging on issues pertaining to the family. The same debate continues to engage politicians, special interest groups and the general public in the twenty-first century.

The mass unemployment and poverty of the 1930s made agitation for equal opportunities and equal pay for women an unpopular cause, though they also forced more married women on to the labour market. Much masked by the general features of the Depression, however, was the further growth of opportunities already discernible from the end of the nineteenth century for office work for young, educated, unmarried women. This was accelerated by the commercial, distribution and financial requirements of large-scale industry, the growth of markets for consumer goods and not least by the considerable expansion of federal government agencies required by New Deal policies and their repercussions at the state level. This increase in female employment was quietly assimilated into the existing segregated occupational

structure which, together with the effects of the increase in marriage
bars, avoided the controversial issues of equality at work.

The Second World War occasioned a substantial increase in the
women in the workforce (from 25 per cent in 1939 to 36 per cent in
1944), three-quarters of which was due to the entry of married
women, but this was easily accommodated as an emergency wartime
measure. While women in the traditional male sector were laid off
to make way for the returning veterans, those in white-collar jobs
in government bureaucracies, the service and sales sectors became
permanent. These sectors became major recruiters of female employees in the late 1940s and 1950s (Gatlin, 1987). The context in
which this quiet revolution occurred militated against an increase in
feminist consciousness and it took more than a decade before its full
repercussions were to unfold.

In Britain the delay in achieving full suffrage till 1928 kept the
momentum for feminist agitation going. Close links with the Labour
Party tended to blur the distinction between legal rights and welfare
provision. In the 1920s, for example, under pressure from the Con-
sultative Committee of Women's Organisations, Parliament passed
twenty laws which improved women's position. This legislation not
only gave women the right of entry to the professions, to sit as JPs and
on juries, to equal rights in divorce, better maintenance settlements
and equal guardianship of children in cases of dispute, but also
improved welfare provision for mothers and infants, unmarried
mothers, civilian widows, school meals and medical inspections in
schools. The publications of feminist organisations like the National
Union of Women's Suffrage Societies (subsequent to the 1928 Equal
Franchise Act), the National Union of Societies for Equal Citizenship
(NUSEC), the Women's Freedom League, and the Six Points Group,
attest to the heated debate on the strategic priorities for women
between equality feminists like Ray Strachey, and the 'new feminists'
led by Eleanor Rathbone (Land, 1990). Yet their respective programmes of reform were barely distinguishable (Smith, 1990) and
reflect the overlap in Britain of feminism with one-nation paternalism
and with socialism.

The much used dichotomisation of the early feminist movement
into equal rights and welfare feminism has its uses for conceptual
clarity and for understanding the divisions within the movement,
but it also has its limitations. In the context of a society still undergoing massive industrialisation, with a class structure and a politics in
flux, with immense wealth living cheek by jowl with ordinary poverty

and profound immiseration, a society coming to terms with the con-sciousness-levelling trauma of the First World War, the aim of improv-ing women's lot inevitably involved improving their lot as wives and mothers. While upper and middle-class women already advantaged by class had benefited most from the legal reforms of the nineteenth-century, working-class women continued to be exploited and abused both at work and in the family. Hence, any feminist reform pro-gramme required both equality and welfare measures. Whatever the criticism of the ideology of 'new feminism', the pragmatic effects of its proposals would as much lessen women's economic dependence on and control by men as they would encourage married women to stay at home. No doubt that is why so many of the so-called equal rights feminists supported them.

Where the differences did emerge more strongly was, as in the States, over employment. Despite the 1919 Sex Disqualification (Removal) Act, the 1920s saw the marriage bar become general practice even in state employment like the civil service, local govern-ment and teaching, with mass dismissals of existing employees. In addition, legislation designed to protect women workers was used by male trade unions to protect male jobs and wages. In 1926 a new Factories Bill proposed further 'protective' restrictions. In alarm and in frustration at the concessionary attitude of NUSEC, a new organi-sation called The Open Door Council (ODC) was set up to campaign exclusively for equal pay, equal status and equal opportunities for women workers. However, its agitation against the Factories Bill was not against protective legislation as such, but against that which was not directly related to maternity, such as shift-work and night-work. Similarly its proposals that the Factories Bill should lift the ban on women working within four weeks of childbirth on the grounds that it was abused on a large scale, was accompanied by a demand for state-paid maternity benefit to enable such women not to work during this period (Banks, 1981). The ODC had little effect because the support for protective legislation and gender-related restrictive practices had its roots in the War Pledge of 1915, by which governments guaranteed to honour male pre-war pay levels and jobs in return for trade union relaxation of obstacles to female employment during the war period.

As the austerity of the 1920s slid into the Depression of the 1930s demands for equal rights seemed increasingly inappropriate. Soaring unemployment reinforced traditional defensive trade union tactics and values. The abject poverty and related physical and mental deterioration of working-class families in the 1930s finally and understandably shifted the energies of feminist organisations firmly behind welfare activism. Their influence on Labour Party policy and consequently on the post-1945 British welfare state with its focus on the family is unmistakable.

It must have been a very dispiriting period for the veterans of the heady days of feminist agitation and mobilisation. On the whole, the organised women's movement in Britain and America was never a mass movement, except for a few years of suffragette activity before 1914, but it did have a highly intelligent, articulate, politically informed following. This support was lost in the inter-war years, partly because it had achieved the goals of many of its middle-class members by 1918 (Pugh, 1992) and partly because the remaining activists were split between the priorities of 'new feminism' and 'equal rights feminism'. The 'new feminist' agenda, precisely because of its pragmatism became incorporated in that of the increasingly interventionist state in the USA and UK throughout the 1930s and later in the post-war welfare settlement, and while very influential in these developments it lost its particular association with feminism *per se* (Wilson, 1980b; Riley, 1983).

In the United States the equal rights strand continued to exert influence in Washington politics through special interest groups, such as the National Women's Party, The League of Women Voters and the National Federation of Business and Professional Women. In Britain, the Fawcett Society, The Women's Freedom League and the Six Point Group survived beyond 1960. However, feminist organisations never regained their earlier levels of support, activity or public prominence and failed to recruit a younger generation of activists. By 1951 the Women's Institute with 7,700 branches and almost half a million members, the smaller Townswomen's Guild and the Women's Co-operative Guild had developed much more in tune with the interests and aspirations of the mass of women and far surpassed the combination of all the feminist organisations.

It is common for post-1960s feminists to blame this decline of organised feminism on 'new feminism' for selling-out to familialism (Banks, 1981; Jeffreys, 1985), but it really does seem that there were no troups to mobilise, a fact that the failure of alternative conceptions and organisations to find a following appears to bear out. The history of feminism is inseparable from the history of the family. For our radical forebears, at least until the inter-war years, emancipation lay in combining personal development, including a career, with family life, while the majority of women believed and felt that women's primary commitment was to children, home and family and defined their interests in relation to that commitment, though this co-existed with strong support for achieving legislative and social equality for women. Not to recognise the specific material, psychological and ideological conditions which set the parameters for the range of questions, issues and action in a particular historical period and to judge them by reference to those of the present day, is a failure of historical imagination and does an injustice to the struggles of women in the past.

2

Sex, the Nuclear Family and Its Radical Opposition

Sex and danger

Much has been written about the profound ambivalence toward sex in the nineteenth-century (Harrison, 1977; Foucault, 1979; Walkowitz, 1980, 1992; Weeks, 1981; Mort, 1987; Coontz, 1988; Bland, 1995). Part of the making of the bourgeois classes was achieved by a cultural distancing from the sexual profligacy of both the aristocracy and the 'dangerous' classes. Hence, a mark of 'respectability' was the domestication of sex in its functional role in reproduction within the family sanctified by religion (Degler, 1980; Gorham, 1982; Rendall, 1985; Smart, 1992). Much has been made of the privatisation of family life and its separation from the world of business, but while true in terms of a general economic and cultural trend it can be overstated and it can obscure the very important way in which the middle-class family traversed the public–private divide. The elaborate rituals of social interaction and etiquette orchestrated by middle-class women provided the social networks for business and professional contacts as well as the marriage circles whereby the hard-earned fruits of middle-class efforts at social improvement and respectability could be consolidated. Status and respectability in both business and social circles, then, depended on middle-class women. Such respectability, however, was precarious, always threatened by potential financial ruin or private scandal. Of the two the latter was the least redeemable since it invariably signalled moral degeneracy.

The conception of sex as dangerous to social order as well as to individual welfare has a long history in Christian theology and in folk belief. Its most prominent symbolic representation is the Garden of

Eden in which carnal knowledge is already present but forbidden in the Tree of Knowledge. It is Woman, Eve, who is the cause of the Fall of mankind from the grace of the Father God, and the banishment from this primeval innocence and purity when, tempted by the Snake, she herself transgresses by eating the fruit of the Tree and tempts Man, Adam, into the original sin with her. This story provides for one strand in Judeo-Christian patriarchy in which the archetype of woman is one associated with primitive sensuality, lack of judgment and self-constraint and a dangerous capacity to seduce men from reason and obedience to the Law. Significantly, the popular nineteenth-century term for a prostitute was a 'fallen woman'.

However, there is a different story in Christianity which provides for another female archetype – the virgin mother, pure, unsullied by male sexual passion, chosen to give birth to and raise the Son of God. Further, the two archetypes, both significantly called Mary – Mary Magdalen, the fallen woman forgiven and 'reclaimed' by Christ, and Mary the Madonna – appear together at Christ's Crucifixion at the hands of men, and it is to them that he reveals himself after he has risen from the dead. By the sixteenth-century, the veneration of female purity and piety and the associated maternal virtues became institutionalised in the 'cult of the Madonna'. And though it was rejected by the Protestant sects along with all the other 'trappings of Papist idolatry', the theme of female virtue persists in their greater stress on spiritual equality.

Further elements in this particular discourse of sexuality were added by eighteenth-century Enlightenment thinking in which rationality and science are opposed to superstition, tradition and intuition as a basis for the ordering of both the natural and the social world. We have already seen how these ideas fed into the bourgeois challenge to aristocratic patriarchy and contributed to subsequent religious, political and cultural radicalism. However, in the process of the Enlightenment project to understand, control and harness the laws of nature to the improvement of mankind, the male sex became identified with Science and Culture, the female with its object, Nature. While the nineteenth-century Romantic movement rebelled against what was seen as the sterile scienticism of technological progress, the destruction of community values and their replacement with calculating individualism, its celebration of the potentially disruptive but essentially creative powers of Nature, human intuition and passion, did little to dislodge the gender dichotomy embedded in the terms of the discourse though it did attempt to redress the balance between them.

In the ambivalences and contradictions of these discourses, was the space for feminists to retell the history of female subordination and to construct a positive identity for womanhood. Bland (1995) describes how nineteenth-century feminists drew upon popular knowledge and experience of male behaviour to revise the narrative with man cast as the sexual predator and seducer, and woman as victim of male lust and sexual excesses. In place of the technical rationality of science and business, they posed the superiority of a moral rationality of constraint and altruism and, drawing on both the madonna theme in religion and evolutionary instinct theory, claimed women to be uniquely endowed with the latter as a consequence of their role as mothers. Hence, in a double reversal, Nature became associated with the essential prere-quisite of reason – self-control – and united with Culture – that which safeguards social and moral order; the association of woman with Nature is converted into a supreme advantage providing her with a civilising mission on behalf of society, while man becomes the epitome of Non-Reason, the carrier of atavistic traits from a primitive past.

The construction of womanhood that challenges bourgeois patri-archy, that enhances women's status within the family and establishes a public voice and role for women, however, hangs on women living up to the strict sexual morality enshrined in the term 'social purity'. Since so much depended on 'respectability' there was no leeway for error. Women themselves were the fiercest guardians of the moral code, and the penalties for transgression were very severe, underlined by the outcast figures of the age – the Unmarried Mother, the Divorced Woman and above all the Prostitute. The grounding of women's new status in 'spiritual motherhood' also led to what nowa-days seems a surprising general hostility toward contraception among feminists. Although part of the reform of men and family life included an end to 'involuntary motherhood', the means by which this was to be achieved had to be supportive of the moral rationality of sex and appropriate to the moral economy of sex – that is, by continence. By severing the link between sex and procreation, artificial contraceptive devices undermined the basis of women's moral superiority and their attempts to retrain men to think of sex as spiritual rather than physical union. More pragmatically, contraception deprived women, in an age when husbands had undisputed conjugal rights, of good reason to reject their nightly advances (McLaren, 1978; Gordon, 1982; Banks, 1986; Pfeffer, 1993; Bland, 1995). Add to this the socialist suspicion of birth control, linked as it was (incorrectly) with Malthus, whose theories of population blamed working-class birth rates and welfare relief for poverty and unemployment rather than the vagaries of the capitalist economic system, and it is perhaps less surprising that it was not until the 1930s that artificial contraception became respectable and assimilated into public population and health policies.

The puritanical prurient repugnance of sex apparently shared by many nineteenth-century women, feminist and otherwise, however, also had other determinants. Prostitution was widespread and its male clients were drawn from all social classes, with the consequence that venereal disease was both common and classless, as husbands passed it to wives with fearful consequences for them and their children. There were attempts to follow European examples and regulate the trade, such as the UK Contagious Diseases Acts in the 1860s and the US experiments in the city of St Louis in the 1870s. However, these were short-lived as a result of the social purity counter-campaigns led by leading feminists like Josephine Butler and the American Frances Willard. They argued that regulation condoned vice and punished women rather than men without whose custom the trade would not exist. In any case men were not subject to medical inspection and treatment and hence were still at large to spread the very diseases regulation was meant to control (Degler, 1980; Weeks, 1981; Bland, 1995; Jeffreys, 1995).

One should also remember that sex for most women meant conception, which until the 1930s carried the threat of death for women of all social classes. Between 1838 and 1935, in spite of improvements in medical knowledge, in general health, in overall mortality and in infant mortality, the maternal death rate in England and Wales remained constant at around 4.7 per thousand live births (Dally, 1982). Today it is about 20 per 100,000 live births (Orton and Fry, 1995).

As well as the fear of their own death, women were likely to experience the grief of several miscarriages, stillbirths and the death of at least one child. In the eighteenth-century only 25 babies out of every hundred live births were likely to survive their first birthday, and though this situation improved dramatically by the late nineteenth-century, still in 1885 sixteen babies out of every hundred died in the first year compared with 0.61 in England and Wales in 1996. In addition many women suffered the life-time effects of multiple pregnancies, poor gynaecological and obstetric care and, amongst the poor, abortions which produced morbidity rates inconceivable today. For poor women these sufferings were aggravated by meagre diets lacking nutrition and by hard heavy housework in primitive, damp and insanitary conditions. Tuberculosis was rife. It would be surprising if the material realities of the consequences of sexual life did not contribute to women's endeavours to reduce the amount to which they were subjected to it by their husbands.

So great was the hegemony of marriage in the context of sex that the possibility of homosexual relationships for women as an alternative was simply unthinkable. Romantic friendships between women were very common and part of the social conventions of a society where there was a strict separation of the sexes before marriage. Relationships such as those described in Thompson's *Dear Girl* (1987) included love letters, gifts, terms and gestures of endearment, extended visits and shared vacations, which today might suggest a lesbian attachment. However, with few exceptions, they do not appear to have been understood in these terms either by the participants or by their peers, partly perhaps because sex and sexual feelings were by definition heterosexual and partly because female homosexual behaviour had no legal category and hence was unregulated. It may well have been difficult for women to differentiate their (lesbian) repugnance of heterosexual sex with men from that expressed by many women of the period.

The only other alternative to conventional marriage and family life was celibacy. Certainly for the talented, well-connected and ambitious, celibacy or spinsterhood was an attractive option, as is witnessed by the reluctance of some famous women, such as Florence Nightingale, Elizabeth Blackwell, the first American woman doctor, Jane Addams, founder of the settlement movement in the USA, and Beatrice Potter (later Webb) to accept proposals of marriage. There were certainly many single women during the period, but how many chose this status in preference to marriage and how many were constitutive of the considerable 'surplus' of women consequent upon the higher mortality rate among infant boys, male emigration which from Britain ran at about 250,00 per year before 1914, and the casualties of war, is a matter of speculation. The alternatives to marriage, then, were few, and the appeal of celibacy limited to the more aspiring and financially independent among women.

There is little evidence, therefore, of any great desire on the part of most women inside and outside the women's movement for emancipation in sexual matters. However, in the early twentieth-century such an interest did develop in a group of feminists that clustered round the avant-garde thinkers in the new science of sex. The ideas of Freud, Magnus Hirschfeld, Havelock Ellis and Edward Carpenter were welcomed as legitimating the right to sexual pleasure for women and questioning the standard medical view of homosexuality as moral depravity. In Britain the new weekly feminist journal, the *Freewoman*, first published in 1911, created much controversy among feminist circles because of the sexual explicitness of some of its articles. The paper also spawned Freewoman discussion circles in a number of cities and generated a much freer discussion of hitherto taboo subjects. Nevertheless, Bland's fascinating study (1995) of feminist engagement with sexual morality in this period indicates that even these radical women appear to reify discussions about sexual pleasure for women into rather speculative spiritual experiences and conceive of passion as being constitutive of mind and soul rather than of physical sensation. There were few who would risk social exclusion and ostracism by living out in practice some of the radical ideas of sexual emancipation.

Mutual conjugal satisfaction and companionate marriage

The ideas of the sexologists gained ground in the inter-war years with the establishment in 1928 of the World League for Sexual Reform and in America the first systematic social surveys on sexual behaviour, anticipated by the small-scale Mosher Survey between 1892 and 1920 which tapped the experiences of American middle-class women born before 1870 and registered general disappointment and the dulling effect of the fear of pregnancy on their sexual interest. Female sexual pleasure as a component of healthy marriages coupled with an emphasis on the need for male restraint gained ground in mainstream medical discourses. Medical journals and advice for the layperson increasingly blamed husbands' failures to consider their wives' feelings and sexual rhythms for the latter's reported frigidity or lack of interest in sexual relations, and the role that positive sexual relations could play in successful marriage became a frequent topic of women's magazines of the time (Weeks, 1981; Pugh, 1992).

This new emphasis on mutual conjugal satisfaction enabled feminists and birth controllers like Marie Stopes in Britain and Margaret Sanger in America to make artificial contraception respectable first among the middle classes but increasingly among the working poor by their positive emphasis on 'voluntary motherhood' and 'family planning' as part of the joys of mutual enjoyment of non-procreational sex.

It is likely that the other impetus for the growing interest in family limitation was the dramatic drop in infant mortality after 1900 ensuring that most children survived, at the same time as compulsory schooling rendered them dependent on their parents for longer and, therefore, less an economic asset than a burden. It is clear from the decline in the birthrate from the 1870s that the middle classes had been limiting their families, but this was also noticable among manual workers by the 1920s, largely through natural methods and reduced frequency of coitus (Degler, 1980; Gittens, 1982). The promotion of the sheath to soldiers in the First World War to protect against VD had done much to reduce prejudice among working men, and the interwar years saw an increasing interest in mechanical methods. The feminist birth controllers always located their work in the context of enhancing Christian marriage and protecting the health of women and children, rather than sexual freedom, and were against any extension to the unmarried. This morally conservative approach finally won over the British Medical Association and the Church of England in 1930, and in the same year Maternity and Child Welfare centres were allowed to give contraceptive advice to married women on request.

This new concern for wives' satisfaction in marital sex completed the success of the strategy of enhancing women's status through increasing that of motherhood and domesticity resulting in the ideal of 'companionate marriage'. Feminist historians are divided on this strategy for the goal of feminism. Sheila Jeffreys (1985; 1995) and Margaret Jackson (1994), for example, believe that the sexology was a negative influence on feminism, in that it deflected feminists from recognising that the root of women's subordination lay not in the particular external framework of marriage but in men's sexual ownership of women within it. In their view, sexology shored up male authority in the face of feminist challenge by achieving 'women's willing subjection to male authority through sexual pleasure', and the hostility to spinsterhood, celibacy and lesbianism should be seen in this light (Jeffreys, 1995, p.203). It is certainly the case that some feminists of the period, like Christabel Pankhurst, did view non-marriage as a form of resistance by women against the sex slavery of marriage.

By contrast, other contemporary feminist historians (Smith-Rosenburg, 1985; Bland, 1995) stress the progressive aspects of sexology for the development of women's ownership of their own sexual feelings and identity. They also note that many of its practitioners were strongly supportive of feminist ideas, and were tolerant of homosexuality – indeed some were homosexual themselves. They argue that with all the limitations of its evolutionary assumptions about a natural heterosexuality and instinct-based behaviour, the discourse of sexology provided a public language for sex, sexuality and sexual relations and the right for women to engage in the debates. It is somewhat ironic that prostitution, which seemed resistant to all the purity campaigns and the volunteer women vice vigilantes, decreased (dramatically from the 1920s) co-incidental with the rise in marriage rates, earlier marriage, an increase in pre-marital sexual activity and the greater endorsement of wives' sexual pleasure.

What in the nineteenth-century has been referred to as a polarity between social purity and sexual reform has its contemporary equivalent in the battle lines to define 'true feminism' around not dissimilar issues: pornography, prostitution, sexual preferences and practices, celibacy, motherhood, the family. Hence, the debate between feminist historians is not merely academic but is fired by current highly charged disagreements between feminists. It is perhaps unfortunate that such principled polarities tend to lead to exaggeration of the distance between the stances rather than the exploration of the inter-relatedness of the issues. Nor do such polarities contribute to positive perceptions of feminism by women outside it, who after all are intended to be the beneficiaries of the movement.

The hegemony of the nuclear family

However interesting, too much can be made of the sexual question in the normalisation of the nuclear family. There are other material factors which some historians believe to have more direct causal effects, in particular the development of domestic consumption as a driver in the economies of America and Britain (Weeks, 1981; Degler, 1980; Gittens, 1982; Clark, 1991; Pugh, 1992; Clarke, 1996; Horrell and Humphries, 1997; Creighton, 1999). Despite the economic downturn in the early 1920s and the slump of the 1930s, standards of living of those in work improved throughout the period, through the combination of a real increase in wages and social welfare and a small redistribution of income via taxation. A major contributor to better living conditions was the massive municipal and private house-building programme of the 1920s and 30s with much improved building standards and density specifications. New suburbs were facilitated by improved urban transport and wired up to the new electric network. These improved homes and their young family-building occupiers were prime targets for the expanding consumer goods industries for home furnishing and domestic equipment, promoted by the expanded number of women's magazines elevating housework into 'home management'.

Along with this went DIY home improvements, family seaside holidays and family leisure pursuits. Gittens's research (1982), which suggests that a critical factor in family limitation was the greater exposure of young single women to new ideas about sex and marital relations occasioned by their employment in urban office and factory work, may also be usefully applied to their exposure to patterns of individual consumption. This pre-marital independence and enjoyment of fashion, cinema, and dancing may well have paved the way for both an increase in marital role partnership (albeit on the basis of the traditional division of domestic labour) and in home consumerism (Rowbotham 1997). It is important to remember that this prosperity was relative and hardly touched substantial numbers of the families of casual, unskilled workers in declining sectors of the economy and those whose adult members were unable to work because of sickness, age, disability or because of domestic and caring responsibilities. Certain state benefits, such as medical services, accrued only to workers who paid contributions; in effect this meant that women and children were not covered.

While the new housing estates provided much healthier, cleaner and spacious environments, they weakened older kinship, neighbourhood and employment-based communities, and hence, in what Lasch has called the 'suburbanisation of the American soul' (1997, p.94), shifted the locus of material, psychological and social support for individuals to conjugal partners and immediate family members. The political solidarities that were part of the older extended and denser social relationships were already weakened by industrial defeats, like the 1926 General Strike in Britain, the failure of the Socialist Party in the USA and the loss of British radicalism with the incorporation of the Labour Party into the British political system. Always stronger in America, individual social mobility increasingly replaced solidaristic class aspirations and provided greater motivation to invest in children: hence the susceptibility of parents to the new child guidance advice emanating from the growing paediatric professionals and developmental psychologists and popularised by women's magazines.

The Second World War occasioned the break-up of many families by the mobilisation of men for military service, and, in Britain, by the mass evacuation of children from the cities to remote parts of the country and indeed abroad to Canada and Australia, against the wishes of at least half the mothers and causing considerable unhappiness to the children (Mass Observation, 1940, cited in Pugh, 1992). With the possible exception of young single women, the assumption that the war brought freedom and fun for women is not warranted. It was an extended period of misery for many in Britain. Apart from coping with the deaths of and severe injury to their menfolk, the women suffered civilian bombing, destruction and damage to their homes, power cuts, rising prices, food shortages and rationing. Many were conscripted, often providing support for the front-line troops as medical, catering and clerical staff; those who were exempt were directed to war work often in the grinding and hazardous munitions factories. Their reaction to the declaration of peace was a general embrace of marriage, children and family life.

The fear of longer-term disruption to stable family life by the war is reflected in key policy documents of the period: the Beveridge Report (1942), the Royal Commission on Equal Pay (1946) and the Royal Commission on Population (1949). In the immediate aftermath of the war, most of the measures to assist mothers to work outside the home were dismantled. The post-war welfare state in Britain and the American social welfare programmes were predicated on a model of the nuclear family with breadwinner father and housewife mother, and on full employment. There was a predictable marriage boom followed by an equally predictable baby boom in 1946–8, though despite government propaganda there was no return to large families. These post-war restorative inclinations were reinforced by medical opinion. For example, the famous World Health Organisation Report, *Maternal Care and Mental Health*, by Dr John Bowlby (1951), published as *Child Care and the Growth of Love* (Bowlby 1953), which studied the effects of maternal separation on wartime refugee and evacuee children and those in long-term institutional care, was widely disseminated by radio, newspapers, women's magazines and in the training of childcare professionals. The popularisers sometimes interpreted the results as evidence that mothers should provide 24-hour care of their children if they were not to end up as neurotic or psychotic delinquents and lifetime criminals.

Riley (1983) has demonstrated that, nevertheless, there was no conspiracy between the state and psychology to reimpose conditions of authoritarian patriarchy and send women back to the home. First, the views of Bowlby (1953) and Winnicott (1957) were genuinely popular with many women who had experienced the traditional middle-class upbringing of nannies and boarding schools or the brutal separation occasioned by evacuation, precisely because their recommendations were actually liberal and permissive and stood in stark contrast to the authoritarian, rigid, conservative child-rearing regimes in which they had been brought up. Indeed I rather agree with Wilson's view (Wilson, 1980b) that the psychoanalytically oriented paediatric advice was attractive because it endorsed pleasure and enjoyment after a decade or so of puritan self-denial, frugality and duty. As Wilson says, whereas this literature has been read by feminists 'as a literature of punishment and the repression of women', it was actually intended as 'a literature of pleasure (which) set about enhancing the joys of motherhood and the intensity of the marital orgasm' (p.190).

Secondly, there were counter-tendencies in national needs: the Economic Survey (1947) reported chronic labour shortages in the British post-war national reconstruction and launched a campaign to persuade women into the labour force, albeit on a temporary basis (Wilson, 1980b). In fact, full employment and rising real wages furnished the means to restart and accelerate pre-war domestic consumerism resulting in the economic boom of the 1950s and 60s, and rising 'affluence'. Better housing with a bath and inside lavatory continued to be a priority together with new labour saving devices for the home. But increasingly fridges, telephones, television sets and even the motor car came within the reach of skilled manual workers (Zweig, 1961). Once again women as the main driver of household budgets were the targets for sales. The demand for continuing improvements to the material environment of the home and opportunities for children outran the capacity of the husband's pay packet, while the supply of jobs in the light manufacturing industries, insurance, finance and commerce and government service provided the opportunity for married women to make up the deficit.

The significant difference in women's employment in this period is that it included a much wider range of social strata and a growing proportion of married women. Perversely, the job opportunities for women deprived domestic service of its traditional source of cheap labour, raised the demand for labour-saving domestic products among middle-class women and tempted some of them into employment to help pay for them. At the same time, the pattern of women's employment for the majority stayed much the same: part-time, temporary and low paid. While the phenomenon of working mothers breaks with traditional assumptions of the desirability of the non-working wife, it cannot be interpreted as evidence of feminist aspirations of independence. Several surveys of the 1940s and 50s (Thomas, 1948; Zweig, 1952; Myrdal and Klein, 1956; Hubback, 1957; Smith, 1961; Jephcott *et al.*, 1962; Lebergott, 1964; Strober, 1977) report that American and British women worked because they wanted to improve the standard of living of their families, not because of feminist aspirations of independence, and accordingly they arranged their work to fit round phases of their family life and their domestic responsibilities. The increased labour market participation of women, then, did not undermine either the ideal or the practice of companionate marriage, at least at this time.

Finch and Summerfield (1991) are right to remind us that neither the pattern of prosperity nor that of companionate marriage was uniform across Britain, citing studies of slum conditions and poverty where authoritarian patriarchal relations prevailed, and certainly evidence from the United States would reinforce this caution (Galbraith, 1958; Harrington, 1963). There were distinctive geographical, occupational, cultural and social strata differences which cut across both the experience of post-war economic prosperity and related consumer boom, and the quality of relations between men and women. Nevertheless it seems incontrovertible that among the younger generations, marriages do become more companionable and families more child-centred during this period. Challenges to this conclusion tend to rest on an interpretation of 'companionable marriage' as meaning one of equal partnership or symmetry of employment and domestic roles, but this would have been largely unthinkable by the vast majority of men and women. The kind of marriage idealised in romantic fiction, promoted by churches, health professionals and welfare workers, counselled by the 'agony aunts' of women's magazines and hoped for by women, was one based on 'intimacy', that is mutual understanding, communication and support, joint leisure activities and sexual exclusivity. The *increase* in general disapproval among *both* sexes of extra-marital affairs in both the USA and the UK during this period reflects this orientation (Richards and Elliott, 1991; Scott, 1998).

The social science literature of the time confirmed the arrival across the social classes of the modern, privatised, child-centred family. In the view of prominent American sociologists of the functionalist school (Ogburn and Nimkoff, 1955; Parsons and Bales, 1956; Goode, 1964), this development was functionally related to the maturing of industrial society, the occupational structure of which required the individualisation of employment based on specialist knowledge, personal competence, geographical and social mobility. This undermined traditional, extended kinship systems based on the authority of elder males, ascribed role structures and on group allegiance. In the process of modernisation, they argue, the family loses its economic, educative and political function to other collective organisations, becoming more specialised in terms of the socialisation of children and meeting the needs of adult personalities. Because the status and income of the family is dependent on the occupational position of adult breadwinners, yet child-rearing requires a relatively long period of responsible nurturing, there is a differentiation of functions and roles within the family between the conjugal couple. At the same time the instrumentality and anonymity of much modern work increases the importance of positive emotional relations at home, hence a greater closeness between husbands and wives. The contemporary sociologist, Anthony Giddens, with even greater hindsight has described this process as the 'transformation of intimacy in which the relations between the sexes become increasingly characterised by a trend toward a "pure relationship"', that is 'a situation where a social relation is entered into for its own sake, for what can be derived by each person from a sustained association with another' (1992, p.58). Empirical studies confirmed this shift across the social classes (Young and Willmott, 1957; Willmott and Young, 1960; Bott, 1957; Fletcher, 1962; Gavron, 1966). The Church of England Moral Welfare Council was so convinced that it concluded that 'the modern family is in some ways in a stronger position than it has been at any period in our history of which we have knowledge' (cited in Fletcher, 1962, p.17).

Flaws in the domestic bliss

However, despite this optimism, there were warning notes. The Report of the Royal Commission on Marriage and Divorce in 1956, while approving of the new partnership in marriage in principle, nevertheless saw in spouses' raised expectations a potential source of stress. Concern about rising divorce rates (from 1.6 per cent in 1937 to 6.7 per cent in 1954 – very low by today's rates!) led others in influential positions in the Church, the social work, educational and medical professions to be more pessimistic, causally linking divorce, the changing position of women and the growth of the welfare state with crime, delinquency and general social indiscipline.

Even the sociological pundits of the modern family registered potential strains. As early as 1942 Parsons warned that the segregation of gender roles increases strain in the family 'since it deprives the wife of her role as a partner in a common enterprise . . . and leaves [her] a set of utilitarian functions in the management of the household which may be considered a kind of "pseudo"-occupation' (Parsons, 1942c; 1954, p.95), a role that had diminished in importance 'to the point where it scarcely approaches a full-time occupation for a vigorous person' (p.98). The other side of Gavron's (1966) findings of marital closeness is the isolation and frustration experienced by the house-bound young mothers in her sample, while Fletcher (1962) acknow-ledged that the family 'can all too easily become a narrow, self-contained little den in which people suffocate each other with their possessive, stagnant and petty emotions' (pp.135–6).

In America, where the advancement of women was more devel-oped, these contradictions were more pronounced. In the early 1960s a mysterious illness afflicting women across the USA reached epi-demic proportions. The symptoms were minor disorders of the skin, digestion, sleeping patterns and behaviour, psychosomatic in nature. It was dubbed 'housewife's fatigue' by medical practitioners as its victims were otherwise healthy wives and mothers of comfortable America. This phenomenon was investigated by an ex-researcher turned journalist, housewife–mother, called Betty Friedan who pub-lished her conclusions in *The Feminine Mystique*, in 1963. The book became an international bestseller and the first major feminist text of the post-war period. Friedan went on to become a founder member and President of what is still the most important women's organisa-tion in the USA, the National Organisation of Women (NOW).

For Friedan, the cause of the 'housewife's fatigue' was the submer-sion of women's identity in that of wife and mother. She argues that while the feminists of the late nineteenth-century and early twentieth-century had made considerable headway in eradicating the formal obstacles to women's equal participation with men, this had been halted in the 1940s and the post-war period by a backlash of tradi-tional male prejudice given respectability by two major intellectual forces in the USA – Freudianism and functionalism. Through their popularisers in the education, health and welfare professions, the mass media and the advertising industry, these two ideologies are said to have persuaded the American public that freedom is bad for women. (As we shall see, these two forces recur as twin evil genii in much of the feminist writing which followed.) Hence, young women still chose to turn their backs on freedom. Such is the power of the feminine mystique, that women are terrified of growing up: 'those who choose the path of "feminine adjustment" – evading this terror by marrying at eighteen, losing themselves in having babies and the details of house-keeping – are simply refusing to grow up, to face the question of their own identity' (Friedan, 1965, p.67).

The detrimental effects of the feminine mystique go far beyond the ill-health and incapacitation that it wreaks on women: women seeking self-realisation vicariously through others, emasculate husbands and induce dependence and emotional infantilism in children, destroying their capacity for fulfilment. In Friedan's view, therefore, it has serious repercussions for the whole American nation.

In the midst of what appears to be the conformist complacency of the 1950s and 1960s, therefore, there were already undercurrents of tensions in and disaffection with family life. These were to explode in the women's liberation movement born of women's engagement and disillusionment with the radical Left student movements of the late 1960s.

Rebellious youth and the sexual revolution

It is generally recognised that some qualitative break – a cultural revolution – occurred in western culture in the 1960s. Closely identi-fied with youth, it expressed itself in symbolic expressions of rebellion in dress, music, manners and ideas. Of course in retrospect there are clear precedents such as the bobby-sox revolt against school uniform in America in the 1940s, and the rock'n'roll craze which swept across Europe from America in the 1950s. But it was in the 1960s that youth became radically marked off from adults, creating a specific status group with a superficially classless identity.

Arguably the most significant thing about youth was sheer num-bers: by the early 1960s there were 20 per cent more young people in the population than in the previous two decades. With a booming economy, they constituted a vast new consumer market and a new social group without clear markers as to their position in society and without an immediate stake in their parents' world. These new free-doms coalesced around sex as a symbol and an activity, and along with its commercialisation both as an industry with its own products and services and as a marketing device to sell other commodities, justifies the attribution of 'sexual revolution' to describe an important feature of this period. The greater knowledge and availability of contraceptive devices, including the new 'Pill', made the fear of pregnancy a less inhibiting factor and parental condemnation less effective in decisions about pre-marital sex. It was finally possible to separate sex from reproduction, and to an increasing degree, to separate sexual behaviour from parental control.

Sexual freedom was one aspect of the celebration of pleasure, spontaneity and living for today in the youth counter-culture (Gouldner, 1971). Any means which enhanced this state – music, dancing, sex, alcohol, drugs – were embraced wholeheartedly. It is very doubtful that the majority of the young actually lived out the 'permissive' culture (Schofield, 1973; Alston and Tucker, 1983). However, the fantasies of the older generation did not allow for a separation between the symbolic and behavioural expression of the cult of freedom. What outraged was the hedonism which violated the work ethic of diligence, respectability and self-restraint in which they had been raised.

Another factor was the dramatic increase in the number of students as a result of government-sponsored educational expansion. New universities and colleges were built and existing ones expanded, and in Britain, free tuition and a statutory means-tested maintenance grant scheme introduced. Among the student population, rebellion became politicised.

A generation brought up in the moral aftermath of the horrors of state fascism and strongly socialised into a democratic ideology which emphasised individual rights, social justice, equality of opportunity and open government, the students reacted against what they saw as the hypocrisy of liberal democratic *realpolitik* and authoritarian underpinnings. The oppression of blacks and Hispanics in America was linked to oppression in the Third World; the Civil Rights Movement identified with the post-war liberation struggles of developing countries – the French colonial war in Algeria and the collaboration of the western allies in the Vietnam war. In 1964 large numbers of white American students from the northern states, flooded into the southern states to assist the largely black civil rights movement. The radicalised student movement spread to and inspired students in Britain and Europe. The students' extension of politics to 'extra-parliamentary' forms and 'direct action' was a reaction to what they saw as the democratic sham of western states. However, it appeared to the Establishment as unconstitutional, illegitimate and potentially violent, especially when they aligned themselves with other more serious and fundamental sections of the population, such as the black radical militants in America and the French proletariat in Paris where the combination almost brought down the de Gaulle government in 1968 (Hobsbawm, 1977; Posner, 1970).

Marxism and Freudianism as revolutionary inspiration

The ideology of the student movement is probably best characterised as 'Left Liberationism'. Unlike previous generations, these young rebels were largely unattached to the established Left parties. Their critique of orthodox Marxism, which was blamed for the degeneracy of socialism in both the East and the West, and the emergence of 'the New Left' in all the major advanced western societies, provided the most exciting intellectual current of the period and the most potent political analysis (Fisk, 1970; Jupp, 1970).

In Britain, *New Left Review* and its publishing house, New Left Books, became a major reference point for radicals in the English-speaking world and for the dissemination of the work of European Marxists, both classical and contemporary. This added to the general and exaggerated impression of the radical movement as a coherent international insurgency organisation, rather than primarily an international network of radical intellectuals and scholars turned activists, often in dispute with each other. *NLR* acted as a catalyst for the subsequent debates between the humanist Hegelian Marxism developed from the Frankfurt, Sartrean and Lukacsian schools on the one hand, and the scientific structural Marxism of Althusser and his followers on the other. The space that opened up for the theoretical integration of psychology, linguistics and cultural theory into the discourses of politics, economics and sociology, was decisive in the development of 'post-modern' theory, which was to become the new intellectual orthodoxy by the end of the twentieth-century.

The United States with a much less indigenous socialist tradition, in the sense of a Left theoretical Establishment, a Left political infrastructure or a mass-based socialist party, was inherently more eclectic in what it absorbed in its radical moment. The principal radicalising influence came from the wave of predominantly Jewish émigré intellectuals who escaped from Nazi persecution in Europe, in particular the arrival in America in 1935 of the scholars of the Frankfurt school of Marxism. Little known at the time, and suppressed during the McCarthy era, the work of Adorno, Horkheimer, Fromm and Marcuse achieved a new eminence in the 1960s when their analysis of totalitarian regimes based on a synthesis of psychoanalysis and Marxism seemed relevant to the imperialist-capitalist states of the West. In particular the views of Wilhelm Reich became extremely popular in the 1960s. His political credentials were impeccable in terms of the criteria of the era: an isolated, eccentric figure, he had antagonised both the leadership of the traditional Left and the psychoanalytic Establishment in Europe.

In his essay, 'The Imposition of Sexual Morality' (1932; 1972), Reich follows Freud in identifying libidinal energy as the universal motivator of human action, but locates it as an element of the Marxist 'base', that is part of the material conditions for life. However, against Freud, Reich argues that the restriction of sexual pleasure is not a condition for the development of 'civilisation', but comes into force only with specific historical conditions, namely the development of private property and the patriarchal family. It is the suppression of natural sexual gratification, its control in the limited legitimated outlets of monogamous marriage and the resultant redirection or 'sublimation' of libidinal energies into socially acceptable channels which provides the key to power over individuals. On the one hand it institutes obedience to authority through internal self-discipline derived from fear, guilt and shame; on the other it sets free psychic interests for a certain form of economic activity, that is the desire to accumulate. Thus the spirit of capitalism developed at the expense of genital gratification.

The family is the mechanism for the integration of cultural demands into the individual psyche, and had become a veritable factory for authoritarian ideologies and conservative personality structures. The claustrophobic, emotionally incestuous bourgeois family is the cause of mass neurosis of which the rise of fascism is only a critical instance. Reich believed that it was possible to break through this repression through sexual liberation. His therapeutic practice was designed to contribute to this by loosening what he referred to as 'character armour' (resistances) to allow for the release of the tension of repressed sexual energy of the body, only fully discharged through orgasm.

Reich's attention to the interaction of the authoritarianism of public and private life, his belief in the efficacy of personal struggle to break out of the straitjacket of repression, and his famous Sex-Pol Clinics for communist youth, appealed to the libertarian, anarchistic, hedonistic tendencies of radical youth of the 1960s. Reich appeared to be speaking directly to them, even to be predicting their own emergence:

Sexual repression has the effect of making young people submissive to adults in a characterological sense, but at the same time, it brings about their sexual rebellion. This rebellion becomes a powerful force in the social movement when it becomes conscious and finds a nexus with the proletarian movement underpinning capitalism. (Reich, 1932; 1972, p.246)

This focus among American radicals on the ways in which social institutions destroy personal autonomy and secure passive acceptance of the status quo, coincided with that of the European Left influenced by existentialism, concerned with the loss of authenticity brought about by the alienating forces of modern society. The importance of sexuality is that it stands proxy for the creative essence of humanity crushed by the economic, political and social developments of the modern world. The radicals shared a common conception of human nature as endowed with a free consciousness rendered unfree and impotent by the social institutions of modern society. Nature is seen as their opposite: spontaneous, uncontrolled, fecund, authentic and thus all things associated with it were espoused. The oppositional stance of the counter-culture involved an immersion in the physical, the sensual, the sexual, but whatever the actual practice, in principle the rationale was that by breaking through the barriers of repression one could get in touch with the inner core of creativity – the rebellion of the liberated individual against the modern Leviathan.

Despite the Freudian influence on the students' gurus, Freud himself was generally rejected as reactionary because it was claimed that he exposed the operations of repression so as to devise an effective therapy to reinforce them. One reason for this interpretation was that most people came into contact with his work through that of his popularisers, many of whom, especially in the United States, became very prosperous by joining the apparatuses of 'social adjustment'. The libertarians believed that while Freud had demonstrated how the repression of sexuality lay at the heart of Civilisation, it was possible to go directly to that sexuality in us all and embrace it; no need for the analyst or transference.

The more fundamental reason why Freud is rejected is because his theory of the unconscious broke with the concept of the unitary Subject, self-conscious and self-reflecting, the author of his acts, which has dominated Western thought since the eighteenth-century. However revolutionary the 1960s radicals were in many respects, they never challenged this classic model of the freely choosing, autonomous, rational individual which lies at the very heart of the liberalism they so detested. Indeed their objection was that it had been distorted, repressed and obscured by modern society and that the revolutionary task was to reconstruct a society in which 'social organisation will be made consistent with the needs of the "free agent"' (Hirst and Woolley, 1982, p.132).

Apart from the empirical problems of an unregulated social life, there are logical contradictions which make this position untenable. On the one hand, the essence of human nature is said to be existential freedom: the free human consciousness. Yet, on the other hand, in modern society that consciousness has been suppressed by a conspiracy of megalomaniac institutions and replaced by a false consciousness amenable to manipulation. First, how is it possible for a free subjectivity to be brainwashed to such an extent that it is unaware of its own freedom? The assertion of free will means that the individual must have *chosen* to be dominated. Secondly, once having acquired the imposed (false) consciousness, how is the individual capable of throwing it off?

It is in the pursuit of recovering this original, pre-given, pre-social individual through liberating sexuality from the straitjacket of convention, that conventional morality and the family became singled out as being the linchpin of political and personal enslavement and thus the main targets for political invective and personal intervention. In the floodtide of the search for personal identity, expressive authenticity and individual freedom through the liberation of the sensual essence of human beings, the family was seen to be the microcosm of the authoritarian, hierarchical, tradition-bound conformism of the larger society. By comparison with the State, the Capitalist Economy and the Military Machine, it was a structure of domination that was within the power of every single individual to oppose.

The assault on the family

The first broadside was fired by a group of young psychiatrists, principally R. D. Laing, Aaron Esterson and David Cooper, who generalised from their work on the dynamics of the families of schizophrenics in which one member's autonomous self was consistently denied, to the functioning of 'normal' nuclear families (Laing, 1965). As the 'anti-psychiatry movement' became increasingly involved in the liberationist politics of the 1960s (Laing himself became a guru of the British radical movement not dissimilar from Marcuse in the USA), a further connection was made between the psychological 'fix' that went

on in families and the greater 'fix' perpetrated by imperialising capitalism. In such a world, it was argued, schizophrenic behaviour can be
seen as the sane, if ineffectual, acts of resistance to brainwashing,
while 'normal' behaviour is, by definition, mad, since it is sympto-
matic of a condition in which human intelligence and perception have
been so stunted and warped as to accept as sane an insane world
(Laing, 1971).

In an analysis reminiscent of Reich, the anti-psychiatrists believed
sexuality to be a residual source of spontaneity and creativity which
could provide the means, in orgasm, of 'evacuating the whole internalised family constellation' (Cooper, 1971, p.124). It therefore constitutes the greatest threat to family stability and attracts the greatest
repression in bourgeois society. The most immediate way that people
can break out of the negation of the family and get in touch with their
existential selves, according to Cooper, is through freely taking pleasure in their own sexuality. The sexual or 'Love Revolution' of the
1960s, then, is not just a part of the psychedelic, hedonistic counter-
culture; it is intended as a death-blow to the family. The only possible
escape from death *in* the family is the death *of* the family.

The other very different influence in left-wing radical thinking was
European structural Marxism. While this too engaged with a revision
of orthodox Marxism in rejecting its economism, it retained a commitment to the *scientificity* of Marxist analysis, drawing on modern
linguistic theory and psycho-analysis as *scientific* discourses to develop
an understanding of those aspects of the social totality which had been
under-developed by the dominance of the economic. In the work of
Louis Althusser, the doyen of French Marxism (1969, 1971), the
social totality was conceived as a complex combination of levels or
'instances': the economic (that is the unity of the forces and relations
of production); the politico-legal; and the ideological. The structure of
the totality exists only as the 'play' of elements – what Althusser
designates as 'structural causality'. The cause–effect distinction is
displaced in favour of a structure which is constituted by the specific
combination and articulation of its elements. Each element operates
relatively autonomously, constrained only 'in the last instance' by the
global structure of the mode of production, an application of the
Freudian concept of 'over-determination'.

In a famous essay (1971), Althusser illustrated how the ideological
level operated through the family and the school in the construction of
human subjectivity, within the context of broader socio-legal and
economic context. Typically, little mention was made of the critical

gender dimension until the publication of a remarkable essay by Juliet Mitchell (1966), a British New Left intellectual. Mitchell conceptualises women's lives as a complex totality constituted by the interaction of four critical elements or structures of women's experience: Production, Reproduction, Sex and the Socialisation of Children. Each is conceived as relatively autonomous from the others; each has its own history, its own pace, its own material conditions. At times these correspond and reinforce each other; at other times they come into opposition or 'contradiction'. The point where such contradictions are numerous or severe enough – an *unité de rupture* – is the moment in which the conditions for a revolutionary change are most propitious. The role of those who would seek to bring such change about, is to identify which of the structures is most beset by contradictions – 'the weakest link in the chain' – and work to increase them and the strain they inflict on the other structures. Mitchell analyses the four structures of women's lives in turn.

Production, contrary to the expectations of the early socialists, had proved no guarantee of sexual equality in the labour market. Industrialisation and the reduced need for physical strength may have provided employment opportunities for women but women's work tends to be concentrated in low-status, low-paid, service occupations. Inequality has been accommodated in the structure of production and hence does not threaten the totality of social relations.

Reproduction did not appear to be the weak link despite the fact that reliable contraception separates sexuality from reproduction and increases the capacity for female sexual enjoyment. Mitchell points to the upward trend in birth rates at the time and argues that the very affluence that encourages technological innovation in reproduction also encourages larger families, and that this is reinforced by familialist ideology. With hindsight, of course, we can see that the increase of births of which she spoke was because of baby-boom women reaching child-bearing age in this period. Underneath, the trend towards smaller families continued, producing the pattern we have today.

Women's role in the socialisation of children, Mitchell argues, has increased because of the extended length of dependent childhood and the importance of the family's 'psycho-social function'. While Mitchell takes issue with the post-war welfarist emphasis on exclusive mothering, she nevertheless warns against easy sloganising about the socialisation of childcare and argues that the interests of the child, especially in the early years, must be an important issue for socialist programmes which take seriously the liberation of women.

Mitchell concludes that it is the structure of sexuality which is the weakest link in the chain of the totality of women's experience, because of the increasing number of people openly ignoring the traditional moral restrictions of its pleasures to the married state. Progressive forces need to maximise the liberating effects of the equality of sexual freedom in the other sites of women's subordination. Neither single-issue piecemeal reforms on the one hand, nor maximalist demands on the other, including the abolition of the family, are effective. Instead, a coherent programme of policies is needed which addresses itself to all four of the structures. It is interesting to note that among the specific reforms she mentions, the free state provision of oral contraception, the decriminalisation of homosexuality and the abolition of illegitimacy have been achieved in Britain and more than half of all undergraduates in the USA and the UK are women.

The essay is ostensibly about the position of women in modern society, but Mitchell herself acknowledges that three of the structures she identifies – reproduction, sexuality, and the socialisation of children – are structures of the modern family, 'historically, not intrinsically, related to each other' (p.31). Her complaint is that the Left has been just as guilty as conventional political positions in treating the family as a 'hypostasised entity', instead of a structure of elements which may often exist in a relation of non-correspondence with each other, as her own analysis of the elements reveals. As a result of this theoretical inadequacy, the traditional demand for the abolition of the family is as abstract as its conception, inhospitable to conversion to specific realistic objectives and, thus, incapable of generating mass support. The essay concludes with a plea for a realistic socialist programme that will not seek to abolish the family, but to free it from its present monolithic idealised form and to recognise and legitimate a diversity of personal relationships.

Reading this essay over a quarter of a century later, one is struck by how relevant it remains. Its Althusserian framework, avant garde at the time, now appears rather dated and, of course, some of the empirical observations no longer pertain. However, it is remarkable overall for its responsible and restrained consideration of the issues, qualities which were soon to be in short supply in the subsequent much publicised debate about the family. This may be the reason why this essay did not receive the attention it deserved at the time. Or it may be that some of the questions raised about socialist theory and practice in relation to the family and to women were too uncomfortable, and the historical moment when they could no longer be ignored (after the election and subsequent re-election of right-wing populist governments on both sides of the Atlantic) had not yet arrived. Whatever is the case, Mitchell's was a lone voice in the Britain of the mid 1960s.

3

The Women's Liberation Movement and the Family

Feminism re-emerged in the late 1960s as part of the vibrant, hedonistic youth culture and radical student movement described in the last chapter. Its immersion in this environment gave new forms to the themes it inherited from its historical antecedents and provoked the new responses which mark out its difference from them. However, it also had good reason to react against the radical movement that gave it birth.

In 1968 a National Resolution on Women was passed by the main students' movement, 'Students for a Democratic Society' (SDS), committing itself to the elimination of male supremacy on American campuses (Roszak and Roszak, 1969), but by that time many of the women had taken their own action. The women felt angry and betrayed by the hypocritical gulf between the men's intellectual commitment to egalitarianism and participatory democracy and their authoritarian and sexist practice in political and domestic life. Sexual liberation in effect often boiled down to greater sexual exploitation of women while the male prerogative and the traditional domestic division of labour was left intact in the counter-culture communes.

The slogan 'the personal is political', first coined in 1962 in the widely circulated New Left document, the Port Huron Statement, took on new meaning when adopted by feminists. They objected to the assumption of the radical movement that class and race were the only forms of oppression and the only dynamic of political struggle. They argued that the oppression of sex was just as profound and at its root lay the interpersonal relations of power between men and women (San Francisco Redstockings, in Roszak and Roszak, 1969). Thus the struggle for women's liberation had to begin by, first, forming a separate movement by and for women which excluded men to create the space for women's political and personal development, and secondly, by fundamentally changing those institutions and practices which bind women into the private life. Foremost among these was the conventional family and even heterosexuality itself:

> From the start, Women's Liberation Movement feminists looked on the family as an oppressive, patriarchal institution... Radical and Socialist feminists in the 1970s were largely united in their rejection of the traditional nuclear family. By the end of the decade, this rejection often seemed to be virtually unthinking. (Lovenduski and Randall, 1993, p. 269)

This rejection was also the aspect that most distinguished the emergent feminist movement from its predecessor in the nineteenth-century and early twentieth-century and those women's organisations to which the latter had given birth. In recent years there has been an attempt to play down the anti-familialism of early post-war feminism, but a thorough examination of the literature of the time, from the classic texts of the movement to political tracts, articles and public statements, and the manifestos of various feminist groupings like WITCH, Redstockings and BITCH (Roszak and Roszak, 1969), does not support this gloss. Certainly early British feminist writing, collected and published as *The Body Politic* (Wandor, 1972), is hostile to the family; the article 'Women and the Family', much reproduced, established in style and content the standard position in the British movement on marriage and motherhood and the preferred alternative of communal living (Williams, Twort and Bachelli, 1970).

This hostility was elaborated and given substance and theoretical legitimacy in a number of texts which linked the everyday, common-or-garden experience of sexism and male chauvinism to an overarching meta-theory of patriarchy. I have chosen to examine in some depth four of these texts, selected first because they all became million-dollar best-sellers at the time and continue to function as landmarks of the period in contemporary discussion, secondly because they articulate common themes and concerns which dominated feminist discourse, and thirdly because they demonstrate the vibrancy, ambition and courage as well as the outrageousness of the period. It may be objected that action is more relevant to a social movement than books and hence a more appropriate object of study. However, liberationists were overwhelmingly articulate, literate and cultured, for whom books were as much weapons in the struggle as any other means.

Anti-bourgeois they were; anti-intellectual they were not. In addition, the organisational features of the movement gave the Book extraordinary importance.

In opposition to what they saw as the overly-cerebral, authoritarian, egocentric and aggressive features of male-dominated political activity, the breakaway feminist movement tried to put into practice egalitarian philosophy and collectivist values. They rejected formal organisational structures in favour of a loose, democratic grass-roots organisation connected by information networks based on personal contacts. A prime purpose of the movement was sharing the commonality of oppression and creating a sense of belonging to a sisterhood in adversity, and hence the importance of the consciousness-raising group which became an icon of the movement.

There were no formal leaders in the feminist movement, but there were 'prophets'. These were women who inspired others because of their ability to generalise limited and specific grievances and convert them into universal oppressions the ending of which was the attainable mission of every individual both in her personal life and through collective action with her sisters. Given the organisational features of the movement, the power of feminist prophets operated largely through the written text, assisted by the propitious entry at the time of the mass-produced cheap paperback in the world of publishing. Thus, the technology of communication overcame both the movement's own organisational obstacles to proselytisation and the geographical dispersal and domestic isolation of its potential sympathisers.

The paperback book, then, was a major force in disseminating the ideas of feminist prophets and hence in mobilising support for the feminist movement. The four best-sellers I have selected, Friedan's *The Feminine Mystique* (1963), Greer's *The Female Eunuch* (1970), Millet's *Sexual Politics* (1971), and Firestone's *The Dialectic of Sex* (1971), were inspirational at the time for the new women graduating in mass from higher education and demanding what they thought they deserved, indeed was their birthright. They were wonderfully outrageous and provided the dreams, style and courage to fire their rebellion. While engaging with social theory of the day, they were primarily exhilarating political polemic. These four texts are particularly interesting in that they demonstrate both the commonality of the issues which concerned the writers and the diversity of perspectives from which they address them.

For example, the most surprising thing about the *The Feminine Mystique* is its insulation from left-libertarianist rhetoric and from the rumblings of the explosion that was about to overtake American politics in the violence of the Civil Rights Movement and the anti-Vietnam demonstrations. Yet it anticipates much of the radical critique of the family and familialism as a socially oppressive and personally diminishing force. It comes independently to this conclusion from other roots. Friedan is a direct link between the women's rights movement of the nineteenth-century and early twentieth-century and the modern movement. She belongs to the generation which directly benefited from the previous struggles, but also experienced directly their limitations. She graduated with distinction from Smith University and enjoyed a successful career in clinical psychology until she married and had three young children, when the difficulties and guilt of trying to continue a career and be a mother came home to her. This personal experience led directly to the research for *The Feminine Mystique* and to her initiative in forming the National Organisation for Women (NOW) to pressure public policy on women's behalf. The book keyed into the frustrations and anger of many American women, providing an alternative to the Civil Rights and New Left movements in raising their consciousness and mobilising their resources.

Germaine Greer, Australian by birth, Cambridge graduate and radical young academic in the UK, was at the forefront of the new wave of feminist thinking, but was never closely associated with the organisations and activities of the movement. However, as much as her colourful iconoclasm, waywardness and flamboyant life-style made other feminists cautious, they made her the darling of the media. She was to British feminism what Brigitte Bardot was to French cinema at home and abroad, and has remained an icon in this respect both in the popular imagination and in media circles, probably as much for her glamour as for her somewhat idiosyncratic views.

Millett and Firestone, by contrast, served their apprenticeship in the American Civil Rights and New Left movements and broke away into feminist politics because of the chauvinism of the male activists. Millett was foremost in the struggle to have the women's movement, and particularly NOW, officially support Gay Liberation. Both Firestone and Millett were active in what became known as Radical Feminism, but represent different positions within that grouping, both theoretically and politically.

The Feminine Mystique has a limited objective: to explain women's psychological condition in the context of their social circumstances at a specific historical moment. The objective of Friedan's immediate successors to fame, Greer, Millett and Firestone, is more ambitious: it is to develop a general theory of women's oppression. This difference in horizons has important repercussions for the place of the family. For Friedan, the infantilisation, stultification and confinement of women to the private sphere was the result of the coincidence of a genuine hunger for the security, warmth and intimacy of marriage, home and children after the trauma of the war years, and the emergence of the home as the single biggest commercial market in the economic boom which followed. Friedan's interest is in women's subordination as an outcome of the post-war idealisation of marriage and the family. For Greer, Millett and Firestone, the family is a central mechanism of the universal, transhistorical oppression of women by men. However, despite their differences, they all devote considerable attention to the role of functionalism and Freudianism and, in echoes of Wollstonecraft and other early feminists, that of their agents, Mothers, in the subordination of twentieth-century women.

The Feminine Mystique

Reference was made in the last chapter to the immediate stimulus for Friedan's text – the mysterious illness afflicting housewives across the United States in the early 1960s – and her conclusions that it was a psychosomatic illness caused by the idealisation of marriage and motherhood and the largely self-imposed restriction of women's talents and ambitions to those of wife and mother. However, the blame for such self-limitation is placed squarely on the socialisation of daughters by their mothers who have uncritically followed the proscriptions of child welfare professionals and educationalists influenced by the work of Freudian psychology and Parsonian sociology.

Friedan readily concedes that the feminine mystique was the creation of Freudian popularisers and cult-setters with all the attendant distortions that have been incorporated into that pseudo-intellectual part of American popular culture. Nevertheless she insists that its basic elements are contained in Freud's work in that he advanced a theory which provides scientific legitimacy for the belief that women's biological destiny is to be wives and mothers and that their psychological health depends on this natural fulfilment. Freud is held culpable for suggesting that for women to strive after goals and activities normally associated with men is a neurotic symptom of the 'masculinity complex'. It is a failure to develop along 'normal' feminine lines by which the young girl comes to terms with phallic absence, abandons her desire for a penis, that is, to be a man, and replaces it with the desire for a child.

Friedan's critique is not limited to admonishing Freud for universalising from his clinical findings with patients brought up in the oppressive socio-cultural conditions of nineteenth-century Viennese society. She rejects what she regards as the fundamental premise of Freud's thought, that is 'his attempt to translate all psychological phenomena into sexual terms and to see all problems of adult personality as the effect of childhood sexual fixations' (p. 94).

Friedan's critique of Freud suffers from many of the same problems as other feminist writers of the period (Mitchell, 1975). Two in particular may be highlighted: the isolation of Freud's writing on femininity from the main concepts of psychoanalysis, and an unrelenting sociological literalism.

Most references and quotes refer to papers or sections of Freud's work dealing with female sexuality with little attempt to locate and understand them in the context of the theory of the unconscious and that of infantile sexuality. This leads to serious misrepresentation and misunderstanding of Freud's enterprise.

For Freud, the content of the unconscious consists of thoughts, wishes, sentiments, and events which provoke such anxiety that they are repressed from consciousness. Most of this repressed content derives from infantile sexuality which, while 'propped' initially by the survival instincts, is not reducible to them. Rather it involves the separation of the sensual pleasure from the bodily need, and its pursuit for its own sake. The child evokes the remembered pleasure in a phantasised image of the means of satisfaction. In Freud's words, 'The first wishing seems to have been a hallucinatory cathecting of the memory of satisfaction' (Freud, 1900:1976, pp. 757–8). As such it is the prototype for the operation of desire and the first instance of erotic representation. Phantasy – conscious, subliminal and unconscious – is therefore the mechanism by which such 'wishes' are expressed and fulfilled. However, such infantile desires cannot be satisfied, partly because desire, unlike need, is insatiable by definition, and partly because they are met with the prohibitions of the social order – Civilisation – experienced by the young child in the first instance in the context of the family. The anxiety engendered is so great that the prohibited desires, both loving and hostile, are driven by a variety of defence mechanisms out of the conscious. Sexual identity is acquired via processes which, for Freud, operate mostly at the level of the unconscious and are inaccessible to consciousness except through the mechanism of transference in analysis.

It was on the basis of the recurrence of common themes in dreams, phantasies, parapraxes, imagery, childhood memories revealed by patients in analysis and by his own self-analysis that Freud developed his theories of what went on in the child's psyche in the context of family dynamics.

In contrast, most of the feminist accounts of the time reduce the concept of sexuality in Freud's work to the physiology of sex, the body, the act, the drive, and thus his account of psychical development to a mere reflection of stages of sexual development. This literalism takes no account of the complexity of the theory of sexual difference Freud developed which is not reducible to simplistic biological principles; nor of the dissatisfaction that Freud himself expressed about his analysis of female sexuality (Freud, 1931:1977, p. 385; Freud, 1940:1973, pp. 149, 169); nor indeed of his insistence that 'all human individuals, as a result of their bi-sexual disposition and of cross-inheritance, combine in themselves both masculine and feminine characteristics, so that pure masculinity and femininity remain theoretical constructs of uncertain content' (Freud, 1925:1977, p. 342).

The other culprit in the causation of the feminine mystique is functionalism, or rather its main contemporary protagonist, Talcott Parsons. According to Friedan, his account of the functional interdependence of sex role segregation in the family and the occupational structure, referred to in Chapter 2, provides justification for maintaining society as it is and for obstructing the further emancipation of women. What is the status of these claims?

It is true that Parsons located the family as one of the major subsystems of the social system and it is also true that he used Freudian insights in his analysis of the role of the family in integrating the personality system and the social system. It is inaccurate, however, to claim that Parsons reduced both to biological imperatives and it is equally misleading to assume that Freud was absorbed intact into the Parsonian edifice.

Parsons identified the irreducible functions of the family as (a) to transmit to the next generation the common cultural ideals, values and mores by which people make sense of the world and which provide the basis for mutual expectations of behaviour in such a way that they become an integral part of their personality and so motivate their social behaviour, and (b) to provide conditions for the stabilisation of adult personalities. It is put very succinctly: 'They [families] are "factories" which produce human personalities' (Parsons and Bales, 1956, p. 16). It was clear to Parsons that any theory of society was inadequate without a theory of psychology, because it was personalities that provided the minimum motivational force and commitment necessary for the survival of the whole social system. At the same time the integration of the personality depended on definitions of behaviour and meanings provided by the social and cultural systems. Thus, Parsons's three systems of action are functionally and dynamically related through the family.

Parsons was interested in Freud's work because he recognised that it provided the theoretical means for escaping the twin orthodoxies of the psychology of the time: biological reductionism and behaviourist reductionism. However, while Parsons's psychological theory is couched in Freudian terminology it is a very different one from Freud's in that it thoroughly sociologises Freudian insights. For example, the notion of drives is converted by Parsons to need-dispositions which are *learnt*. Whereas for Freud the *id* is the prime reservoir of instinctual psychical energy, (sometimes referred to as *libido*), Parsons identifies it as one of the four sub-systems of the personality, that which is responsible for the adaptation of the needs of the organism to its environment, the others being the ego, the superego and the identity, all of which are derived from the social and cultural sphere. Hence, Parsons retains no space for the operation of pre-social desires. Whereas for Parsons the integration of the four sub-systems constitutes a coherent, unified personality system, albeit with built-in socially induced strains, for Freud the personality exists as a fragmented disunity characterised by highly charged conflicts between the structures of the psyche.

Friedan, however, seems immune to these important differences. She assumes that the Freud in Parsons is the Freud that has supplied the modern world with the psychological justification of the feminine mystique. Parsons compounds his sin in her eyes by adding a sociological justification. In Chapter 2 we noted that for functionalists the modernisation process had resulted in a differentiation of functions and roles within the family along the lines of instrumentality-expressivity. Parsons is clear that the problem is not that this order of differentiation exists, 'but why the man takes the more instrumental role, the woman the more expressive' (Parsons and Bales, 1956, p. 23). Parsons is no biological determinist. He is insistent that:

> If...the essentials of human personality were determined biologically
> ...there would be no need of families...It is because the human person-
> ality is not 'born' but must be made through the socialisation process
> that...families are necessary. (p. 16)

Thus, the expressive nature of women's function is not a simple and
direct function of their biology, especially in complex modern societies
where many of the traditional differences between the sexes have
diminished, but derives from the *coincidence* of their reproductive
capacity and social convenience:

> For simplicity we will refer to mother and child, but recognising that 'agent
> of care' is the essential concept and that it need not be confined to one
> specific person; it is the function which is essential. (Parsons and Bales,
> 1956, p. 63)

I also pointed out in Chapter 2 that Parsons was aware of the
potential for strain within families of the segregation of gender roles
in an age of greater educational equality and wider opportunities for
women. In a society where prestige is entirely defined by success in the
public sphere, domesticity carries little status, yet at the same time
wifely and motherly devotion is a *sine qua non* of womanliness and
social respectability. Parsons reveals here an important contradiction
at the heart of familialism and women's experience of it: it entails
qualities and activities which rank lowest in economic status and yet
highest amongst moral values.

Parsons indicates yet another dimension of this contradiction which
may help to explain what tips the balance for most women: 'the
pattern of domesticity... offers perhaps the highest level of a certain
kind of security' (ibid, p. 99). This is precisely the feature that some
modern feminist writers (Dworkin, 1983; Campbell, 1987) have isolated to explain the large number of women who form the social base
of the conservative, anti-feminist backlash in contemporary politics.
In a world where the promise of sexual equality has materialised as the
opportunity to compete with men on *their* terms, they argue, many
women have consciously or unconsciously opted for the security of the
traditional pattern.

Parsons observing this 'identity crisis' among women in the 1940s,
identified two main modes of emancipation from domesticity: the
'glamour' pattern and the 'good companion' pattern, yet both may
create further strains on the marriage. On the one hand, the glamour
pattern 'tends to segregate the elements of sexual interest and attrac-

tion from the total personality', may introduce jealousy into the relationship and is difficult to sustain with increasing age. On the other, the community involvement of the 'good companion' mode may detract from the marriage relation, because of the limited ability of the working husband to participate. In this situation, says Parsons, 'there is quite sufficient strain and insecurity so that widespread manifestations are to be expected in the form of neurotic behaviour' (Parsons and Bales, 1956, p. 99). It may be that Parsons correctly predicted the epidemic of symptoms in the late 1950s to which Friedan's book is addressed. Parsons readily admits that there is another pattern of behaviour open to adult women, which is to pursue careers of their own in the public sphere, but he notes that despite the considerable progress towards the emancipation of women, few have pursued this strategy. He adds prophetically that its general adoption 'would only be possible with profound alterations in the structure of the family' (ibid, p. 96), a point with which few feminists would take issue.

A serious reconsideration of Parsons's work suggests resonances with feminist analyses of the family and attempts to explain its continuing attractiveness to women despite the well-known statistics on divorce. It is also easy to see why Betty Friedan, witnessing the stultifying effects on women of the idealisation of the family so prevalent in the immediate post-war period, interpreted Parsons's observations as a celebration of the 'feminine mystique'. It is easy to see why her anger at college textbooks and college courses in marriage and family life which trained young women for their future domestic role, should have got displaced on to Parsons for providing them with their scientific justification. And it is true that Parsons's prose has the ponderous, paternalistic tone and old-fashioned turn of phrase that one might expect from someone born in 1902, whose entire professional life was devoted to academic study often of the most arcane type and whose social milieu rarely extended beyond the most elite university campuses. But, like Freud, the man's work cannot be reduced either to his biography or to the work of his worst popularisers.

With hindsight, Parsons's observations on the family and on the gender roles in America in the 1940s can be seen as astute estimations of (a) the forces engendering gender-role congruence and those reinforcing gender-role segregation, (b) the strains and conflicts these impose on men, women and the marital relation, (c) the predominant responses to these strains, and (d) the fundamental change in family structure likely to occur if more radical responses were to be adopted. This is not to say, however, that there are not substantial and even devastating critiques that can be made of Parsons's whole conceptual edifice (Rocher, 1974; Savage, 1981), for example those relating to its profoundly teleological character and its cultural determinism, but these are not those advanced by Friedan, nor for that matter by other radical critiques of the time.

A major theme of *The Feminine Mystique* is that the coincidence of these two major intellectual currents of twentieth-century social science – Freudianism and functionalism – put American women into a 'deep freeze' in the 'comfortable concentration camps' that were their homes. How, then, was it possible for women to break out of them?

Fundamentally for Friedan the 'problem that has no name' is a crisis of personal identity occasioned by status deprivation. Women 'can find identity only in work that is of real value to society – work for which, usually, our society pays' (Friedan, p. 301). She recognises the importance of the voluntary work that housewives do, but insists that it does not provide the self-esteem and self-confidence nor the external status necessary to bring real and lasting satisfaction. In the 'new life plan' that women must devise, housework, marriage and childcare must be seen as they really are – a part of one's life – and not ends in themselves.

Friedan believes the greatest obstacle to obtaining paid work to be the lack of higher education and professional training. Many of the related policy proposals put forward by Friedan in the closing pages of the book are now established equal opportunity practices in many of the universities and colleges in the United States and have begun to characterise much of higher education in Britain. These include the expansion of the part-time mode of study, the introduction of 'credit accumulation' and 'independent study' which aids the problem of discontinuous study and geographical mobility, the accreditation of prior learning and work experience, the encouragement of 'mature' students particularly women with support systems geared to their needs, the revision of academic curriculum to change the 'macho' image of some subjects and to introduce 'women's studies' to compensate for the omission of consideration of the other half of humanity by most academic disciplines. The steadily increasing numbers of women in higher education and the professions since the 1960s stand witness to the vast untapped pool of talent and aspiration in the population which Betty Friedan helped to identify and set free.

The Feminine Mystique focussed on the psychological damage to women, their husbands and their children occasioned by the confinement of women to the family, but while it is anti-familialist, it is not anti-family. Indeed, it is Friedan's belief that the liberation of women from the straitjacket of familialist ideology will actually lead to a more fulfilling relationship with men. This belief is inscribed in the aims of the National Organisation for Women (NOW), the largest women's organisation in America which Friedan was instrumental in founding in 1965: it aims 'to bring women into full participation in the mainstream of American society now, exercising all the privileges and responsibilities thereof, in truly equal partnership with men' (quoted in Hole and Levine, 1971, p. 85).

It was this view that brought Friedan into direct conflict with some of the younger, more radical adherents to the cause, for whom nothing short of total destruction of the family would set women, and humanity, free.

The Female Eunuch

While most intellectual feminists would regard Simone de Beauvoir's *The Second Sex* (1949) as the first major feminist text of the post-war period, the one the general public reward with this accolade is *The Female Eunuch* (Greer, 1970). While *The Feminine Mystique* created an earlier stir and mobilised many women to the cause of feminism, Betty Friedan could not rival Germaine Greer as a media personality. The press fell in love with her sheer eccentricity and vivacity, and no doubt her beauty, a love affair that continues to the present day. And in those heady days of radicalism, she exhilarated and inspired many young women, keying into their sense of defiance against the constraints of their parents, particularly their mothers, as much as their anger with and justifiable envy of young men.

The title of the book refers to the way in which the sexuality of women, defined as 'life force', the source of their creative powers, is suppressed from birth. The artificially produced exclusive relationship with the mother ensures that the external environment is only admitted by degrees. Closeting continues for girls inducing dependence and fear of the world beyond the security of the home, a passivity and timidity further reinforced by the gender expectations of schools. The outcome of female socialisation is 'the female eunuch' rendering

women unable to avail themselves of the opportunities that the twentieth-century has brought.

Love, Greer claims, is possible only between equals. Since women
are regarded and regard themselves as the second sex, the heterosexual relationship is always tinged with condescension or contempt on
the man's side and hollow self-interested self-sacrifice on the
woman's. The incompatibility of relations between men and women
is obscured from youth by the myth of romantic love and the com-
mercialised accentuation of sexual difference. This emphasises certain
aspects of the difference between the sexes making them fascinating to
each other, until familiarity replaces novelty and they are confronted
with the reality of their incompatibility. Of course this happens within
marriage and family life.

The end to which both sexes have been so systematically trained
turns out to be a closed, self-centred prison of boredom in which the
male–female couple are neurotically dependent on each other. With
the father absent from the home so much of the time, there is an
enforced emotional and physical intensity in the relationship between
mother and child. Mothers are jealous of anything which threatens
their monopoly of the children and their husbands:

> Every wife must live with the knowledge that she has nothing else but home
> and family, while her house is ideally a base which her tired warrior-hunter
> can withdraw to and express his worst manners, his least amusing con-
> versation, while he licks his wounds and is prepared by laundry and toilet
> and lunch-box for another sortie. (Greer, 1970, pp. 232–3)

This authoritarian compulsive family more often than not leads not to
the romantic idyll of happy-ever-after, but to resentment, misery,
loathing and abuse. Greer documents in detail the undoubtedly
worst aspects of domestic life.

Greer has little faith in the efficacy of working within conventional,
or indeed feminist politics to empower women. Instead she recommends women to liberate themselves by refusing to marry, and if
already married, they should threaten to leave home to gain better
conditions. For those with children, this requires more courage for it
means either impoverishment in most cases or leaving without the
children. In the latter case, Greer offers the cheering thoughts that 'it
is probably better for the children in the long run to find out they do
not have undisputed hold on mother' and 'the husband is consoled by
being allowed to retain the children and can afford to treat them better
with less anxiety than a woman could' (p. 323).

Having cleared the conventional family out of the way, Greer offers the following recommendations to prevent its re-emergence. Women should not promise monogamy to their male partners and maintain independence by indulging in a bit of promiscuity. They should form household co-operatives, sharing household appliances, housework and childcare, but they should also break with the ideology of work and routine. Above all they should refuse the meek and conciliatory roles into which they have been socialised and go to war against male supremacy, the most effective method of which, she claims, is 'simply to withdraw our co-operation in building up a system which oppresses us, the valid withdrawal of our labour' (p. 329).

The Female Eunuch is both the most breathtaking and the least rigorous of the texts under discussion. On the face of it, the breadth of Greer's allusions and references, which cover anthropology, psychology, sociology, history, literature, and aesthetics, is impressive, as is her ability to integrate them and bring them to bear on what was, at the time, a new field of enquiry. However, a more sober and insistent reading suggests that this breadth is superficial and the application more a matter of personal whim and opportunist expediency. A cavalier treatment of texts and a disregard of the basic requirements of scholarship leads not only to obvious bias but also to careless lapses of logic and coherence in her own work.

For example, in relation to the family, there is the most obvious contradiction between the description of the 'real' Oedipal situation in the home with the father an absent figure and the veiled incestuous, feverish relationship between the mother and the children (pp. 224–5), and the claim that the nuclear family has become 'a locked-off unit of male–female . . . threatened by its children! Contraception has increased the egotism of the couple . . . in these families where children must not inconvenience their parents, where they are disposed of in special living quarters at special times of day' (p. 230).

The text also suffers from an ahistorical idealisation of traditional family life of the past. This is supported by some dubiously selective use of Peter Laslett's evidence to support Greer's claim that a new pattern of family life was established in seventeenth-century England by religious reformers. Now the question is not whether she is right or wrong about the emergence of modern marriage and the family but whether her use of Laslett's work is valid, given his claim that the nuclear family has always been the main family form in the kinship structure of North-West Europe (Laslett, 1971).

The same idealisation is found in her treatment of family life in the Calabrian hamlet where she sojourned. The singing of a twelve-year-old girl doing the family wash at the well is presented as the epitome of childhood happiness. Greer seems unaware of the contradiction entailed in the fact that *The Female Eunuch* is devoted to decrying the castrating upbringing of girls in the nuclear family of advanced industrial society, yet the same gender socialisation in a poverty-stricken village in a romantic part of the world, where family life is actually being destroyed by North–South economic inequalities, is not only acceptable but actually extolled. The impression of patronising condescension is reinforced when Greer tells us that the same village had given her the idea of a way in which 'brilliant women might be more inclined to reproduce'. They could buy a farmhouse there, or in one of the many similar, where their children could be born and in which they could live when it pleased them. The fathers could visit, 'as often as they could, to rest and enjoy the children'; the children could grow up in freedom from restraint, even from knowing who their 'womb-mothers' were, while the brilliant mothers would be able to enjoy their work or their children as they pleased. Of course, 'the house and garden would be worked by a local family who lived in the house' (pp. 234–5).

There is also the sense in the book of skin-deep acquaintance with some of the theoretical inheritance to which she lays claim. For example, there is no systematic presentation of Marxism in general or with reference to the family, yet out of the blue we are told that the function of the family in capitalist society is that it 'immobilises the worker, keeps him vulnerable, so that he can be tantalized with the vision of security' (p. 232). Consumer capitalism addicts him to alienated work, and if he threatens to resist, his wife will strengthen his habit. On the basis of this slimmest of analyses, Greer is certain that if women's liberation – the only true proletarian revolution – abolishes the patriarchal family it will simultaneously abolish the authoritarian state, and 'once that withers away Marx will have come true willy-nilly' (p. 329).

Finally, Greer provides us with no theoretical mechanism for the conversion of this population of castrated women into a potent revolutionary force which is to overturn the family, the state and capitalism. To be fair this is not a problem exclusive to Germaine Greer but is endemic to models of human behaviour which attribute to humans on the one hand an essential freedom of spirit and on the other an apparently infinite capacity to be brainwashed.

Greer betrays throughout the book an ambivalent attitude towards men. It is the 'masculine' virtues that are praised and the vices are very often seen as provoked by women. Indeed Greer is hardest on women; in particular her worst invective is reserved for Mothers, for it is in the web of control, recrimination and guilt that they weave around their daughters that the castration takes place. In the exploration of her early life in *The Female Eunuch* and in a later book (1990) triggered by the death of her bullied father, there is nothing but hostility expressed for her mother. It is perhaps surprising that her experience of the omnipotent power of the Mother, both at home and in her convent education, did not make her wary of the totalising theory of patriarchy she adopted.

Sexual Politics

If Greer's text is lacking in systematicity, Millett's more than makes up for it. Millett is in no doubt about the definitional and ontological status of patriarchy:

> a disinterested examination of our system of sexual relationship must point out that the situation between the sexes now, and throughout history, is a case of that phenomenon Max Weber defined as 'Herrschaft', a relationship of dominance and subordinance. What goes largely unexamined . . . in our social order, is the birthright priority whereby males rule females. Through this system a most ingenious form of 'interior colonization' has been achieved. It is one which tends moreover to be sturdier than any form of segregation, and more rigorous than class stratification, more uniform, certainly more enduring. However muted its present appearance may be, sexual dominion obtains nevertheless as perhaps the most pervasive ideology of our culture and provides its most fundamental concept of power. (Millett, 1971, pp. 24–5)

Millett identifies eight aspects of patriarchal rule in recorded history: ideology, biology, the family, class, the economy-education couple, force, mythology, psychology.

Central to patriarchal domination is the 'conditioning to an ideology' which legitimates male supremacy in three respects: status (the political dimension), role (the sociological dimension) and temperament (the psychological dimension). While in the past religion and myth has provided divine justification for the inferiority of women, in modern times God has been replaced by Nature as the creator of the sexual order. Science has attempted to assert biology as the basis for human sexual divisions, from early ideas about physiology and brain size to contemporary sociobiologists and ethnologists who emphasise genetic and endocrinological differences. Millett argues that in fact scientists are in 'hopeless disagreement' about the nature of sexual differences and concludes that these are not natural but induced by the socialisation process by which patriarchal ideology is 'interiorised' in both sexes.

This takes place in the first instance in the family which Millett regards as 'the fundamental instrument and the foundation unit of patriarchal society' (p. 33) for two reasons. First, it reflects in its structure the authority of the husband–father, and secondly, it 'effects control and conformity' of its members in accordance with the state. This is guaranteed by the 'chattel status' of women which persists in the customary adoption of the husband's surname, his domicile and the exchange of domestic and sexual services for financial support assumed in the legal contract of marriage. It is also provided for by the boundaries drawn around the nuclear family by the principle of legitimacy and the corollary of the wife's sexual fidelity. Thus, the child is socialised into 'patriarchal ideology's prescribed attitudes toward the categories of role, temperament and status' (p. 35) both by the cultural values transmitted in the normal process of child-rearing and by the model provided by the role structure in its own household. Millett recognises in passing that the family also serves as a 'citadel of property and traditional interests' (p. 36) but this economic function is secondary to those of reproduction and socialisation in her theory of sexual politics. It is clear to her that as 'the fate of the three patriarchal institutions, the family, society, and the state are interrelated' (p. 33) any serious radical change to the family would result in societal disintegration.

Other social institutions reinforce patriarchal ideology and women's subordination. Women's education limits them to paid work of low value and low pay or to unpaid work in the home, both rendering them dependent on their husbands. It may appear that some women have a greater economic and social status than some men, but, says Millet, this is an illusion. Women's relation to class is an indirect and also a precarious one: widowhood, divorce or desertion often result in a sudden and dramatic drop in class and status position. For this reason, women tend to be susceptible to conservative ideas because 'they identify their own survival with the prosperity of those who feed them' (p. 38).

Finally, Millett argues that beneath these mechanisms to induce conformity to patriarchal ideals and structure, lies brute force. In past times this was much more to the fore, but in the modern age it remains celebrated in pornography and semi-pornographic media. Indeed, Millett believes this has been encouraged by the increasing permissiveness and decline of censorship in the twentieth-century. This appears to be the thesis of the large sections of *Sexual Politics* which analyse the work of D. H. Lawrence, Henry Miller and Norman Mailer. She finds in them evidence of a profound misogyny which is not accountable by idiosyncratic quirks of personality but are truly reflections of the fear, disgust and hatred of women which lie behind patriarchy.

Millett recognises that there have been some male champions in the battle for women's liberation, specifically John Stuart Mill and Frederick Engels, though she tends to minimise the important differences between them drawn out in Chapter 1. However it is the reactionaries, like Freud and functionalism, who provoke most attention.

Millett's account of Freud suffers from the same literalism as we saw in Friedan: the largely unconscious processes are thought of as conscious, interactional ones and are sometimes assumed to involve rational calculation and intentionality. For example, she reduces Freud's account of female dissatisfaction to 'a *literal* jealousy of the organ whereby the male is distinguished' (p. 183), and his account of the development of heterosexuality in the female to a crudely rationalistic process whereby 'the little girl at first *expects* her father to prove magnanimous and award her a penis. Later, disappointed in this hope, she *learns* to content herself with the aspiration of bearing his baby' (p. 184) (emphases added).

Millett takes the referents in Freud's theory to be the behaviour of the child and its parents as given external objects, while what is actually crucial for Freud are the psychical structures and processes which develop in interaction with the parents and others but which are not necessarily formed through a simple correspondence with external objects or events. What is important is the child's active though unconscious desires in relation to the parents and siblings and the ways in which the psychical structure and 'economy' develops through such processes as defence, repression and sublimation. While there is an important link between this psychic work and the actual interpersonal interaction in the family, no direct one-to-one relation is assumed in Freudian theory.

Another misreading of Freud is Millet's assertion that:

The gravest distortion in Freud's theory of female psychology stems from his incapacity, unconscious or deliberate, to separate two radically different phenomena, female biology and feminine status. By inferring the latter is as much, or nearly as much, the product of nature as the former, and somehow inevitable, rather than the product of a social situation, he seems to convince us that what a man's world has made of woman is only what nature had made of her first. (p. 190)

In fact, Freud persistently adhered to the existence of an innate bisexual disposition in human beings, the expression of which is characterised in infancy by 'polymorphous perversity'. This situation may continue into adulthood (and indeed there is abundant evidence that it does, for example in fetishism, transvestism, voyeurism, sado-masochism, but also in the case of the 'foreplay' which is regarded as a normal part of heterosexual sex) but for the intervention of Culture, which prescribes norms of behaviour and legitimate sexual objects along the sexual polarity male–female. Now it is quite true that this opposition is one in which the male category is endowed with more highly valued characteristics than the female. It is a patriarchal opposition: Freud has no doubts about that. But it is not, according to Freud, one given by biology. When Freud speaks of feminine and masculine, he is referring to certain attitudes and traits which are *conventionally* associated with female and male, but which are found in both female and male individuals. While anatomical sexual difference is given to us by biology, the meanings imputed to this difference are not:

> In mental life we only find reflections of this great antithesis; and their interpretation is made the more difficult by the fact . . . that no individual is limited to the modes of reaction of a single sex but always finds some room for those of the opposite one . . . For distinguishing between male and female in mental life we make use of what is obviously *an inadequate empirical and conventional* equation: we call all that is strong and active male, and everything that is weak and passive female. (Freud, 1940:1973, p. 45. Emphasis added)

Written at the very end of Freud's life, this quote (which can be best supplemented by the fuller discussion in the essay 'Femininity' (Freud, 1933:1973), stands out in stark relief against Millett's claim which once again appears to be the consequence of the literalism common to the texts under discussion,despite their other differences.

Psychoanalysis, for Millett, is no other that a giant auxiliary mechanism to the family: where the latter fails to elicit conformity, psychoanalysis steps in to effect secondary adjustment. Freud is the arch-patriarch whose 'intent is not only to limit female life to the sexual-reproductive, but also to persuade us that women live at a low cultural level because this is the only one of which they are capable' (Millett, p. 200).

On the contrary, the aim of analysis, for Freud, is not adjustment to society, but 'to give the ego back its mastery over lost provinces of his mental life' (Freud, 1940:1973, p. 30). Such statements are substantiated by Freud's recurrent insistence that normality is a value judgement, only an 'ideal fiction', and by his well-known resistance to parents' requests to cure homosexual offspring. In the light of this necessary professional commitment to moral impartiality, Freud's account of the feminine condition should be understood as a *description* of the specific cultural demands a patriarchal society makes on women, and not the *prescription* to conform to those demands imputed to him by Millett.

As to that other agency of reaction identified by Millett, sociological functionalism, there is a similar over-simplified account of Parsons to that found in Friedan. In fact Parsons is no match for the perfect circle of functional social reproduction found in *Sexual Politics*. Every institution in society functions to maintain and reinforce the material and ideological conditions required for patriarchal rule. Even those forces which appear to challenge it, such as the 'first phase' feminists, merely add to its stability by reforming its worst excesses.

Where does all this get Millett in terms of a political programme? First, there should be a complete refusal to participate in sexual relationships which have any economic exchange, and sexual permissiveness unhampered by traditional inhibitions and taboos should be adopted. Second, women should have complete economic independence and refuse the traditional role attributed to them. Third, women and minors should have complete legal independence. Fourth, the care of children should be removed from individual mothers and given over to professionals.

These demands are quite consciously calculated to destroy the family. The first would 'threaten patriarchal monogamous marriage'. The second and third would 'undermine both its authority and its financial structure'. The fourth would 'undermine family structure' (Millett, p. 62). It is clear from this that of all the institutions which make up the patriarchal edifice it is the family that is singled out for destruction. Private property, the patriarchal state, the universities, science, religious hierarchies, even the literary elite, all the targets of Millett's invective, appear to have been spared the annihilation that is to come.

This conclusion is vindicated by Millett's vision of what will replace the present regime: 'a permissive single standard of sexual freedom'; a single sexual mode of status, role and personality consisting of the integration of the 'best' qualities of the current polar types; complete individual autonomy and freedom from any kind of dependence; the separation of reproduction from socialisation; and the possibility of 'voluntary associations, if such is desired'. There is no indication of what economic, political, ideological and psychological structures will be necessary to sustain such an association of individuals. And that, of course, is the point. In this scenario there is no society, only a loose association of atomistic, freely choosing, rational individuals with not an unconscious between them, a scenario uncomfortably similar to that of the radical libertarians of the 'New Right' yet to appear. However, in the late 1960s, it offered the unstructured, humanistic, autarchic utopia which suited the predominant personalist politics of the time.

The Dialectics of Sex

As part of their revolutionary strategy, Greer and Millett wished to undermine the patriarchal proprietary family by separating sexuality from reproduction. In *The Dialectics of Sex*, Shulamith Firestone proposes to abolish reproduction in its present form altogether. Firestone argues that the destruction of patriarchy required the abolition of not only the social family but also the biological family itself. Contrary to Friedan, Millet and Greer who, as we have seen, were at pains to prove that almost all the distinctions between the sexes were culturally induced, Firestone insists that 'it was woman's reproductive biology that accounted for her original and continued oppression' (Firestone, 1971, p. 83).

While strongly influenced by Marxism, Firestone believes that Marx had gone wrong in attributing the fundamental basis for human life to the production of the means of subsistence. Rather there was a 'sexual substratum' which Marxists were too blinded by their obsession with the economy and their own sexism to see. Biological reproduction, not economic production, was the fundamental material reality and the biological family the basic unit of all social relations. It was biological reproduction that necessitated economic production. However, the very nature of human reproduction imposed an 'inherently unequal power distribution' because women have always been at the mercy of their reproductive system and this has resulted in their dependence on men. The inequality of this division of labour is the basis of the conflicting interests between men and women. They constitute two sex classes and the relationship between them has always been characterised by a sex war, however obscured this may have been by subsequent ideologies such as romantic love. The modern nuclear family is only a more concentrated manifestation of the original biological family.

This situation, unfortunate for women though it might have been, was inevitable and unavoidable. Adapting Marx, Firestone argues that the social relations of reproduction will persist until the forces of production develop to such a point that the former are burst asunder. That time, says Firestone, has now arrived. The technologies exist which can make human reproduction in its present form a thing of the past. These include the means of safe and reliable contraception and abortion, but more importantly, the potential of modern embryology which makes artificial reproduction a reality.

Firestone warns that men will not be prepared to accept such a revolutionary change because they benefit directly from the sex class system. It will not be brought about, therefore, without a struggle. She is scathing about the ability of either what she calls 'conservative feminists' such as Betty Friedan and the National Organisation of Women (NOW) or the 'politicos', that is, those feminists affiliated in some way to Left politics, to achieve any serious headway in the class war. The first group is doomed because their concentration on eliminating 'superficial symptoms of sexism – legal inequities, employment discrimination and the like' (pp. 36–7) in order to achieve equality with men, does not challenge the very root of the patriarchal system and so will always end up being incorporated by it. The second will always be diverted by other struggles prioritised by male Left politics because underneath they have 'lingering feelings of inferiority as women' (p. 41) and so still need male approval. Only 'radical feminists' are capable of the enormity of the task because only they have truly confronted the oppression of women as the universal oppression on which all others are founded and thus have the courage to confront the universal oppressor – men.

The chief target in the sex war is to be the family. The main broadsides are familiar ones: the socialisation of childcare; complete economic independence for women (this to be aided by the complete cybernation of economic activity); the abolition of all sex segregation in society; complete freedom from any sexual inhibition, taboo or prohibition. Firestone is more radical than most in that she extends all of these freedoms to children, but her most original contribution to sexual politics is the demand that the family's function of reproduction is replaced by technologically sophisticated artificial means. In her view nothing short of this will destroy the family.

It is to be replaced by a combination of 'single professions', people who 'live together', and 'households' of about 15 consenting people under limited renewable legal contracts of terms of about seven to ten years which would include a regulated one-third percentage of children for whom responsibility, like that for all household jobs, would be shared, but in whom there would be no rights of possession. While she concedes there would be considerable difficulties in the transitional period, once the power psychology of the possessive, repressive biological family had diminished and a restructuring of our psychosexuality had taken place as a result of the changes in the material conditions of living and working, this New World would constitute 'a paradise on earth anew' (p. 274).

Such ideas had already some currency within radical feminism. However, it was not until the publication of *The Dialectic of Sex* that the idea to replace natural reproduction with the new reproductive technologies received widespread publicity (Gatlin, 1987). Outrageous though it was thought to be, it was in some ways a logical conclusion to the demands to abolish the family so fervently adopted at the time. Whether the role of the family was seen as repressing natural spontaneity and creativity in the interests of modern totalitarian technocracies, perpetuating private property, the social division of labour and possessive individualism in the interests of capitalist imperialism, or controlling women and socialising children into sex roles, statuses and temperaments for patriarchy, Firestone is right in that reproduction does lie at the heart of familial organisation. Most of the discussions avoided the issue. It got deflected into questions of preventing reproduction or slid into the issue of collective childcare. Only Firestone, probably out of naïvety, walked in where the wised-up feared to tread.

The issue, however, was to emerge later with the public availability of reproductive technologies associated with research into infertility. The irony was that the later debate centred on the demand being made on these services by single lesbians and lesbian couples who wished to put themselves through the 'violence' and 'brutality' of pregnancy and childbirth from which Firestone appeared to think all women would wish to escape. But by then the lesbian community, culture, theory and practice had gone a long way in recognising the complexity of human desire.

Feminist activism and division

These authors, whatever their differences, had no doubts that it was patriarchy that was at the root of the oppression of women and that its overthrow meant changing institutions and practices in both the private and the public spheres. Whatever academic aspirations the authors had for the four texts I have considered, they were primarily intended as political rhetoric – a call to arms – to mobilise women to the feminist cause.

A programme of demands was adopted by the women's movement in the USA and Britain. In America, NOW functioned as the main co-ordinating organisation. A women's Bill of Rights was drawn up in 1968 covering legal rights gained by the enforcement of Title VII of the 1964 Civil Rights Act, employment rights, equal pay, publicly funded childcare, the removal of sex discrimination not covered by the Civil Rights Act, reproductive rights, the Equal Rights Amendment, and in 1971 sexual preference rights.

A similar programme was adopted at the first national conference of the British women's movement, held at Ruskin College, Oxford in 1970. While two of the demands – equal pay and equal opportunities in education and jobs – reflected the traditional claims of feminism, the other two – 24-hour nurseries, free contraception and abortion on demand – reflected the new identification of sexuality and relations between the sexes as the source of women's subordination. This direction was reinforced by the other demands made in subsequent years – financial and legal independence, an end to discrimination against lesbians and the right of women to define their own sexuality, freedom from intimidation and violence from men.

However, it should not be thought that these manifestos were achieved easily. Indeed in the process the theoretical, political, socio-economic, racial, ethnic and sexual differences which had always existed between women, emerged as claims to different interests and different priorities based on an inverted hierarchy of oppression. The ideology of sisterhood which inspired the movement in the first place became unsustainable over time.

In 1970, at Ruskin, we felt we had one goal, we were unified . . . you did feel
you could have one feminism. One 'women's liberation' . . . It was an illusion, but you have to have those illusions to build a party, a political group.
(Mitchell in Wandor, 1990, pp. 111–12)

The first major rift within the movement was triggered by the
emergence of 'radical feminism' of which Millett and Firestone were
major spokespersons. Male dominance and the subjection of women
was regarded as endemic to heterosexual relations *per se* so that the
only way women could free themselves from male power was to reject
heterosexuality. For this faction, heterosexuality was neither natural
nor a choice for women: it was imposed on them by the instruments of
male power to ensure male sexual access to women. For it to become a
choice, the current patriarchal organisation of society would have to
be dislodged, and for that separatism was essential. This was first
articulated as the strategy of 'political lesbianism' by New York Radicalesbians (1970) but developed during the 1970s into a much
broader exploration of woman-centred culture which Adrienne Rich
was later to call 'lesbian existence' (Rich, 1981, p. 23).

This tendency within the movement also became associated with
the assertion that male violence was at the root of women's oppression
(Bouchier, 1978; Feminist Anthology Collective, 1981; Gatlin, 1987).
Early feminist studies on pornography and rape (Griffin, 1971;
Brownmiller, 1975) claimed that such inclinations were not confined
to pathological males, as conventionally thought, but were inherent
elements of all heterosexual relationships. By the 1980s Robin Morgan's statement, 'Pornography is the theory and rape the practice'
(Morgan, 1980), epitomised a dominant position in academic feminism and during that decade was to become a slogan for a series of
political campaigns and mass demonstrations sensationalised by the
media.

It was the attempt to make these developments identical with the
women's movement that led to the conflict with other feminists. In
America the liberal feminists, by far the largest group, represented by
NOW, the Women's Equity Action League (WEAL), the National
Women's Political Caucus (NWPC) and the Coalition of Labor
Union Women (CLUW), remained ascendant but under pressure
incorporated some of the radical agenda (Morgan, 1970; Freeman,
1975; Bouchier, 1978, 1983; Eisenstein, 1981; Elshtain, 1981;
Friedan, 1983; Gatlin, 1987). In Britain, by the time of the Birming-
ham Conference in 1978, the conflict between the radical feminist
faction and the socialist-feminist majority was so severe that no further

nation-wide conferences of the movement took place (Costain, 1980, 1981; Allen, 1982; Randall, 1987; Lovenduski and Randall, 1993).

Whatever the limitations of radical feminism as a theoretical perspective, it has to be said that its impact in practical terms was to force the public to recognise the problem of male aggression and violence (Gatlin, 1987; Lovenduski and Randall, 1993). In the early 1970s, feminists in the USA set up and staffed rape crisis centres offering 24-hour telephone help-lines and counselling to women victims of sexual assaults, and these were developed in Britain along with high-profile public campaigns, including 'Take Back the Night' marches and demonstrations through cities. The revelations of this work about the prevalence of sexual assault and rape, particularly that perpetrated by male relatives and intimates of the victims, shocked the public and made the authorities take the issue seriously.

The other major practical initiative developed by radical feminism was the women's refuge movement. This began in Britain in the early 1970s with a few houses offering sanctuary to women who were victims of domestic violence, and was soon adopted in America. The refuges were organised on the non-hierarchical, self-help and personal development principles of the Women's Liberation Movement (WLM). They were funded by a variety of sources, but came to rely on public funds bringing with it a tension between the kinds of management control required by statutory authorities and the looser democratic processes of the refuges.

There is no doubt that practical activity of radical feminists has brought long-term benefits in revealing the prevalence of male violence and abuse of women and children, and in so doing, significantly reducing the public's tolerance of it. This has led to major changes in public policy in legislation and legal procedures, in police policy, practice and training, in the establishment of local authority and charity-run refuges and of special advice and counselling units, epitomised by government-funded Zero Tolerance campaigns.

Further acrimonious disputes within the feminist movement were provoked by differences of race, ethnicity, class and religion. Feminism was accused of prioritising the issues of white, middle-class, well-educated women and negating the experience of other groups of women. This was felt particularly strongly by black women and led in the USA to a breakaway movement, The National Black Feminist Organisation, in 1973 and in Britain, The Black Women's Group in 1974. Black women's views are captured well by the black American feminist, bell hooks:

No other group in America has so had their identity socialised out of existence as have black women...When black people are talked about the focus is on black *men*; and when women are talked about the focus tends to be on *white* women. Nowhere is this more evident than in the vast body of feminist literature. (hooks, 1982, p. 7)

The feminist movement's uncompromising stance on the family did not accord with the experience of black women. Since they were often the main breadwinners in black households, they did not share the forced financial dependence on men. Indeed black women, before and after the abolition of slavery, had always been part of the labour force; few had the luxury of being able to be 'just a housewife'. Also, their families did not resemble the isolated cells of suffocating domesticity which drove educated white women to feminist mobilisation but were part of extended communities bound by ties of mutual obligation and dependence, psychological and material, which protected them in a generally harsh, exploitative racist environment.

In addition, many black women were uncomfortable with the dominance of sexual issues in feminist politics. Abortion and contraception were suspect partly because of the mark left in black consciousness by the eugenicist-inspired compulsory sterilisation laws in some US states in the early twentieth-century, and partly because of black women's greater attachment to evangelical religions which took rather fundamental positions on these issues, as well as on homosexuality. Further, black women could not understand white feminism's insistence on the separation of female identity from that of being a mother. In their culture, women embraced motherhood. Unlike white feminism which focussed on the interests of women themselves as the goal of equality struggles, for many black women, feminism was about gaining the conditions in which they could achieve their ambitions for their children (McLeod, 1999).

The radical legacy of the search for identity and the assertion of the incontrovertibility of personal experience led to a politics of identity susceptible to division, partition and secession. This diversity of identities and assumed interests limited the development of any national unifying umbrella organisation and confined feminist politics to fragmented political activity.

In addition there was a tension between feminist goals and organisational means. The need for effective and sustained political action to achieve strategic objectives drew part of the movement into more formal organisational structures and involvement with the conventional political processes. This was particularly the case in the USA where, as we have seen, there already existed many established 'equal rights' women's organisations.

Such organisations were well-acquainted with the lobbying system and had many influential contacts in mainstream politics. With the inclusion of the criterion of sex, albeit on the back of race in the 1964 Civil Rights Act, and the establishment of the Equal Employment Opportunity Commission, the climate was ripe for the advancement of women, and the older feminist organisations were well placed to assist the new movement. This opportunity was taken up by the two largest feminist groups: the National Organisation for Women (NOW) established in 1966, and the National Women's Political Caucus founded in 1971. However, this strategy required the kind of hierarchical organisation, permanent offices, a written constitution and national co-ordination, that was dissonant with many of the movement's original values and organisational principles based on direct democracy. Consequently, there was considerable criticism of these developments and some defections (Freeman, 1975; Costain, 1981; Gelb and Palley, 1987; Gelb, 1990; Boles, 1991).

In Britain, partly because of the historical weakness of a discourse of equal rights, and the dominance of Marxist feminism in the new movement, no similar organisation to NOW developed. Similar antipathies to 'bureaucratic incorporation' prevented the establishment of a national co-ordinating body and fuelled debate between those feminists who were also members of established political parties and others who eschewed them. National co-ordination was limited to annual conferences and on-going campaigns, such as the National Abortion Campaign (NAC). These organisational strains were partly resolved by the leftwards shift of the Labour Party in the 1970s and the growth of women's committees and sections in local government and in the large white-collar trade unions. This provided more acceptable organisational avenues for the advancement of feminist goals and consequently socialist feminists entered Labour politics in substantial numbers (Flannery and Roelof, 1984; Goss, 1984; Segal, 1987; Lovenduski and Randall, 1993).

As Costain (1980) points out, the differences within feminism limited it to *ad hoc* coalitions mobilised in relation to specific campaigns, but this did have some advantages for effective action. It allowed for rival groups to co-operate for a limited period of time for a common cause, for groups legitimately not to participate on certain issues and for minimum dispute over leadership. It also provided a greater diversity of strategy and tactics by which the media, the general public and the politicians were made aware of the issues (Boles, 1979; Costain, 1980,1981; Gelb and Palley, 1987; Mathews and de Hart, 1990), and thus must be credited with raising the profile of and public support for the advancement of women. It also provided an image of the feminist movement as more united than it was in reality.

Hence, from outside feminist politics it appeared that the movement was united in anti-familial ideology, and the various campaigns associated with it were taken to be components of a coherent and concerted project to radically undermine the foundations of family life. The media's tendency to sensationalise and trivialise can be held partly responsible for this perception. However, there can be little doubt that it was the feminist critique of the family, clearly articulated in the writings and media interviews of the major spokeswomen of the WLM, rather than the demands for equality of opportunity, that provoked the mobilisation of another social movement with women as its dominant constituency.

4

Pro-Family Reaction

The radical and feminist movements and their assault on the family provided the media with an endless source of delight. The personalist politics, the celebration of the individual, the sense of immediacy, but above all the theme of liberated sexuality, appealed to the press thrilled by the sheer exhilaration of a new cultural phenomenon which broke free of Establishment conventions. It is not surprising that the new irreverence, audacity and enthusiastic experimentalism should have found a welcome in field of artistic production. In addition to the commercial media the movements created their own alternative media, through street theatre, 'events', campus and local radio, and film, but above all in the underground press. These short-lived, ever-changing, iconoclastic publications were hugely popular with young people and were the main disseminators of alternative politics, values and fashions.

The well-publicised anti-familialist proclamations by feminists and their libertarian predecessors coincided with a tranch of 'permissive' legislation in the moral field, pressure for which had been building up during the twentieth century (Weeks, 1981). By the late 1950s and early 60s it had developed into single-issue lobby groups for the reform of the laws on censorship, divorce, abortion, family planning, prostitution, homosexuality and suicide. The elections of 1964 and 1966 produced a Labour government under Harold Wilson with a mission to modernise Britain, and with inclinations toward reform (Pym, 1972). The wave of new Labour MPs, who owed either their own or their parents' livelihood to the post-war expansion of the public sector, were characteristically 'causalists' or 'short-term negative utilitarians'; less concerned with punishing moral failings than pragmatic solutions to minimise suffering and, hence, sympathetic to the reformers (Davies, 1980).

The reforming legislation was not a package under a 'family' label, but promoted by private members and passed by a free vote in the House of Commons. Each Bill was aimed at a single illegal activity unrelated to any others and was informed by the liberal principle of the separation of the public and private spheres, wherein it is held that the state should intervene in the latter sphere only where harm is inflicted or a minor is involved. The legislation, therefore, is best understood as part of a mopping-up operation by which the post-war liberal democratic state concluded its business of separation of moral and legal codes of conduct.

In the United States, John F. Kennedy's similarly reforming Democrat administration initiated the 'Great Society' programmes, such as Medicaid, Medicare, the Civil Rights Act, job creation and training schemes, urban regeneration and educational projects. Both he and the British Prime Minister, Harold Wilson, were sympathetic to improving the opportunities for women in the public sphere: in 1961, the former established the President's Commission on the Status of Women which led *inter alia* to the introduction of anti-discriminatory employment policies in all federal agencies and their contractors, while the latter is notable for his promotion of able women politicians to ministerial jobs and for two major pieces of anti-discriminatory legislation – the Equal Pay Act (1970) and the Sex Discrimination Act (1975). While no challenge to the family was intended in these measures, neither administration was interested in preservation politics. Thus, we can see that throughout the 1960s, despite media attention to the anti-familial propaganda of the radical and feminist movements and their traditionalist opponents, the family did not become part of the national political agenda because the political constellation ascendant at the time was not particularly sympathetic.

Early reaction

It was both the media celebration of the counter-culture and the apparent collusion of the politicians that most disturbed those in the population to whom the radical world-views were alien and offensive. The potential damage to young minds goaded them into forming the first organisations to defend traditional norms and values against what was seen as subversive influences destructive of the very fabric of society. There can be little doubt that it was traditional Christian morality that was outraged and that it was the ideal of Christian marriage and Christian family that was identified as its bedrock.

There are interesting differences at this point between the British scene and that in the United States. The earliest reactions emerged in Britain in a number of organisations formed to defend Christian standards of social and personal behaviour, amongst them the National Viewers and Listeners Association (NVALA) founded by a schoolteacher, Mrs Mary Whitehouse, who was to become the best known of the British moral crusaders till she died in 1997. This started life in 1963 – the same year as the publication of *The Feminine Mystique* – as a campaign, 'Clean Up TV', to raise public consciousness about the moral degeneration of broadcasting and its detrimental effect on the family and society. These pressure groups were to combine in the launch in 1971 of a national populist crusade, the Festival of Light, and culminated in the Longford Report on Pornography and a major public petition.

However, this was the period of the Cold War and many campaign leaders had links with the American anti-communist organisation, Moral Re-Armament. For these crusaders the 'permissive' legislation of the period, the commercial promotion of sexually explicit material and the radical counter-culture were part of a greater communist-inspired conspiracy of older men in high places to undermine the moral foundations of western societies (Whitehouse, 1977; Tracey and Morrison, 1979; Sutherland, 1982). It is easy to see how, with this world-view, the family becomes the last bulwark against the red peril. Ordained by God for the procreation and protection of children, the family symbolically replicates the Holy Family in human consciousness and so transmits the mystery of Creation. The very exclusiveness of the family makes it the least susceptible of all social institutions to infiltration and, hence, the most important to defend.

The gay and women's liberation movements were seen as the ultimate weapons in the plot to destroy the family. Mrs Whitehouse argued that it was women's lib that had turned women into 'female eunuchs' and was responsible for the upsurge in homosexuality, the increase in pornography, and in violence to women. There is a deep fear of sexuality in the statements of NVALA members which extends beyond simple prudery. This fear is articulated best, as always, by Mrs Whitehouse:

Sexual anarchy is the forerunner of political anarchy. Political anarchy is
the precursor of either dictatorship or destruction. (1977, p. 186)

While the same sense of moral outrage can be found in the United
States, the issues were overshadowed in the 1960s by one overriding
topic of public debate – the issue of the black family. Interestingly, the
American debate was articulated in terms resonant of nineteenth-
century moral concerns and presaging the dominant contemporary
discourse on the family, that is the relationship between sexual indulgence and economic fecklessness, or to put it another way, between
family form and poverty. The question of the disintegration of the
family in post-war United States, first arose inscribed in the politics of
race and poverty in the controversy over the Moynihan Report.

The Report, *The Negro Family: The Case for National Action* (1965),
was written by a key adviser to President Lyndon Johnson, to mark a
new government initiative in the civil rights field. Daniel Moynihan, a
successful social science academic from a deprived background himself, had been part of the team behind Kennedy's 'War on Poverty'
project.

The Report addressed the problem of squaring the improvements in
the legal status of black Americans from the school desegregation
ruling of the Supreme Court in 1954 to the Civil Rights Act in
1964, with the actual deterioration of the socio-economic position of
American blacks relative to the white population. While the Report
has no doubts that the fundamental cause is 'the racist virus in the
American blood stream', it nevertheless insists that family dysfunction
among the black population itself reinforces the structures of discrimination and disadvantage. At the heart of what Moynihan calls 'the
tangle of pathology', is the absent father. He argues that the greatest
victim of racism is the adult black male. Feared more than the female,
the elderly or children, he has been deprived of regular, adequately
paid employment and hence often been unable to support a family.
The long-term result is demoralisation, reduced self-esteem and a
drift to shiftlessness and irresponsibility. The individual incapacity to
perform the role of the strong father becomes, over time, a cultural
characteristic of the whole social group.

In this situation, the mother takes on responsibility for the family's
economic survival. This reversal of the normal familial role affects the
children. Moynihan cites evidence of the better academic performance of black girls, their greater representation in white-collar and
professional occupations, their higher pay levels and the greater

benefits obtained from federal equal opportunities policies. There is no doubt in Moynihan's mind that the matriarchal structure of the Negro family is one of the reasons for its pathology.

While Moynihan accepted that there was no inherent reason why one family form should be preferred over another, he believed that:

> it is clearly a disadvantage for a minority group to be operating on one principle, while the great majority of the population, and the one with the most advantages to begin with, is operating on another... Ours is a society which presumes male leadership in private and public affairs. The arrangements of society facilitate such leadership and reward it. A subculture, such as that of the Negro American, in which this is not the pattern, is placed at a distinct disadvantage. (Moynihan, 1965, p.29)

It was certainly the case that throughout the 1950s and early 1960s, to which Moynihan's statistics relate, most white American women remained housewives throughout the years of childbearing, a situation which found favour with the majority of women according to numerous opinion polls of the time, such as the National Manpower Survey in 1957 (Gatlin, 1987, p. 262). Nevertheless, the sexist assumptions and male presumptions which abound in the Report did not go unremarked, particularly by black women anxious that it would justify sexual discrimination in the labour market (Rainwater and Yancey, 1967).

To be fair, Moynihan focused on the problems of the black family because he believed it was the starkest example of the failure of the traditional approach in American social policy which was characterised by a plethora of different programmes each with their own objectives and administered by a variety of different agencies, often overlapping, inconsistent and contradictory. Moynihan favoured the less individualistic, family focus of European taxation and welfare systems. Economic and social policies, in his view, should be geared to ensuring the stability of families for he believed that these were much more effective in ensuring the stability of individuals than anything governments could devise. Taking the welfare of the family as a reference point, he argued, would make it possible to integrate a range of strategies, programmes and projects coherent and consistent in both their goals and their administration.

Readers will make connections between Moynihan and Charles Murray (1990, 1994), the American ideologue of the New Right who has almost become a household name on both sides of the Atlantic. However, there are important distinctions. First, Murray does not come clean on the race dimension unavoidable in the context of US demographic and income statistics, but subsumes it coyly in the concept now most associated with him, the 'new underclass'. Secondly, both Murray and Moynihan focus on the absent father as a factor in poverty and its associated culture. However, Moynihan's associated problem is 'independent working women', the consequent reversal of roles in the family and the effect this has on masculine identity, while Murray's problem is welfare mothers. This, of course, may reflect the difference in the employment market in different economic climates. Thirdly, and most important, Moynihan's proposal to deal with the situation was to change the strategic direction and organisation of social policy such as to integrate and increase employment, housing and welfare provisions, not, as Murray intends, to cut them back.

The Report was commissioned by the White House, and President Johnson himself intended to make it the basis of a major civil rights speech to be followed by proposals for reforms. However, the Report was leaked before the appropriate consultation had taken place with both the permanent civil servants and the civil rights leaders. Mangled versions of it appeared in the press and before long it was at the centre of a major political controversy. There are a number of theories about why what was to have been a major government initiative ended in a fiasco (Rainwater and Yancey, 1967; Steiner, 1981). Among these one can list the emergence of a major foreign policy crisis in the Vietnam War, stonewalling by White House dissenters, bureaucratic rivalries, political miscalculation, professional arrogance and complacency and, finally, downright administrative incompetence and bungling.

There is little doubt that had Moynihan Report been implemented along the lines Moynihan intended, millions of American children would have benefited. However, whether it would have been successful in its aim to strengthen a particular type of family – that of two resident married parents with a breadwinning father and a housewife mother, – is less certain. The same intention lay behind the 1942 Beveridge Report on which the foundations of the British welfare state was built, but it does not appear to have been able to withstand other socio-economic and cultural changes running counter to that goal.

We see here in 1965 a rehearsal of many of the themes of the contemporary debate over the family: the blurring of the distinction between moral and social behaviour; the association of sexual indulgence with economic fecklessness; the pattern of roles within the family; the absent father; welfare mothers; working mothers; illegitimacy; the best interest of the child; the burden on the public purse of welfare families. It also exposes the complexity of the process by which a social phenomenon becomes transformed into a social problem and, depending on a number of contingent factors, may or may not become a political issue. In addition, it suggests that if an administration is looking for a new vote-catching issue or for a vehicle to pursue a major change in policy direction, the family is a high-risk gamble. It is certain to achieve media publicity and public attention but it is most unpredictable to calculate in terms of response.

Anti-feminist ideologues

In the event, the issue of the family was submerged in the absorbing American tragedy of the Vietnam War. When it emerged again as an issue of public concern in the early 1970s, it was in the context of an articulate and confident feminist movement. There were well-publicised attempts to discredit the arguments and evidence which supported feminist demands for equality, notably those of Midge Decter (1973), George Gilder (1973) and Steven Goldberg (1973). Their views circulated in the popular press, articulating anxieties and fears as well as provoking reaction in a broader public, but they also contributed to right-wing think-tanks in America and Britain which became central in the construction of a new conservative political force in both countries. Together these texts provide a useful map of the terrain of counter-feminist arguments, the themes for the battle over the family that was to follow and the battleground for the contemporary act of this grand drama.

These three authors are united in the view that there are fundamental differences in nature between men and women and that the family merely reflects these. Goldberg's position in *The Inevitability of Patriarchy* is a version of natural selection theory: neuroendoctrinal differences between the sexes interact with the social environment which is characterised by universal social hierarchy producing a dominance tendency in human males. This leads to systems of organisation and authority in which the overwhelming number of high-status positions in hierarchies are occupied by males and in which deference is paid to males in familial and dyadic relationships.

Gilder does not attempt to be so technical. He stakes his claim on a broad but fundamental difference between male and female sexuality based on their different role in reproduction. Male primal sexual impulses are characterised by self-gratification, impulsiveness and transitoriness, while those of the female are characterised by a concern with intimacy, security and durability. This apparent incompatibility, however, is tempered by the fact that while the female is provided by her own body with a secure sense of psychological identity, the male is not, and therefore, is always dependent for it on his relationship with the female. An important element of that confirmation of his own identity is the production of progeny by which he can be assured of his own biological continuity and social immortality. Gilder believes that such processes are likely to be unconscious and instinctual but they have their expression in what humans experience as love. Therein lies female power: the woman can offer or withhold sexual, psychological and social affirmation which the male needs more than she does. 'Women domesticate and civilise male nature' (Gilder, 1973, p. 23). In return, the male protects and supports her and their offspring.

For Decter, too, procreative relations are the source of life itself and, as such, the prototype for all other caring, responsible and sustaining relationships in society. While she accepts the legitimacy of equal opportunities for women to develop the full range of their potential and welcomes women's increased control over their lives, she argues that it is motherhood which provides women with a unique role and a unique relationship to which men can only ever approximate. However, motherhood in Decter is a combination of biological and psycho-social elements and hence less biologistic than the two male writers. It is the overriding importance of the relationship with the child that accounts for the different meaning and value that women attach to employment, sexuality and marriage. Both marriage and motherhood, therefore, are institutions which are valued, maintained and protected mainly by women, not men.

All three writers believe that, contrary to feminist claims, women wield a considerable measure of power and status, much of it derived from their role in the family, and that the attempt to abolish the family, therefore, will not liberate women because there is no other institution which can satisfy their essential needs, and a great deal of damage will be done to women, children, men and society in general in the process. Goldberg warns against upsetting the balance of nature and culture achieved by gender role differentiation: 'the reduction in feminine behaviour desired by the feminists would force women to deal with men on male terms, which would inevitably lead to a reduction in women's real power' (Goldberg, 1973, p. 22). Gilder claims that feminist demands for economic equality mistake power in the market-place for real power, and are leading to the emasculation of men and the masculinisation of women. He believes that the influence of feminists and others is leading to a situation of 'sexual suicide', by which he means mass failure to reproduce the species, to provide adequate psychological security for child-rearing and for adult personalities, to sustain the very conditions for civilised life itself. This is a theme echoed by Decter in her view that feminists who promote women as the victims of patriarchy and advocate withdrawal from relations with men, non-phallic sex and political lesbianism, represent the ultimate flight from the freedom and responsibility of making difficult choices in life and creating their own destiny, hence the title of her book *The New Chastity*.

Of the three, Gilder is the most interesting in that he states the case for traditional moral conservatism which, while it strongly emphasises the 'social consequences' argument, contains at its heart the 'spiritual essentialism' that also characterises the attitude of the British anti-permissive lobby. Indeed his work was so admired by its members that the title of his book, *Sexual Suicide*, became a major theme in their rhetoric. Gilder shares the same conception of sex as a destructive and depraving force if not confined within monogamous marriage where its sheer sensuality can be converted to 'a transcendent unity'. This notion of a 'transcendent bond' is one which recurs in conservative philosophy, unites its conception of the individual, society and the state and explains why the family is central to it: 'Paramount [to a civilised society] is the worth of the human individual, enshrined in the home and in the connection between a women and child . . . the most primary and inviolable of human ties' (Gilder, 1973, p. 245). On this bond depends all the other moral, religious, aesthetic and social values which characterise civilisation. This has profound implications for the conservative view of state intervention and distinguishes it from other philosophies of the Right.

Hence Gilder is critical of political philosophies which see society as 'an aggregation of individual units' (p. 140) instead of 'an assemblage of families, family aspirants and unmarried units within the familial order' (p. 142). Nor is he in favour of the extension of the ethos of the market-place to other spheres of life, or the ideology of exchange to other social relationships. Indeed, one of the great values of marriage and why it is at the core of civilised values, he argues, is because it is not a contract of exchange but 'escape[s] the psychology of exchange altogether' (p. 72).

Rather, he believes society, through the state, has a responsibility to strengthen the family in its traditional form, particularly among the poor. He acknowledges Moynihan as providing the blueprint for his own ideas, in that a primary policy objective must be job-creation, training and apprenticeship for all poor males, and the promotion of small businesses, entrepreneurialism and home ownership for the better-off. This would be accompanied by a coherent package of family policies, including a negative income tax adjusted for family size and child allowances, which together would operate as an incentive to work. Such apparently progressive policies, however, are predicated on disadvantaging women, because they are to be funded by diverting resources from schemes which support lone mothers, train welfare mothers, provide child care to enable mothers to work, and promote positive discrimination in federal employment. Welfare is not seen in terms of citizens' rights or of meeting needs, but in terms of a mechanism to restore the autonomy and self-sufficiency of the family. It was the issue of welfare in a time of economic recession, that was to enable an alliance to develop from the mid-1970s between traditional conservatives and a new vibrant brand of radical liberalism despite fundamental differences in philosophical outlook.

This examination has revealed that what antagonised these and other traditionalists about feminism was less the demands for equality of opportunity than its refusal to accept the traditional relationship between men and women and its proclaimed objective of promoting the abolition of the family. It is precisely because of the emotional and moral investment in the family as a way of life for many women that such texts, despite their failure to provide convincing evidence for the biological basis in which they root their claims about the necessity and universality of monogamy and the domestic confinement of women, had such popular impact.

The other women's movement

While the ideas of these counter-feminists created quite a stir in public debate, they were not in themselves responsible for the whirlwind of public protest that burst out in the United States in the mid-1970s. This was triggered off by two events in the legislative field. One was the *Roe* v. *Wade; Doe* v. *Bolton* decisions of the Supreme Court in 1973 which liberalised abortion. The other was the revival in 1971 of the Equal Rights Amendment (ERA) to the United States Constitution, which proposed that 'equality of rights under the law shall not be denied or abridged by the United States or by any State on account of sex' (Section 1).

Pro-life organisations and anti-ERA pressure groups sprang up. Their collaboration was such that they increasingly became seen as a mass pro-family movement. Probably the most outstanding feature of this movement was that its rank-and-file members were overwhelmingly women, the strength and level of their activism all the more remarkable given the generally low level of female political participation (Granberg, 1978, 1981; Ehrenreich, 1981, 1982a; Harding, 1981; Luker, 1984; Marshall, 1991). It is ironic that the feminist slogan 'the personal is political' was appropriated and practised by women to assert the importance of those very aspects of women's lives that feminists believed to be the essence of their oppression. (Schlafly 1977) It is equally ironic that in doing so they were compelled to leave their kitchen sinks to attend meetings, address mail-shots, organise fund-raising events, leaflet and lobby, and act as delegates at out-of-town conventions. There were no doubt many neglected husbands and children as a result.

Women activists of the pro-choice and pro-ERA persuasion were surprised by the ferocity of belief and behaviour of the participants:

> Feminists expected *men* to resist their efforts, but they were largely unprepared for the extensive mobilisation of *women* against their reforms.(Harding, p. 57)

Most surprising of all was that the 'enemy' had borrowed their own forms of rhetoric and unorthodox, eye-catching direct action tactics. The nature of the conflict was obvious to the media: in 1977 a major television network presented a special report called *ERA: The War Between Women*.

It is all the more surprising, then, that for most feminists writing about the action, the significance of this 'other women's movement' was somewhat underestimated. In some Left publications there is no recognition at all. For example, Marshall (1985) argues that while in the period of economic expansion of the 1960s it was in the interests of the capitalist class to encourage the liberalisation of life-styles built around individual consumption, with the recession of the 1980s, 'freedom of choice defined by the market withers away as the market shrinks' (p.28). In the changed economic conditions the traditional family comes to the fore to absorb the casualties of recession for the

capitalists free of charge. Any support for the pro-family lobby, therefore, is simply a false consciousness induced by the capitalist media
industry. Marshall does not note any gender characteristic of this
support, despite the fact that she specifically addresses her piece to
questions of women's rights, sex and the family.

Eisenstein (1981) does note the large numbers of women campaigners in the pro-family army in the United States, but puts it
down to married women voters between the ages of 45 and 64 who
were frightened that ERA might remove what security the traditional
family provided them. In her view, pro-family politics were manipu-
lated by the Right to reinstate patriarchy as a central plank in a
militaristic and authoritarian agenda. Again, in Gordon and Hunter's
(1977/8) account of the role of sex and family in the New Right, only
one small paragraph registers the importance of women in the campaigns. They see the pro-family movement as part of a shift in strategy
on the part of the Right from periodic electoral manipulation to
systematic generation of conservative mass movements, and that to
this effect the family has been added to busing as a highly symbolic
and emotive issue. As we shall see, this rather oversimplifies the
oppositional forces and the importance that constructions of women's
interests and their relationship with the family played in their mobilisation.

An anti-abortion lobby existed prior to the Supreme Court's
decision, dominated by the powerful and male-dominated Roman
Catholic Church. When the Church failed to influence the elections
of 1974 through the normal lobbying process, the American
National Conference of Catholic Bishops launched a 'Pastoral Plan
for Pro-Life Activity' in 1976 outlining a strategy for a parish-based
network to co-ordinate the recruitment and fund-raising activities
of the local churches, and advised parishioners to elect and vote for
pro-life candidates in local and national elections (Petchesky, 1981;
Tribe, 1990).

An unlikely alliance developed with other fundamentalist religious
groups, particularly the traditionally anti-Catholic southern evangelical Protestants. These latter groups propagandised through the
13,000 radio stations and 36 television shows of the 'electronic
church', of which Jerry Falwell's Moral Majority is probably the best
known. Nevertheless, this pro-life movement was markedly different
from pre-1973 anti-abortion groups in that at the regional and local
level it was characterised by a mass grass-roots movement of local
women. At this level, according to Luker (1984), the ready-made

organisational and communication systems of the Catholic Church were more important than its bureaucratic leadership or financial assistance.

In 1971, the feminist lobby got the ERA through the House of Representatives and the Senate with little opposition. Many liberal states had already introduced similar legislation and the Supreme Court had been using the Fourteenth Amendment to bar discriminatory practices against women. The importance of the ERA, therefore, was to establish the principle of according to women equality of rights under the Constitution, and to provide a device to force recalcitrant states and reactionary judges to act in a manner consistent with that principle (Boles, 1979; Steiner, 1985; Berry, 1986; Mansbridge, 1986; Mathews and De Hart, 1990).

To become part of the United States Constitution, the ERA had to be ratified by 38 states by 1979. Thirty states ratified by early 1973 but then the process ran into difficulties. Pro-life propaganda made the connection between the ERA and the liberalisation of abortion laws emphasising the leading role of the National Organisation of Women (NOW) in both. The fact that both were also products of decisions by relatively liberal, cosmopolitan federal institutions, also goaded parochial state legislators and voters. Pro-ERA activists did not have effective campaign coalitions to defeat the opposition and the ERA failed to be ratified by three states.

The interesting thing about the anti-ERA campaigns was that they quite clearly set out to attract support by constructing women's interests as antithetical to the ERA. It was claimed by leaders of the anti-ratification organisations, like the veteran campaigner, Phyllis Schlafly (1977) that ERA would abrogate the federal and state laws that require men to financially support their wives and families and make illegal all differences of obligation, treatment or provision between men and women. Because of the broader nature of the issue the anti-ERA movement was able to attract a greater cross-section of support than the pro-life lobby. The ERA was represented as threatening the way of life of a substantial section of the population regardless of their doctrinal attitude to abortion. The latter responded by providing a women's army of tireless, volunteer foot soldiers.

The development of pro-family organisations in Britain was a much quieter affair than its counterpart in the USA. The single most important factor was probably the much greater secularisation of British culture and social organisation. Ninety per cent of Americans believe in a personal God compared with 31 per cent of British; 79 per cent of

Americans report comfort from their religion compared with 46 per cent of British; Americans attend weekly church at twice the rate of the British (Gallop and Castelli, 1989).

However, there was a slow but consistent development in moral crusading organisations in Britain from the mid-1960s. The 1967 abortion reform legislation triggered off two anti-abortion pressure groups, the Society for the Protection of the Unborn Child (SPUC), and its militant breakaway, LIFE. While a large proportion of their memberships is Catholic, the organisations themselves have no formal association with the Roman Catholic Church, and receive no funds or other material assistance (Marsh and Chambers, 1981). The moral market place consisted of the pro-life groups, the traditional religious moral orders, and long-established women's organisations such as the Mothers' Union and the Women's Institute; groups of secular moral entrepreneurs such as those who rallied round Lord Longford's 'Festival of Light' campaign. Since Britain has no written constitution, there was no equivalent to the ERA in the politics of the family. However, there were a number of heated controversies which generated fierce differences in public opinion: around the regulation of sexuality – divorce, prostitution and homosexuality; the representation of sexuality – obscenity, censorship and sex education; the regulation of human reproduction – abortion, family planning to single people and under-age girls, embryo research.

These failed to deflect the modernising Labour and Conservative governments of the 1960s and 1970s, but they did catch the ear of a faction of the Tory Party searching for a populist hook on which to hang their vision for the Party and for the Nation. Public confidence in the government faded following the world oil crisis of 1973–4, the fiscal crisis and the involvement of the International Monetary Fund in the management of the British economy. In the build-up to the General Election of 1979, the revived Tory Party with its new leader, Margaret Thatcher, used the family metaphor to establish a link in the public's mind between Labour governments and moral permissivism, industrial unrest, the failing economy and the loss of Britain's place in the world.

Pro-family organisations in Britain blossomed after the election of Mrs Thatcher and a Conservative government in 1979. The Conservative Family Campaign, Family Forum, Family Concern, Child and Family Protection, Christian Social Action, the Campaign for Family and Nation, the National Family Trust, and Concern for Family and Womanhood joined the older social purity organisations to pursue the cause of 'traditional values' in public policy. As in America, the rank-and-file membership of these moral crusading organisations was composed largely of women.

Explanations of the emergence of the pro-family movement

It is appropriate at this point to consider the explanations that have been offered for the development of this mass pro-family women's movement mobilised to challenge feminism's claim to speak on their behalf.

It may seem odd to the reader to employ social movement theory in this context because we have become used to linking the term 'social movement' with those 'progressive' causes of the post-war period associated with centre-left politics and the object of much Marxist analysis (Touraine, 1971; Castells, 1977; Aglietta, 1979; Melucci, 1980; Jameson, 1984; Bowles and Gintis, 1986). However, the distinguishing features of social movements is primarily their organisational form, the relationship of the members to the organisation and the overall political objective. In contrast to orthodox political organisations, social movements tend to be informally organised on a network basis with few permanent officers, a fluid membership and income derived from small, voluntary individual donations and *ad hoc* fund-raising events. Movements tend to be historically short-lived, either dissolving or mutating to a more formal political organisation. Members have a greater emotional commitment to the movement through which they derive an experiential belongingness and common sense of identity. They are informed by a wider, less pragmatic vision of the 'good society' and are willing to adopt unorthodox methods to achieve their aims.

On this basis there can be little doubt that pro-family organisations constituted a social movement. First, the membership, on average, had little previous experience of organisational activity. Second, while there were major national umbrella organisations, vast number of *ad hoc* local groups were organised, funded and supported by grass-roots members' activities. Third, with some notable exceptions, there were few national leaders; little national co-ordination or funding; no permanent bureaucracies, organisation being mostly based on networks. Fourth, their strategies and tactics were split between traditional lobbying, and forms of direct action such as parades, demonstrations, mass rallies, street theatre, even civil disobedience. Fifth, they were united by a common cause beyond that of the immediate issues, to which they were profoundly and emotionally committed. The similarities with the women's liberation movement are evident.

Explanations for such social movements have tended to concentrate on the general social class and status composition of their members. For example, on the basis of their research on the earlier American Temperance Movement and the anti-pornography campaigns in the USA respectively, Gusfield (1963) and Zurcher *et al.* (1971) suggested that social groups which enjoy a social status and material privilege, respond to the threat of new social groups by distancing themselves on the grounds of moral superiority and by attempting to use the state to impose their morality as a national standard.

In Britain, Wallis's research (1976) on the National Viewers and Listeners Association (NVALA), also concluded that moral crusades were primarily a phenomenon of the entrepreneurial middle classes squeezed by the dominance of corporate capitalism and the huge expansion of interventionist state, and the concomitant shift in ideology from individualism, production, thrift and self-denial to collectivism, consumption, credit and hedonism. Wallis argues that the isolation of the traditional middle classes in their occupational, suburban and rural ghettoes was undermined by the advent of television. These changes in moral values and lifestyle seemed to be epitomised by the new permissive treatment of sex on television and it was for this reason that it became the major target for a crusade.

Berger and Berger (1984), directly addressing the emergence of a strong pro-family movement in the United States in the 1970s, sees it as evidence of a growing alliance between the business, lower-middle and working classes in response to the threat of the new 'knowledge class' with its base in the 'production, distribution, and administration of symbolic knowledge' (p. 49). This opposition focused around symbols of a pre-modern American way of life, of which a most emotive one is the American family. They detect 'an unmistakable undertone of class resentment and class hostility in the rhetoric of the neo-traditionalists', and thus conclude that 'the current war over the family is but one battle in a much larger conflict between classes in America' (p. 50).

Others (Morrison and Tracey, 1978; Cliff, 1979) did point out that while the membership of the NVALA was predominantly rural and suburban middle class, this covered diverse status groups, only some of which could be said to be in decline. Further, the opposition of the NVALA was to a whole way of life summed up as secularism rather than to any specific class or social group in British society. They concluded that the most salient factor was religious conviction of a fundamentalist Christian character. This emphasis on the independent power of moral conviction is one which has particular interest when we turn to social movements which have women as their major constituency and the family as a major mobilising symbol.

The most prominent hypothesis in the American literature was that the most significant factor that divided the radical women's movement from the other women's movement was the relationship of women to paid employment. However, empirical research based on various General Social Surveys, the National Election Study and a number of systematic national and local state studies suggests perhaps surprisingly that the situation is considerably more complex.

Of course, there are recognised difficulties with the categorisations of social class and gender which have been well rehearsed, particularly in the British literature (Goldthorpe, 1983; Stanworth, 1984; Goldthorpe, 1984; Heath and Britten, 1984; Crompton and Mann, 1986; Lee and Turner, 1996). However, most of the American studies used multivariate analyses sensitive to the complex determinants of women's socio-economic position. While the problems are not eliminated by these techniques, the results are sufficiently indicative to demand re-examination of certain widespread assumptions.

Of particular interest are the similarities between the activists of both camps who were generally younger, more urban, scored higher on education and socio-economic indicators, and had higher participation rates in public and community life relative to their respective supporters. Anti-abortion, anti-ERA activists were less likely to be in full-time work, but in comparisons between full-time homemakers and women employed outside the home, only weak differences were found in attitudes toward abortion (Granberg and Granberg, 1980). Himmelstein (1986) suggests that the battle was 'less a struggle between polarised social classes and more one between contending elites with quite different world views' (p. 4).

When it comes to supporters among the general population, the data is simply inconsistent for age, class and race where regional differences produce opposite effects. Differences are attenuated over time for education levels. Further, the data does not support a political polarisation of women in relation to the family issue on the basis of marital status or whether or not they are in paid work (Staggenborg, 1998). Indeed one fear of anti-ERA women was that the availability of traditional women's work would be undermined by equality by forcing them to compete with men.

In fact the empirical evidence points to the importance of the role of religion in the women's lives as the overriding differentiator (Granberg, 1978, 1981; Harding, 1981; Bolce *et al.*, 1982; Luker, 1984; Wood and Hughes, 1984; Himmelstein, 1986). When religious affinity and related social and cultural networks are controlled, other variables, such as socio-economic status, educational profile, racial diversity and political experience, are considerably reduced in significance, but holding the latter constant does not diminish the effect of the former (Tedin *et al.*, 1977; Huber *et al.*, 1978; Boles, 1979; Burris, 1983; Berry, 1986; Mansbridge, 1986; Mathews and De Hart, 1990).

This is not to suggest that socio-economic factors are unimportant, but that their effects may be mediated or overdetermined by other factors. In this case ethico-religious elements stand out. This may go some way to explaining why the housewife–employee dichotomy did not turn out to have the level of predictive value that might have been expected. While not denying the objective obstacles to the full parti- cipation of women in paid employment, there is sufficient evidence to suggest that the effect of women's 'prior orientations' should not be discounted. Thus, among working women there may be two 'qualita- tively different types': those for whom paid work is always secondary to their family life and those with a greater employment commitment (Hakim, 1991, 1992, 1995; Crompton, 1996). In this context, the concept of 'gendered moral rationalities' developed by Duncan and Edwards (1999) to explain the labour market behaviour of lone mothers, is interesting. Their investigation into women's perceptions about the relationship between motherhood and paid work took account of class, cultural and ethnic differences, the influence of different types of neighbourhoods and of different labour markets and social policy regimes in the UK, USA, Germany and Sweden. They conclude that while economic and social policy assumes that people are motivated by economic rationality, for the women in their sample 'it is socially negotiated, non-economic, understandings about what is morally right and socially acceptable which are primary factors in determining what is seen as rational behaviour' (p. 18). This con- cept may be usefully extended more generally to the behaviour of pro- family women.

The critical factor in the American evidence seems to be a set of interlocking beliefs and values about what constitutes a fulfilling life for a woman. For pro-choice, pro-ERA activists, this may include but is not exhausted by marriage, children and family life. They may be part of a life strategy, planned to include active participation in the public sphere and not subject to the whims of Nature or the shackles of tradition. For those women with a religious orientation, self-esteem and respect in the community derive primarily from their role as wife and mother. They therefore find any diminution of the status of either, or of the foetus, a direct threat to their very identity. However, contrary to the general labelling of pro-family women as anti-feminist, many of them responded positively to other feminist objectives, such as equal opportunities in education, employment, pay, public office. Even among evangelical Christian women only one-third could be categorised as anti-feminist and more were likely to support NOW than the Moral Majority (Wilcox, 1989). It was the identification of feminism with anti-familialism that constituted the substance of the opposition to abortion and the ERA (Mason and Bumpass, 1975; Bolce *et al.*, 1982; Pohli, 1983; Luker, 1984; Wilcox, 1989).

Much has also been made of the links between moral and political conservatism (Crawford, 1980; Petchesky, 1981; Pankhurst and Houseknecht, 1983; Peele, 1984). There is certainly no doubt that right-wing orchestrators of the Republican revival operating from the Heritage Foundation in the mid-1970s saw in the politics of the family the opportunity for appropriating social and moral values for the Conservative cause and getting vast numbers of non-voting moral conservatives to the ballot box (*Conservative Digest*, 1979, 1980). Nor is there any doubt of the importance of the success of this strategy in helping Ronald Reagan into the White House in 1980.

However, the view that the pro-family movement was a creation of the New Right (Gordon and Hunter, 1977/8; Eisenstein, 1981, 1982; Ehrenreich 1982a, Dworkin, 1983; Faludi, 1992) fails to take account of the fact that a genuine grass-roots movement existed independently of political groupings and prior to the mobilisation of moral conser-vative forces in the run-up to the presidential election. Indeed, it might be said that it was precisely because concern about abortion and the family was genuinely broad-based and had already polarised women that the Democratic vote was undermined and that rather than being a pawn of grander machinations, the pro-family movement took advantage of the changing political currents to pursue its own quite specific ends (Hunter, 1991). Further evidence for this view, for example, is found in the subsequent distancing of factions within the 'right-to-life' movement from the political elements. The rift within the priesthood over the alliance between the Bishops and the Republican Party was much publicised in the Catholic press. Many within the Church were dismayed at the association with a party which in its rightwards move was preparing to dismantle much of the poverty programmes which the Catholic Church supported, a view shared by the lay Catholic population (McKeegan, 1992).

The membership of the British moral conservation movement was also primarily women. They shared a similar pattern of socio-economic, geographical location, age and marital status with their American counterparts, and again the most significant factor is their religious beliefs and related social values and mores (Morrison and Tracey, 1978; Cliff, 1979; Weeks, 1981, 1985).

Similar assertions have been made about their politics and their anti-feminism (David, 1983, 1986; Fitzgerald, 1983; Marshall, 1985; King, 1987) and the overlap between many of the leaders of the British pro-family movement and well-known activists on the Tory right has been well documented (Durham 1989, 1991). However, leading British social purity campaigns were never as close financially or in personnel with right-wing politics as their American equivalents. Analysis of grass-roots supporters and sympathisers suggests a varied political affiliation and an ambiguous relationship with the ideals and goals of feminism (Segal, 1983; Bland, 1985; Campbell, 1987; Wilson, 1987; Durham, 1986, 1989, 1991; Somerville, 1992a). Long before the media exposure of sexual scandals among pro-family Conservative politicians in the mid-1990s, there was a cooling of the relationship as it became apparent that the family rhetoric of the Tory government was not materialising in practice.

What we have, then, are social movements predominantly composed of women, relating to and engaging with mainstream political agencies in pursuit of their goals but remaining independent of them as a social force. Social movement theory would tend to explain these movements and the war between them in terms of their location in the class and status configuration of society and the 'interests' derived from that configuration. In fact what divides them seems much more broadly related to what Hunter (1991) has called 'cultural re-alignment', cross-cutting gender, class, political, denominational, racial and ethnic divisions, in which differences and their associated 'interests' are constructed in a struggle over the symbols of public culture and their embeddedness in the institutional framework of public policy.

The question of women's interests

It is precisely this element of political activity in the construction of group interests and subsequent mobilisation that has been the focus of 'resource mobilisation' theorists, like McCarthy and Zald (1973; and Zald and McCarthy, 1987). They do not reject the importance of class and status as potential sources of frustration, resentment and conflict. Nor do they, unlike the rational choice model which they developed, neglect the fact that people organise in support of causes beyond their most immediate rational self-interest. However, they do shift our attention from predisposing factors to the social movement itself, the characteristics of its organisational structure and behaviour and of others in the field, the resources by which it mobilises public support and the strategies and tactics it adopts relative to its objectives.

Hindess (1987) has taken this further in arguing that interests are always construed by specific organisations, what he conceives as 'collective actors', in the process of assessing reasons for taking or not taking particular forms of action. They are very important in politics as conceptions on which rest important policy decisions for the organisation, in their role in political polemics on which public support for the organisation may depend, and in their effectivity in achieving desired ends on which hangs the credibility of the organisation. Such assessments are shaped by the political, ideological and organisational traditions in which politics is conducted in any given society, and change over time.

The importance of interests in political discourse and political action, however, should not be confused with their ontological validity, which can never be known, and therefore cannot determine the support of their imputed constituencies. Which interests individuals recognise will not just depend on their class or their social situation which may produce contradictory criteria, but on the means of calculation available to them. This will include the range of ideological discourses accessible to them. Critical in how they define their interests, therefore, will be the argument, form and practice of intervening agencies. Such an approach is missing from much of the literature on women's organisations involved in the politics of the family. However, if this argument is to be granted any validity, it not only points to the inadequacy of a class analysis but also to any other analysis that is predicated on the assumption of ontological interests as the basis for social movements. And this challenges some of our basic assumptions about the feminist movement.

Biological sex appears to provide one of the clearest cases of a pre-given constituency of interests. Women, by the very dualistic categories of social organisation based on sexual difference, would appear to contain within their own bodies the basis for the generation of common interests. Hence attempts at theorising the question of women's interests have asserted 'reproduction' as the basis for a legitimate claim to the representation of women as a group, on the grounds that the gendered division of labour in both the private and the public spheres is a consequence of 'reproduction' in much the same way as the social class division of labour is a function of 'production' (Eisenstein, 1981; Sapiro, 1981). This issue received its most rigorous theoretical airing in the fiercely debated 'domestic labour debate' within Marxism, with the attempt to establish whether or not women's work in both the biological and social reproduction of the worker under capitalism, contributed to the exchange value of commodities and hence to the creation of surplus value. On this issue rested the question of whether women's domestic labour was 'productive labour', and therefore central rather than marginal to capitalist economies (Harrison, 1973; Seccombe, 1974; Dalla Costa and James, 1975).

Even those unhappy with the term 'interest' because it draws feminism into the ideological terrain of liberal democracy which is at root patriarchal (Pateman, 1988), nevertheless based their preference for the concept, 'need', on the same foundationalist premise of the common female experience of reproductive biology (Diamond and Hartsock, 1981). And indeed it was on this basis that the common cause of feminism was constructed. It also explains the transposition of the term, women, from its profane use in the empirics of everyday life, to Women, a sacred symbol, a collective emblem of its individual entities, endowed as a totem with the power to mobilise and empower those who recognise it.

However, the examination of the two women's movements illustrates that this hyposthetised ontological reality did not engender self-evident common interests. Both groups claimed that their theory and practice was based on women's interests as grounded in women's experience. Both regarded themselves as simply organisational expressions of the reality of women's lived experience of marriage and family. Faced with the failure of the first-order determinant – reproductive biology – to explain the lack of common perception of interests, feminists tended to resort to the second order – the stratification of women in social classes and status groups. But as we have seen, this is not the main distinguishing feature between the two groups.

An illuminating way of conceiving this issue may be to follow Parks's (1982) assertion that in liberal democracies with their 'politics of choice' the concept of interest functions 'to persuade, to assert and to deny claims that an action or policy increases one's control over the conditions of choice' (1982, p. 549). Jonasdottir (1988) has pointed out that this aspect of interest, what she calls 'form', is neglected by social scientists who have focussed primarily on 'content'. In the case in point, the debate centres around the question of whether or not abortion reform or the ERA would result in public policies in the interests of women. The 'content' aspect of interests clearly is always subject to conflict and cannot be resolved by recourse to first principles. Instead, the common experience of reproductive biology might provide for a shared interest in increasing women's control over their choices, however defined, by influencing public policy.

This may make sense of the evidence from the USA of an increase of 'gender identification' among women of all demographic groups since the 1970s, that is the extent to which they identify with the category, woman, and among such women a growing concern with public policy (Gurin, 1985). There is no evidence, however, of a concomitant growth in the level of endorsement of the women's movement. Miller *et al.* (1988) look to a longer-term increase in 'gender consciousness' or solidarity, as more women come to view continuing gender inequalities as unacceptable, but they also admit that group identification cannot be taken to imply policy cohesion.

What we may be witnessing, therefore, is a growing of interest among women in having their views represented in political forum so to increase their control over the conditions of choice in areas that they value or for which they calculate they derive benefit, but also a polarisation in the content of their views. Hence Phillips's (1991) endorsement of Jonasdottir's formulation that 'since segregation is a fundamental ordering principle of gendered societies, women can be said to have at least one interest in common. They need improved access to every sphere' (Phillips, p. 73) misses the point. Access to the decision-making sphere may be desired by some women precisely to attempt to ensure the continuation of gender segregation. And large numbers of them mobilised against ERA for this reason.

The above analysis of the two women's movements suggests that how women understand their experience depends on the different access to and engagement with discourses through which meanings are constructed about the nature of individual and social relations, of social hierarchies, of sexuality and sexual difference, of personal identity and social responsibility, of the sacred and the profane. It is these which make sense of lived experience and create vulnerabilities to specific moral and political ideologies. In this case it was the ideologies of feminism, marxism, liberalism, Christianity and conservatism, and the organisational forces which promoted them which constructed the interests of the family and those of women. The construction of the family as antithetical to women's interests by one group of women, particularly when it appeared to be supported by the policy actions of government, mobilised another group of women around a counter-formulation. The interests of women were thus articulated in the process of political struggle itself.

5

The New Right:
Anti-Feminism in Power?

The ability of the pro-life movement to interpret the changes in the organisation of domestic life as the breakdown of the family, link them with the economic uncertainties of the 1970s and attribute both to the effects of the anti-familialism of feminism and the 'permissive society', was effective in increasing their influence among anxious elements of the public. As we have seen in the case of the Kennedy and Wilson administrations, mobilising public opinion in itself is no guarantee that an issue will be adopted in the formal political arena. It was, therefore, the emergence of two further factors that led to the full politicisation of the family. On the one hand, the effects of moral pluralism and family diversity began to make heavy demands on public funds and, on the other, family issues became increasingly important in the internal ideological politics and for the political ambitions of the Conservative and Republican Parties in Britain and the USA.

This chapter will describe how the public expenditure dimension of the family issue was of particular interest to an emerging political constellation committed to massive reductions in public spending, indeed to dismantling the institutions and instruments of post-war welfarism. In addition it was a political constellation for which the family was especially important, both as a central concept in its belief systems and as a symbol uniting different constituencies within its own social base and potential sympathisers. In my view, it is these two factors which were more important than any anti-feminist backlash in moving the family from the moral battlefield on to the formal political stage, and in propelling the two superstars of a regenerated conservatism, Margaret Thatcher and Ronald Reagan, into the national and international limelight.

The public expenditure dimension

The extent to which people are able to maintain moral autonomy in their private lives, has always been dependent on the extent to which they are able to financially maintain their personal and family circumstances independently of aid from outside agencies, such as the church, charitable organisations or the state. In an age where income supplement, direct and indirect, is largely the responsibility of the state, the right to privacy becomes contingent on the discretion of public agencies. It is in the context of public expenditure, then, that the disintegration of families and the liberalisation of moral and legal codes becomes a concern of governments. It was the 'public burden' costs of moral pluralism which became a major factor in the politicisation of the family and which will continue to make family norms and organisation an issue for governments in the future.

Steiner's (1981) account of the American experience is illuminating in this respect. In the case of abortion, the pro-life lobby was unable to prevent the Supreme Court's ruling in 1973 which provided for early abortion as a constitutionally protected exercise of the right to privacy, but it was successful in 1976 through the Hyde Amendment in persuading Congress to severely restrict the use of federal Medicaid funds to finance this new constitutional right.

Similarly, the concern about teenage pregnancies was not seriously taken up by national politicians until the 1970s, although the rate was by then 20 per cent lower than in the 1950s when the common solution to the problem was the quiet adoption of illegitimate babies by childless couples. The reason for the change in politicians' sensitivity to the issue can be found in the increasing numbers of adolescent mothers keeping their babies, consequent on the intervening change in moral climate reflected in professional definitions of 'the best interest of the child', and the shift from private to public support of illegitimacy.

Family income support also became a political issue in the 1970s as the numbers of single-parent families receiving public assistance (Aid to Families with Dependent Children – AFDC) increased, in particular the numbers of families with 'absent' as opposed to dead fathers. Indeed, it was claimed that AFDC itself incited family disintegration since it encouraged fathers to abandon their family responsibilities in the knowledge that the state would substitute. This led to the reform of AFDC allowing states to pay it to families where the father was unemployed (AFDC-U). What is noticeable about the debate, however, is that it was not conducted in terms of children's needs, but of how best to use federal funds to secure two-parent families whose dependence on public assistance could be expected to be short term. This extension of welfare to indigent two-parent families was accompanied by a policy of federal enforcement of child support by fathers of one-parent families, which made co-operation of an AFDC applicant in establishing paternity and the whereabouts of the absent father a condition of benefit. As Steiner (1981) notes, there was no comparable attempt to use federal power or funds to compel child support payments from absent fathers whose families were not public dependants. He concludes, 'to the extent that a system can be devised that deters fathers from shifting the burden of child support from themselves to public assistance, family dissolution declines as a public issue' (p. 113).

In Britain, too, the costs of moral pluralism in an age of economic recession and fiscal crisis became apparent. The Finer Report (1974) on One-Parent Families established the scale of the problem in terms of both the increasing numbers and the level of demand on state income support as a result of non-payment of maintenance by fathers and the inability of many lone mothers to support themselves and their children. A one-parent benefit was introduced and a number of other state benefits and provisions were subsequently adjusted to take into account the special circumstances of the lone parent.

Concern about the increasing public expenditure on welfare and tax allowances attendant on family dissolution made politicians begin to consider the costs of liberalism in personal life. The traditionalists' moral arguments for the restriction of individual freedom of choice in personal life became supplemented by claims that such restriction would also be economical in terms of public expenditure.

First, there are the costs of divorce itself; much is paid for by state-subsidised legal aid. Secondly, in the context of an employment structure in which women's work is predominantly low-paid and part-time relative to that of men, an ethical climate in which mothers normally are awarded custody of the children, and fathers are reluctant to pay adequate maintenance, divorce has meant the impoverishment of a great number of women and children. This, and the growth of never-married mothers, has had the well-known consequence of the 'welfare mothers' phenomenon. In the USA the racial dimension of the welfare costs of lone parents makes the issue particularly sensitive. Thirdly, the decline in the numbers of informal carers for the disabled and the increasing numbers of elderly occasioned by trends in female

employment, family formation and dissolution has serious implications for public expenditure in social and health services. George
Brown of the Society of Conservative Lawyers estimated that in
Britain, 'The financial cost to the country of family turmoil probably
amounts to well over 2 billion a year, including the indirect costs to
industry' (Brown, 1987, p. 143).

The public expenditure dimension of family pluralism, then,
exploited by the moralist lobby, increasingly became a focus for political concern as governments tried to deal with the fiscal crises of the
mid-1970s. The liberal democrats in the USA and the social liberals
in Britain were forced to introduce deflationary policies which made
them unpopular with their electorates and which brought into sharp
relief the economic consequences of family dissolution. As a consequence of both, prominent political figures became sensitised to
the electoral implications of the war over the family. The family
moved onto the political agenda.

The family and the US Presidency

The first major politician to capitalise on the public concern for the
family issue was the Democrat President, Jimmy Carter. In 1976, he
initiated plans for a White House Conference on the American family
with representatives from a wide range of organisations, as a prelimin-
ary to a coherent family policy for the whole nation. However, the
whole project ended in much the same debacle as its precedessor, the
Moynihan initiative, for at least some of the same reasons (Steiner,
1981; Friedan, 1983).

First, it is clear that there was no agreement within the bureaucracy
about the specific objectives of a national family policy. A Family
Impact Seminar concluded that the enormous differences between
families preclude any generalisations about the effects of government
policy on 'the family' and indeed question the viability of a single
unified national family policy altogether. Secondly there were disputes
about the appointment of the senior conference staff leading to the
resignation of the initial executive director, a black woman divorcee.
Thirdly, and perhaps most damaging of all, however, was the inept
handling of politically sensitive interest groups. The organisers
ignored attempts of a coalition of nine national black organisations
to contribute relevant personnel and a black dimension to the conference programme and policy development. Equally inept was the

cavalier treatment of a similar consortium representing Catholic organisations. Even an influential coalition of national voluntary and professional organisations which normally work closely with government departments was cold-shouldered.

The eventual outcome was three conferences in 1980, none of them at the White House. Very little was achieved by way of developing a national family policy, and a large number of religious, professional, ethnic and special interest groups were frustrated, alienated and disaffected as a result. Having taken up the problem of the family at a Presidential level, the failure to deliver even an effective conference contributed to the drawing of lines between the contending factions in what was to develop into a war over the family.

Following the Carter debacle, the traditionalists found a new champion in the Republican candidate, Ronald Reagan, a known opponent of abortion. Restoring the strength and independence of the 'traditional' family was a central plank in his overall strategy to get the American economy back on its feet. America's loss of pre-eminence in the world economy and politics was blamed on liberal welfarism, the mammoth bureaucracies that grew up to carry out its interventions and the dependency culture that it encouraged. Reducing taxation and cutting federal spending would restore the incentive and the ability of families to look after themselves and restore American pride and spirit of independence. Familialism and nationalism were the twin themes in Reagan's rhetorical repertoire. Both were sweet music to the moral crusaders. Most commentators (*inter alia*, Crawford, 1980; Petchesky, 1981; Pankhurst and Houseknecht, 1983; Peele, 1984; Abbott and Wallace, 1992) agree that a key factor in Reagan's triumph was the alliance that was built up during the 1970s between the political Right and the evangelical Christian movement.

The historical association of the Protestant fundamentalism of the Southern states with racist, anti-Catholic, anti-communist right-wing politics is well known, but whereas in the past its adherents were largely poor whites, this was transformed by the wealth of oil and rich grain farming of the 'sun-belt revival'. The fundamentalist churches became an influential part of community and political life, their message liberated by the new communication technologies. For example, the Christian Broadcasting Network, founded by the Baptist evangelist, Pat Robertson, was reported as grossing some $230 million a year (*The Observer*, 28 February 1988) and operating a satellite network reaching cable systems and television and radio stations across the United States. It was this aspect of their propaganda work which was effective in mobilising their followers in the pro-Life and the anti-ERA campaigns. These Christian demagogues of the 'electronic church' exerted a powerful influence on the imagination of millions of Americans, experiencing their first recession since the Second World War, confused by the apparent ability of small Middle East nations to hold the West to ransom, and exposed to daily reminders by the media of the increase in crime, drug abuse, divorce rates, teenage pregnancies and abortion.

This did not go unnoticed by those on the right of the Republican Party, in particular, the infamous 'Gang of Four' – Paul Weyrich, Richard Viguery, Terry Dolan and Howard Phillips – who saw in it the opportunity for a coalition of morally conservative forces which could be won to the Conservative cause. In the mid-1970s they founded the Heritage Foundation, a think-tank for Reagan, the main objective of which was to turn the plethora of right-wing policies into a popular political agenda, the National Conservative Political Action Committee, which was to target individual politicians, and the Conservative Caucuses, which were to mobilise at the local level.

One of their key objectives was to broaden the electoral appeal of conservative politics by activating non-voting groups in the population. Among these were religious congregations which traditionally repudiated politics as a corrupting secular activity. Weyrich, in the *Conservative Digest* (1979), estimated that 'there may be nearly 100 million Americans – 50 million born-again Protestants, 30 million morally conservative Catholics, 3 million Mormons, and 2 million Orthodox Jews – from which to draw members of a pro-family, Bible-believing coalition'. It was to this end that a strategy of incorporating the Protestant fundamentalists was adopted. A meeting with Jerry Falwell led to the establishment of the organisation 'Moral Majority', made up of three subsidiaries: the Moral Majority Foundation, Moral Majority Inc., to which was charged the lobbying function, and the Moral Majority Action Committee charged with finance and funding political candidates. Moral Majority was intended as an ecumenical movement drawing on all religions with orthodox positions on moral values and channelling their energies and resources to propel a new theocracy into the White House.

The televangelists ensured that the right connections were made on the national radio and television networks between moral concerns and the stances of political parties and their representatives while the pastors urged their congregations to vote for candidates who stood for family values. This conservative coalition also ensured that right-wing interests were well represented in all organisations which held a brief for social and moral issues. The *Conservative Digest* itself (1980) provides profiles on the leadership of pro-family organisations which reveals the intersection of personnel between it and right-wing politicos. It is ironic that the reforms following the Watergate scandal, which limited the amount of money that individuals could contribute to political campaigns, provided the means both for the rise to power of experts in mass fund-raising, and for the growing importance of the 'little man and little woman' in American politics.

The full significance of such a block vote is realised only when one remembers two important facts about the American political system. The first is that, given the low turn-out in American elections, they can be won on very small margins. Getting a previously non-voting section of the electorate to the polls, therefore, can have a major impact on the result. This certainly seems to have been the case in both the 1980 election for the Presidency and that for Senate. The second is that after the election is won, the President brings in with him a whole new administration. Political power in policy-making resides less in the permanent civil service, as it does in other Western democracies, than in the White House bureaucracy. In theory this makes possible a wholesale revolution in political vision, government agenda-setting, policy objectives, and in governmental structure itself, though, of course, in a federal system like the USA, the considerable independence of individual states is always a counter-balance. The stakes involved then for the pro-Reaganites were very high.

The credibility of some of the most famous TV preachers, such as Marvin Garmon, Jim Bakker and Jimmy Swaggart, was undermined in the late 1980s when their ungodly lust after each other's financial empires led to mutual public denunciations of adultery, consorting with prostitutes, and addiction to pornography, and revealed multi-million dollar fraud. Nevertheless, a decade of persuasion through the construction of a network of interchange between religious bodies, moral pressure groups and politically conservative organisations enabled the moral majority movement to survive the scandals sufficiently for Pat Robertson to remain a serious contender in subsequent rounds for the Republican Presidential nomination.

There can be little doubt about the importance to the Right of the American family as a crusading symbol, and the communication techniques of the electronic churches and the moral crusading organisations for mobilising conservative opinion. However, it must be emphasised that it was precisely because concern about abortion and the family was genuinely broad-based that it could be used to undermine the Democrat vote. The politics of the family which had already polarised women, was crucial in the Right's appropriation of social and moral issues for the Conservative case and was important in enabling them to emerge as the dominant force in American politics and society. It was certainly a factor which helped to put Ronald Reagan into the White House, feeding in as it did to serious concerns about the Democrats' ability to manage the economy effectively.

British politics and the family

On a lesser scale, pressure groups developed in Britain in the 1970s with the aim of raising the profile of the family and related social and moral issues with the government, with little success except in relation to family poverty. The Labour government was embarassed by pressure from an uneasy coalition of Tory and Labour backbench MPs of compatible moral and religious persuasions, special interest organisations, the churches, women's organisations, the TUC and the media, into introducing Child Benefit in 1977, an untaxed non-means-tested cash benefit paid direct to the mother which replaced family allowance and child tax allowance which accrued to fathers, and an interim One-Parent Benefit which subsequently became regularised as part of the benefit system (Field, 1976; Jacobs and Kellner, 1976; Land, 1977; Field, 1977). However, such measures were specific and discrete and not the outcome of a thorough interdepartmental review of changes in family life and their implications for government policy (Phillips, 1978). In general, the Callaghan government was unresponsive to the moral crusaders. However, there were those in the Conservative Party whose hearing was more attuned to new issues.

Sir Keith Joseph, often regarded as Margaret Thatcher's mentor and a prominent member of the Tory Shadow Cabinet, was one of the first to launch the theme song of the revived Tory Party: that all Britain's economic and social ills and its demise as a great world power were due to the trendy philosophies of the 1960s, which had weakened the family and hence undermined the moral fibre of the British people. For some of the Tory leadership, deviant motherhood had a particular responsibility. In an article in *The Times* (21 Oct. 1974), Joseph acknowledged the influence of the moral crusader, Mary Whitehouse, before issuing an indictment of working-class lone mothers: 'They are producing problem children, the future unmarried

mothers, denizens of our borstals, subnormal educational establish-
ments, prisons, hostels for drifters' (Joseph, 1974). For Patrick Jenkin,
who was to become Minister of State for Social Services, it was working mothers: 'Quite frankly I don't think mothers have the same right
to work as fathers do. If the good Lord had intended us to have equal
rights to go out to work he wouldn't have created men and women.
These are biological facts... The pressures on young wives to go out
to work devalue motherhood itself' (Jenkin, 1977).

Certainly the defeat of Ted Heath and the victory of Margaret
Thatcher in the fight for the Tory Party leadership in 1975 opened
the way for a more populist and demagogic style of leadership, more
conducive to the moralist lobby. The issue of the family was the
subject of the social policy session at the 1977 Party Conference,
followed up the subsequent year by a paper entitled *Family Policy*
published by the Conservative Party Research Department. The
family was also the overriding theme for the Conservative Women's
Conference in 1978.

It would be misleading to suggest that the pro-family lobby was as
important to Mrs Thatcher's electoral success in the 1979 General
Election as it was to Reagan winning the US Presidency. Despite the
political prominence of the family in both Labour and Conservative
public utterances in 1978 and the predictions in some of the national
press (*Sunday Times*, 14 May 1978) that it would be a key election
issue, it faded from view and the 1979 General Election was fought
and won on the economy and industrial relations. Most commentators of the political scene agree that the Conservative victory was in
large part the result of the votes of substantial numbers of skilled and
semi-skilled male workers who calculated that they were more likely to
improve their personal lot with Tory promises of tax cuts and free
collective bargaining than with Labour.

Nevertheless, the family was an effective political weapon as a
metaphor in the populist language developed by the new Tories to
explain their radical plans to change the direction of British public
policy and economic fortune. The national economy was likened to
the household budget, national identity and unity were identified with
a family pulling together in difficult times; law and order legislation
with family discipline; welfare cuts with disincentives for family disintegration. The family, in the deft hands of Mrs Thatcher, united
economic with moral concerns.

It was this appeal to the common-sense of ordinary people over the
heads of the so-called experts that persuaded enough of them that the

Labour Party was an out-of-date, class-conscious organisation with an obsession with bureaucratic centralisation which stifled individual initiative, effort and choice, and that the Conservative Party would return power to the people as individuals through their policies of privatisation, deregulation and decentralisation. It was an appeal to people as individual and family consumers, not as members of corporate, social, cultural or economic groups, and certainly not as members of progressive social movements.

Interestingly enough, it was in the 1980s, *after* the Conservatives came to power, that the moral crusading groups grew in number. Those with a particular brief for the family included Family Concern, Child and Family Protection, Christian Social Action, the Campaign for Family and Nation, Concern for Family and Womanhood, the National Family Trust, the Conservative Family Campaign, Family Forum and probably the most influential, Family and Youth Concern, previously,The Responsible Society. These were regularly given a platform by various organisations on the political Right, such as the Monday Club, the Salisbury Group, the Freedom Association, the Adam Smith Institute, the Centre for Policy Studies, the Institute for Economic Affairs and the Social Affairs Unit (Cockett, 1994).

Durham (1993) provides rich data of the close relationships (including wedlock) between the leaders of the main British moral lobbies and Conservative MPs, including several members of the government itself, and a fastidious account of the attempts to move legislation towards greater consistency with traditional Christian sexual ethics. Both Durham (1985, 1993) and Abbott and Wallace (1992) date the pro-family movement in Britain from the founding of the Conservative Family Campaign in 1986, whereas it seems to me that this can be justified only by the use of very narrowly defined boundaries of the political. Such a group did not appear out of a political vacuum and its main sponsors were all long-serving activists in moral conservation.

As early as 1976, Conservative MPs formed a Lords and Commons Family and Child Protection Group many of whom were members or supporters of the anti-abortion organisations. It was also Tory MPs who agitated for the 1973 National Health Service (Reorganisation) Act to make it a statutory obligation for local health authorities to require parental consent before providing contraceptive advice or devices to under-age children. The campaign on this issue, led by another rural housewife, Victoria Gillick, sparked off a national controversy and led all the way to adjudication in the House of

Lords. While Gillick's deep involvement in this and other moral campaigns no doubt derives primarily from her devout Catholicism, she was also an experienced political activist with involvements on the extreme right of the Conservative spectrum (*The Guardian*, 31 January 1984; *Searchlight*, February 1984). Certainly the campaign consolidated the growing partnership between MPs, mainly Conservative, and energetic moralist organisations. Again it was the influence of Valerie Riches, the National Honorary Secretary of Family and Youth Concern (ex-The Responsible Society) which was behind Mrs Thatcher's decision to radically curtail the Health Education Authority public campaigns warning of the danger of Aids (*The Sunday Correspondent*, 21 January 1990). This included censoring a TV campaign, preventing the distribution of Aids information packs to schools, the disbanding of a special Aids unit, and vetoing a major survey of sexual behaviour in Britain which would have provided invaluable information relevant to the study of the disease.

The infrastructure of the Conservative Party facilitated such organisations. For example, the Conservative Political Centre at Smith Square provided publishing facilities for a number of pro-family groups such as the Society of Conservative Lawyers and the Conservative Family Campaign. Party connections were invaluable in the successful battle for the inclusion of a clause in the Local Government Act of 1988, which made illegal the award of public funds to any organisation or event that might 'promote' homosexuality, and for the clause in the 1986 Education Act which insisted on the incorporation of traditional family values in any sex education programmes in schools.

The point here is that while the moral conservatives in Britain were never so numerous, well-organised and well-funded as in the United States and their organisations never so politically integrated into a far-right strategy, it is a mistake to underestimate their political importance in Britain. While there are many importance differences between the US and British situations, for example in the role of religion and race, forms of nationalism and political culture, there are also important similarities in the philosophical, political, socio-economic and moral elements out of which both the New Right and the pro-family movement grew. Indeed there was a great deal of cross-Atlantic fertilisation in these respects even before the 1979 and 1980 elections. Reference has already been made in Chapter 4 to the links between the American Moral Re-Armament organisation and

British moral evangelism and the impact of American anti-feminist ideologues such as George Gilder. Cockett's fascinating study (1994) of the strategy, activities and influence of international free-market think-tanks developed after the Second World War as a counter to the prevailing orthodoxy of Keynesianism, reveals the importance of the regular and substantial exchanges in personnel on lecture tours, conferences, consultancies and sabbaticals, most particularly between the politically aligned American Heritage Foundation and the Centre for Policy Studies in Britain established only one year apart in 1973 and 1974 respectively.

These crusading organisations and their political links were behind every attempt in Britain to reinstate Christian sexual morality and the 'traditional' nuclear family. There is, of course, nothing outrageous in this activity. The process of persuasion and lobbying through organisational and personal contacts is part and parcel of the mechanisms of interest group politics accelerated by the arrival of television as a key electioneering medium and by the decline of class-based politics. Pressure group politics was more novel to Britain and was to some extent encouraged by the move to a quasi-Presidential form of government ushered in by Mrs Thatcher. While not constitutionally able to take in a hand-picked administration, she more than any other prime minister promoted her 'own men' to the most important and influential posts in the permanent Civil Service and the British Establishment beyond. In addition, she abolished or emasculated a whole intermediate layer of elected institutional power, disbanded independent quangos and established new ones, with key positions filled by fellow-travellers. The opportunity for lobbying in this situation was greatly facilitated.

In Chapter 4, I pointed out that this apparent affinity between moral conservationism and right-wing politics led many radical and feminist commentators to assume in varying degrees an identity between them (Gordon and Hunter, 1977/8; Eisenstein, 1981, 1982; Fitzgerald, 1983; Marshall, 1985; David, 1986). There is here the assumption of a more or less unambiguous and necessary 'fit' between the Reagan–Thatcher economic strategy and the objective of strengthening the traditional family. In her international bestseller, *Backlash*, the American journalist Susan Faludi (1992) articulates the most cynical view of New Right policies. For her, the pro-family movement 'allowed New Right men to launch an indirect attack on women's rights...by using female intermediaries'. Behind it lay a misogynous male anger at women's growing independence: 'Under the banner of "family rights" these spokesmen lobbied only for every man's right to rule supreme at home' (p. 270). In fact, a closer examination of their policies suggest that such views overstate the parallel between rhetoric and action and confuse economic principles with political expediency.

There can be no doubt that concern about the family became a mandatory aspect of political rhetoric in Britain and America. There is rather more doubt, however, about whether this concern matured into anything very concrete in terms of a range of policy objectives, instruments and mechanisms. In these respects the success rate of the moral re-armers has not been high. Measures often regarded as pro-family successes are better understood in the more general context of the ideological aim of 'rolling back of the welfare state' and the practical objective of reducing public spending to which both American and British administrations were committed (Krieger, 1987; Wilson, 1987; Hoover and Plant, 1989; Brenner, 1993; Pascal, 1997).

End-of-era impact analysis: the Thatcher years

In the Thatcher period the pro-family campaign's greatest triumph was probably Clause 28 of the Local Government Act. There were many near misses of course. In Britain, the Gillick case to remove medical confidentiality in the case of under-age minors seeking contraceptive advice was not finally defeated till it reached the House of Lords. The attempt to reduce the time limit on abortion, which piggy-backed on the Human Fertilisation and Embryology Bill (1990), was successful in that the limit was reduced to 24 from 28 weeks. However, the argument that won the day was the view of the Royal College of Obstetricians and Gynaecologists that advances in medical technology meant that 24 weeks was now the age of independent foetal viability. It is ironic that the effect of the Bill was actually to liberalise abortion legislation by removing any upper limit for cases of grave permanent risk to the physical and mental health of the mother or in cases of severe foetal abnormality, and by separating the Infant Life Preservation Act of 1929 from the 1967 Abortion Act so ensuring that doctors no longer run the risk of prosecution for carrying out a late abortion. It is also notable that in law the father, whether married to the mother or not, was eliminated from considerations in the case of terminations, the decision about which was confined to the woman and her doctors.

Public spending cuts have been described as anti-feminist or designed to strengthen the traditional family. Much has been made of the 5 per cent reduction in the number of childcare places in publicly funded nurseries between 1980 and 1991 as evidence of the Conservative government's determination to return women to the home. However, in the same period the numbers of daycare places in private nurseries went up by 259 per cent and with childminders by 137 per cent. In fact the decade saw a dramatic rise in the provision for under-five child care in Britain (Randall, 1996). In the context of anxieties about labour shortages, positive support came from the CBI, a number of large employers and House of Commons Committees. The government responded with a number of initiatives including expanding under-5 places in primary schools, sponsoring voluntary sector provision, improving regulation of child-minding, encouraging employers to provide childcare facilities by waiving the tax on work-place nurseries and introducing a childcare tax allowance. While not in any sense a coherent national childcare policy, it is difficult to see these measures as part of an anti-feminist backlash. Rather one is witnessing once again an economic policy in which the costs of child-care are shifted from public to private resources.

The British government made it more difficult for mothers of pre-school children to get unemployment benefit by requiring them to state the child-care arrangements which would enable them to be available for work. It also introduced, with the active support of the lone parents' lobby, the Child Support Act of 1991 to ensure realistic child maintenance orders and enforce their payments by fathers. However, the operation of the Child Support Agency which reduced benefit in line with the increased maintenance and encouraged lone mothers to work by reducing the working week qualification for family credit, made it clear that the overriding concern was not with the poverty of children in lone parent families but to transfer their financial support from the public purse to that of their parents. The government's estimate of the gain was a cut of £3.2 million off the benefit bill for lone parents. It is not lone parents *per se* that have been the target for government and media censure, but poor lone parents who rely on state support (Isaac, 1994). This underlines my assertion that it is the public expenditure dimension rather than a commitment to reinforce the 'traditional family' that really drove public policy during this period.

The promotion of care in the community rather than residential care for the elderly, infirm, those with disabilities and special needs and the mentally ill is often seen as another way of forcing women back into their family duties (Gardiner, 1983). In fact while community care does increase the workload of women, it has also increased the number of paid jobs in the domiciliary and other back-up services in the health and social care sector and these have largely been taken up by women (Pascal, 1997). It has also made visible and set a value on the work of informal carers, such as in the increase in married women's financial entitlement by the extension of the Invalid Care Allowance, though the latter was achieved only via recourse to the European Court (Finch, 1990). It is therefore unlikely that, in aggregate, community care has operated to confine women to the home.

Similarly, reductions in the entitlement to benefits of post-school adolescents and publicly funded accommodation for the young homeless, forcing them back on their families, may seem on the face of it to concede to the family evangelists. However, they may be more appropriately understood in the context of high youth unemployment in the 1980s and the failure of the various youth training programmes to recruit. It is not youth in general that are affected by government edict, only those who claim state support. Unfortunately many of their families are in poverty themselves. The result is the cardboard-box communities that nestle in the commuter byways of major cities, where the youngsters are prey to all the subversive influences from which family policy is supposed to safeguard them.

The Report of the Law Commission on divorce reform (1990) resulting in the Family Law Act of 1996 met some of the traditionalists' concerns, ending the 'quickie' divorce of three-to-five months based on adultery or unreasonable behaviour by introducing an initial 'cooling off' period of three months in which couples are offered the services of marriage counsellors, followed by a further nine months for reflection and 'mediation' and by requiring the resolution of financial and child-related matters before the marriage can be formally ended. However, the Act did not concede the principle of 'no fault'. Indeed, it removed the difficulties which arose for individuals whose spouses contested the basis for divorce, extended legal protection against domestic violence to cohabiting couples and introduced controversial measures to treat pensions as part of financial settlements. It had plenty critics among the moralists inside and outside Parliament.

At the end of three terms of Thatcherism, government policy in relation to the family contained little more than was indicated at its start, apart from a new child support agency to pursue maintenance from absent fathers. Mrs Thatcher's tone also moderated: she continued to express unease at trends in family life, but conceded that 'we must be supportive of lone parents' (Thatcher, 1990). She concluded that it was not part of the state's role to determine whether women worked or not. Despite fluctuations in the rhetoric, Mrs Thatcher's policies were entirely consistent with the general accommodation of governments since the 1960s to the desire and need for married women of school-age children to take up paid work. Government Statistical Service reports showed that the trends towards births outside marriage, co-habitation, divorce, and remarriage had not been halted, indeed had become more widespread, during the decade of a government committed to strengthening the traditional family.

Despite the pro-family's lobby to support full-time housewife-mothers, government policy in fact encouraged and facilitated more working mothers. On the one hand, there were employment, fiscal and social security changes which supported well-educated women, single and married, in the primary sector of the employment market, and the strengthening of professional development programmes and outcome targets in the civil service and the NHS. On the other, there were exhortations as well as practical initiatives to get lone mothers off welfare and into work. The overall effect of government policies was to accelerate the growing heterogeneity of employment and income among women workers rather than do anything to dissuade them from working (Martin and Roberts, 1984; Walby, 1999).

End-of era impact analysis: the Reagan years

Trends in the United States, where the traditionalists are much more numerous, better organised, and well resourced, and where the virtual autonomy of each of the states allows for greater local control, showed a similar general pattern. Indeed, while President Reagan introduced savage cuts in the American welfare system, he seems to have been no more able to effect policies to strengthen the traditional family than Mrs Thatcher.

In the Reagan period the pro-family campaign's greatest triumph was preventing the ratification of the Equal Rights Amendment (ERA); the nearest miss was the 'Laxalt' (Family Protection) Bill which sought to have the traditional family as the final authority over all moral questions, to reintroduce Christian worship in the state schools, to censor sex education in schools and to prohibit the 'advocacy' of homosexuality in any form. Its clauses were debated during the 1981 and 1982 sessions but it never got out of committee stage. The anti-abortion movement was successful in eroding the public funding of abortions through the Hyde Amendment in 1976 and the *Harris* v. *McRae* judgment which upheld it in 1979 but did not succeed, despite the packing of the federal courts by the appointment of pro-life judges, in overturning *Roe* v. *Wade*, and indeed provoked many states into passing their own pro-choice legislation (Hoover and Plant, 1989).

According to end-of-era evaluations of the impact of the Reagan–Bush administrations (Krieger, 1987; Kymlicka and Matthews, 1988; Pierson, 1994; O'Connor, 1998), Reagan managed in the first two years of office to create such a massive deficit through the slashing of taxation at the top and middle of the income levels and the huge expansion of the defence budget, that whichever party held the balance of power in Congress it would be forced to hold down if not cut back social spending, a legacy that was to undermine Clinton's later policy ambitions. It is also true that Reagan's 1981 Omnibus Reconciliation Act which reduced funding of a whole range of human resource programmes mainly by changing eligibility criteria, along with the Economic Recovery Tax Act of the same year which lowered the tax thresholds for those on low incomes, resulted in a deterioration of the living standards of the working poor and a year-on increase in the total number of families in the poverty trap (Krieger, 1987; Gottschalk, 1988; Weaver, 1988; O'Connor, 1998). The Family Support Act of 1988 was introduced to reinforce policies in relation to ensuring that absent fathers paid child maintenance and encouraging workfare schemes combining training and employment aimed particularly at lone mothers, and worked largely on the basis of an incentives-to-work hypothesis, that is a cut in benefits but a rise in earnings disregard. Many states introduced compulsory 'workfare' schemes for all welfare recipients with children over six-years-old (by 1990 reduced to children of three and in some states to one-year-olds).

Reaganite policy programmes certainly reduced federal spending on certain types of welfare, but they can hardly be described as positive in relation to supporting the traditional family, since it was precisely working families of the poor which were most disadvantaged by them. Nevertheless they have been interpreted as such by feminist writers (Abramovitz, 1982; David, 1983), on the grounds that they provided a disincentive for women to seek paid work, given the related losses in benefits both in kind and cash transfers, and thus succeeded in the aim of returning women to the home.

Since there is no systematically collected data on a federal basis, it is difficult to produce conclusive evidence one way or the other. However, Power (1988) reports that research carried out in 1984 by The Center for the Study of Social Policy on women in Georgia, Michigan and New York City who had been victims of the AFDC cuts, indicated that they were not leaving the workforce. On the contrary, many had either increased their hours or taken on a second job. Handler's evidence (1996) also suggests that reduced benefits have not driven women out of employment, though they may have driven them into the informal and illegal economy. Analysis of *monthly* rather than *annual* data reveals a dynamic movement of the welfare population in and out of welfare as they move in and out of work for reasons of their vulnerable position at the bottom end of the labour market. The real cause of welfare dependence, says Handler, is the overall lack of jobs providing a decent living as a result of global economic changes. Hence for large sections of the population, work and welfare are not alternatives; they are both complementary and essential.

However, even more telling are the less well known items of Reagan's legislation. Tax allowances for childcare expenses were raised as were the tax incentives to employers for providing workplace nurseries or a package of fringe benefits which serve the same purpose (for example, longer holidays, childcare vouchers, etc.). This led to a large expansion in privatised and voluntary sector childcare services which has probably increased the numbers of working mothers by providing a paid female workforce to service them. Pension legislation was reformed to make private pension schemes accessible to women; all formal inequities by gender were removed; benefits during maternity or paternity leave were protected; states were able to divide pension benefits on divorce. Legislation introduced retirement equity and insurance equity (Tobias, 1997). Banks were required to apply the 1974 Equal Credit Opportunity Act to business women seeking loans. Laws against discrimination in education and employment and which provided redress for discrimination were strengthened. Tougher child support orders and collection from fathers was introduced. Brenner (1993) points out that the failure of the Equal Rights Amendment (ERA) to be ratified had greater negative symbolic impact for women than practical significance. Many states enacted their own ERAs as a result and anti-discrimination legislation existed anyway in most states. The failure did not signal either a decrease in support for them or an assault on them. Indeed, Gelb and Palley (1987) argue that with the rightwards shift of the federal government

in Washington, the states became more central arenas for the achievement of equity goals and support for women's issues.

What is noteworthy is that, first, many of the above policies primarily benefit college-educated full-time women workers in large organisations and hence increase differences and divisions between women
employees. Secondly, they do not require significant increases in
public spending. However, even in the case of poor women it does
not seem that Reaganite policies have returned women to the home.

The harshest of Reagan's measures did not run for long, as opinion
polls began to show that public support for 'chiselling welfare' began
to cool. Many of the programmes were liberalised by subsequent
legislation: in 1984 income and assets thresholds were raised and
both social security and welfare programmes such as AFDC were
exempted from the mandatory cuts in government spending introduced to reduce the federal deficit. In addition, further tax reforms
reversed the trend and reduced the tax liabilities of lower-income
people. However, the aforementioned deficit and the general rightwards shift in political culture forbade return to high spending on antipoverty programmes.

The successors: Bush and Major

Reagan and Thatcher, the two great ideologues in the politics of the
second half of the twentieth-century, were replaced within two years
of each other: Reagan in 1988 by the Republican, George Bush, in the
normal process of the American political system; Thatcher in 1990 by
John Major, more dramatically by a palace coup within the Conservative Party primarily over the issue of Europe and the collapse of her
economic miracle. Larger than life Reagan and Thatcher were hard
acts to follow and neither of their successors were up to it, especially in
the context of a cooling of the public's enthusiasm for neo-liberalism.
Both largely carried on the policies of their predecessors though in a
more subdued form until, threatened by unpopularity at the polls,
they resorted to the more dramatic ideological clothing of their predecessors – to their cost.

Bush inherited both a very substantial budget deficit from Reagan
and a hostile Congress dominated by Democrats which opposed
many of the cuts in welfare programmes he proposed. He turned
to moral exhortation, inviting the voluntary sector and the churches
to increase their provision to the needy. When this met with little

success, he squeezed the states' budgets further, but allowed them further leeway to request exemption from federal requirements, by proposing alternatives in welfare benefits and services. Hence the plethora of state-level welfare experiments we have seen in the USA which have interested both the Conservative government and the Labour opposition (Handler, 1995; O'Connor, 1998).

He also inherited a political situation in which the Republican Party was in hock to a coalition of politically and socially conservative forces both inside and outside the party organised by its extreme right wing which had delivered resounding victories in both the Presidential and Congressional elections in 1980. Bush, a representative of the affluent, Ivy League, northeastern Protestant elite which dominated mainstream Republicanism, had to achieve 'street cred' with the nouveau elite in the Party to gain the Presidential nomination. The price he paid was to renege on his record of support for family planning programmes in the US and overseas, and become a born-again pro-lifer.

With the conservative version of 'the personal is political' spiralling when he won the White House, and the abortion issue at its centre, Bush accelerated his predecessor's policies of appointing pro-life candidates to key posts in health administration and in the federal and district courts. One of those appointments was the Supreme Court nominee, Clarence Thomas, a black Yale law school graduate around whom broke a national controversy when he was accused of sexual harassment by a former employee, Anita Hill, a professor of law, also African-American and a Yale alumni. Thomas just squeezed nomination with his credibility shaken.

It therefore came about that Bush presided over a series of Supreme Court decisions which eroded reproductive rights in the USA but which also eroded the support of mainstream American opinion. Poll after poll showed an inverse relation between each of these decisions, especially the 1989 *Webster* decision, and public support for the *Roe* principle (McKeegan, 1992). While only 12 out of the 600 anti-abortion bills which were introduced in 44 states were passed, the attempts by the flying squads of the National Right to Life Committee hitting the legislatures of one state after another was sufficient to trigger off a pro-choice backlash that began to turn the discomfort of average Americans at the rhetoric, tactics and successes of the anti-abortion movement into votes by the 1990 elections. McKeegan records how this in turn provoked both moderation by the pragmatists within the pro-life movement, and extremism by the doctrinaire, with the Catholic bishops shifting from exhortation of its flock to the threat of excommunication and Operation Rescue stepping up its terrorist activities. The fragile coalition that brought the Republicans to power began to come apart.

Having alienated his natural allies among Republican moderates, Bush had nowhere to go but to hang on in with the far-right politicos and moral fundamentalists. He vetoed a series of policy reversals in Congress on public funding in the field of human reproduction, such as for abortion in the case of rape and incest victims, for UN population policies, and for fetal tissue research; and on the 'gag' rule of 1987 which forbade advice or counselling about abortion in federally funded family planning clinics. He endorsed the adoption of 'family values' as the theme for the Republican Convention and as the main plank of his platform in the Presidential campaign in 1992. This was his final undoing. It is likely that the main reason for Bush's failure in that campaign was the economic recession, restructuring and downsizing of public and private sector organisations, and the attendant growth in unemployment and job insecurity across a much wider range of occupational groups than America had seen in the past. But Bush was also judged on the failure of his social policies: the total welfare bill had not been reduced; crime rates had risen; the drug problem was worse; there was no dent in the abortion statistics; the number of teenage pregnancies and lone parents had increased, as had the incidence of sexually transmitted diseases and the transmission of AIDS to heterosexuals, women and the newborn. Election polls and opinion surveys indicate that, on top of practical policy incompetence, Bush and his administration appeared to the public also to be out of touch with the majority of the American people on matters of morality and the individual's right to privacy in personal life.

In Britain, John Major was certainly perceived as more sympathetic to women than Mrs Thatcher. As Chancellor of the Exchequer, he had insisted that the decision of mothers to work or not was one in which the government should not intervene. As Prime Minister he gave his public backing to Opportunity 2000, an employer-led initiative to support women's career tracks and to the Employment Secretary, Gillian Shepherd, setting up a senior level working group to address the obstacles faced by working women. He presided over the expansion of places for four-year-olds in primary schools, preschool and after-school care provided by the voluntary sector. He introduced a childcare allowance for low income mothers and reversed Mrs Thatcher's freeze on child benefit by both increasing and index-linking it. During his premiership, he also removed one of the fiscal supports of the traditional family by phasing out the married couple's tax allowance.

On the other hand when it came to economic policy he pursued the Thatcher agenda. He abolished the wages councils which protected the wages of the lowest paid, the majority of which were women, and refused to comply with European Union Directives to extend employment and social security rights to part-time workers, again most of which are women, though the latter was overruled. He resisted the Equal Opportunity Commission's pressure to update and strengthen equality legislation in the employment field and dragged his feet in implementing Recommendations and Directives of the European Community Council to improve support for working parents, such as parental leave, public childcare, extended maternity leave and pay. (Kavanagh and Seldon, 1994). Given Major's more sympathetic stance on women, his record in government reveals even more than Thatcher's that New Right policies are not uniformly anti-women or anti-feminist. There is little in the above analysis that provides evidence in support of the view that the aim or consequence of these policies was that women were returned to the home. Indeed it is ironic that at the start of this period, lone mothers, the very group targeted by the Tories to get off welfare and into employment, were more likely to be in paid work, full-time than were married mothers; it is now the reverse.

Morally conservative forces both within the Tory Party and outside it were incensed by the continued failure of the government to strengthen the traditional family brought into the public spotlight once again by a series of media cases of 'dysfunctional families'. The public's horror was whipped up into moral panic by the case of the toddler, James Bulger, abducted, tortured and murdered by two pre-teen boys. Lone mothers on welfare came in for the full brunt of this generalised anxiety, a theme orchestrated by the Conservative Family Campaign at the 1993 Party Conference. Major was driven into appeasing the Party moralists and their audiences in the general public by initiating the Back to Basics campaign to raise the moral standards of public and private life. Unfortunately for him, one by one the loudest proselytisers of this theme fell from grace under the scrutiny of investigative journalism in an orgy of revelations of adultery, illegitimate children, abandoned families, covert homosexual liaisons, 'kinky' sex and suicides. This coincided with a series of public accusations about the involvement of some senior Conservative politicians, including ministers, in financial irregularities, corruption, breaches of parliamentary privilege and professional conduct. The combination of hypocrisy and sleaze was too much for the public. The government's credibility sank. It limped along stretching out its full term of office to receive its punishment at the ballot box in 1997 with the massive landslide Labour victory.

Jordan (1995) argues that Major's 'back to basics' strategy was not only a response to pressure from the traditionalists within his party and the country, but an attempt to shore up with moral exhortation and punishment the failures of the economic policies of the Thatcher years. It is an analysis that, on the basis of evidence assembled above, would seem also relevant to the USA.

First, cutting back on universal provision in favour of targeted benefits increases administrative costs, unless they can be offset by the reductions in public spending achieved. This was done by tightening eligibility criteria and transferring the costs of these transactions to the claimant by delaying or suspending payments during investigations and appeals. This had two effects: claimants didn't bother applying, hence the low take-up rates, and/or they took on undeclared work for cash. This rational behaviour on the part of individual claimants' not only increases the costs of benefit administration and decreases tax and insurance contributions to the government, but also reinforces the casualisation of the labour market and depresses the wages of the unskilled. This in turn makes the illegal economy all the more attractive since it pays better than the formal or informal economy – hence the rising tide of crime that has been associated with right-wing administrations on both sides of the Atlantic, incurring further costs to the public in enforcement. As Jordan says, the irony of this is that a major factor in the lack of decently paid, regular, stable employment has been the very policies of privatisation, deregulation and 'labour flexibility' by which the New Right sought to reduce government spending. Without material incentives and rewards for 'straight living' to offer the poor, the government increasingly resorts to exhortation and coercion and winding up the moral righteousness of the other two-thirds of the population to intimidate them.

However, an increasing number of the better-off also became disaffected as a consequence of the working through of other aspects of New Right policies, in particular the impact of competition and deregulation on administrative, professional and middle-level management employment particularly in the public sector. This frustration began to be reflected in levels of government unpopularity in opinion polls:

> The majority coalition of the comfortable is eroded by the competitive forces unleashed by government policies. So long as a majority of house-holds could be seen to be gaining economic advantages over the minority, even if this involved increased transaction and enforcement costs, the new systems might well have been sustainable. Once it became clear that the parental generation cannot act so as to secure access to job assets and their attendant advantages for their offsprings' generation, then the ideological basis of the 'property-owning democracy' is undermined. (Jordan, 1995, p. 378)

Despite a deep commitment by US and UK governments to rescue the two great nations from the morass of sloth, dependence and moral uncertainty induced by decades of liberal-democracy, there is little evidence of any substantial success in restoring the traditional moral bedrock on which, it was believed, they had been built. In the next chapter we will examine why.

6

New Right Impasse on Family Policy

The previous chapter outlined the process by which moral issues in relation to sexuality and the family became major items on the political agendas of conservative administrations in America and Britain. I argued that a main trigger for this attention was less an anti-feminist backlash, though that was an element, than the sensitivity to governments committed to major reductions in public expenditure of the increasing material repercussions of moral pluralism and family diversity. Equally important was the role morality played in bonding disparate elements of conservatism into a new populist right-wing force. However, I also argued that ultimately these governments failed in their crusade to reinstate 'traditional' values and institutions at the heart of their economic revolution. In this chapter I explain this unorthodox conclusion.

Why the lack of success?

Probably the greatest obstacle to the success of the Great Crusade is the sheer weight and momentum of the major demographic, economic, social and cultural shifts in western societies in the twentieth century. These include the reconfiguration of the population profile consequent upon improvements in living standards, public health, medical science and technology; the changes in the relation between different sectors of the economy and their impact on the nature, volume and structure of occupation; the fragmentation of the class structure and the emergence of social groups which cut vertically across traditional class criteria and develop new forms of organisations and cohesion; the penetration of the ideology of equality of opportunity and liberal freedoms in the public consciousness with the resultant raised expectations about material, social and personal fulfilment. These changes, of course, have had enormous impact on women and consequently on the family. It is highly unlikely that these underlying trends will be reversed.

However, these generic changes are not in themselves sufficient to explain the overall lack of success of the moral conservatives.

Another reason was the considerable strength of the opposing camp in the war over the family. Feminist and other special interest organisations were effective in relation to particular campaigns, but also important has been the day-to-day activity of those whose professions and occupational responsibilities involve finding solutions for the casualties of poverty, ill health, ignorance, prejudice, urban pressure, psychological instability, and family breakdown. Berger and Berger (1984) have suggested that they act as a buffer against the extremes of the 'critical' and the 'neo-traditionalist' camps, evolving pragmatic solutions to the realities of the problems facing them and remaining detached from the evangelicalism of the other two. Their importance lies both in their general sympathy to issues of gender equality, and in their pivotal role in the formulation, implementation and evaluation of policy.

Yet another obstacle has been the difficulty in aligning governments' economic objectives with policies to strengthen the 'traditional' family. The family campaigners' proposals for financial inducements substantial enough to return women to the home, such as allowances which might compensate for the forgone earnings of informal carers of children, the elderly or those with special needs, could not be afforded. As it is, women's income earned outside the home is critical for a large number of families and vital for the Exchequer in keeping down benefit claims.

The dual-earner family is now the norm. The suggestion that this could be balanced by the reduction in unemployment consequent upon men acquiring the jobs vacated by women, takes no account of the gender-segregated structure of the labour market nor the 'flexible employment markets' of the American and British economies. In Britain the ratio of full-time to part-time jobs shifted from 25:1 in 1951 to 5:1 in 1981 (HMSO, 1984). In November 1989, a National Economic Development Office/Training Agency survey reported that between 1971 and 1989 total male employees had fallen from 13.4 million to 11.7 million, including almost a million part-time workers.

The numbers of women working in the same period rose from 8.2 million to 10.2 million, but significantly with a rise from 2.7 to 4.3 million of them working part-time (NEDO/TA, 1989). In other words, the increase in part-time jobs accounted for most of that percentage increase. While this growth has slowed since 1996 and been overtaken by full-time jobs, it remains the case that any significant decline in the availability of female labour would have serious consequences for the economy.

Indeed, faced with a 20 per cent decrease in school-leavers in the 1990s, the Conservative government in Britain actually introduced measures to encourage married women back to work. Following some US work-fare schemes, the Department of Employment initiated an Employment Training Scheme which provided £50 per week towards childcare costs for participating lone parents. There was a great deal of government propaganda exhorting employers to accommodate their work practices to the needs of working mothers. Some employers, such as the National Westminster Bank, Marks and Spencer, BP Oil, the Department of Trade and Industry, Abbey National Building Society, were applauded for their initiatives in developing retainer, returnee and flexitime schemes. Praise and publicity was also lavished on enterprising companies which responded to the market for private childcare provision particularly in the form of workplace nurseries. These initiatives, however, tended to benefit only better-paid women in permanent, skilled and full-time employment. In terms of direct government action, the only contribution was tax relief on workplace nurseries introduced in the 1990 Budget to act as an incentive to employers, while local authorities, the traditional providers of good-quality nursery provision, were starved of funds and were reduced to offering places only to a very restricted category of parents. The Conservative government had a great deal to say about the 'dependency culture' which they claimed had induced citizens to expect the state to provide, but it had less to say about a similar attitude among private employers. There is very little evidence that the private sector was either fully aware of the impact of the demographic 'dip' on future recruitment (NEDO/TA, 1989) or that it was willing to fill the childcare gap left by the withdrawal of public funds. Indeed the CBI informed the government that it was unrealistic to expect employers to foot the bill (*The Guardian*, 25 April 1990).

The US government faced a similar dilemma in the contradictory demands of the economy for increased female labour, of elements within its own power base for policies that strengthen the traditional family, and of its own anti-public spending rhetoric. Its response was to introduce childcare tax credit for working parents and to leave provision to the private arrangements of individuals and employers, a strategy undermined, as in Britain, by the failure of the market to adequately respond to the demand for childcare provision (Skold, 1988). A special report of the *Wall Street Journal* (21 June 1993) reviewed the response of corporate America to new demands for family-friendly employment practices. While many examples of new attitudes and good practice were in evidence among some of the largest companies such as Johnson and Johnson, Xerox Corp., American Express, Chevron Corp., and UNUM Life Insurance Co., three factors were identified as inhibiting factors for private industry delivering on a mass scale: the view of 70 per cent of companies that work-family programmes were too expensive to implement; the persistence of a corporate culture based on the family structures and division of labour of the 1950s; and the negative attitudes of managers lower down the corporate ladder. Few companies were interested in contributing to solve the problems of poor single mothers, which are left to state work-fare schemes using largely public sector employers.

In the case of the scheme to enforce child maintenance paid by fathers, developed in Wisconsin, USA, adopted in Australia and enthusiastically seized upon by the British government, research indicates that it may not reduce government spending. First, the gains from the enforced contribution have to be set against the administrative costs of pursuit and enforcement, wasted in many cases where payment merely reduced second families to income-support levels. Second, there was little incentive for women to disclose the father's name since with no maintenance disregard and income support reduced pound for pound, only the Exchequer benefited. Third, since the attachment of earnings order worked only where the father had permanent, full-time, regular employment, and was not linked to the Inland Revenue data banks, many fathers avoided detection and payment. Fourth, and this really offended the moral as well as the economic principles of Thatcherism, there was the possibility that setting the maintenance at an effective level for getting lone mothers off welfare, would so impoverish low-paid fathers that it would act as a disincentive for them to work at all. The political outcry and legal challenge from groups of fathers experienced at the onset of the Child Support Agency's implementation of this policy in 1993, underlines some of the problems outlined above. It is not surprising that the Labour government on coming into office, despite its strongly principled view that parents of both sexes should take responsibility for the support of their children and its commitment to stick to the public expenditure targets of its predecessor, ordered a root-and-branch review of the CSA.

However, perhaps as important a reason for the failure of the moral campaigners to make any great headway in practice lay in the nature of the New Right itself.

Ideological differences in New Right attitudes to the family

The political regime that emerged on both sides of the Atlantic at the end of the 1970s and which claimed the family as its own has been the subject of a great deal of political and academic commentary in which it is generally referred to as the 'New Right'. There is considerable disagreement among political scientists about the appropriateness of this term (Bosanquet, 1983; King, 1987; Green, 1987; Hoover and Plant, 1989. See also the debate about 'Thatcherism': Hall and Jacques, 1983 vs Jessop *et al.*, 1984). Certainly in the work on the politics of the family, it is not always clear what is meant by this nomenclature. It appears to have been first used in the US in early 1970s to refer to the morally conservative element in American politics and more specifically to those on the right of the Republican Party who are involved in the social purity organisations (Crawford, 1980; Peele, 1984). This has been also adopted by some British writers. For example, David (1983) regards the New Right in the USA as 'represented chiefly by the Moral Majority, and in Britain by right wing pressure groups on the present Tory government' (p. 31). It is on this definition that the claim, common in feminist writing, that the New Right constitutes a patriarchal reaction to the successes of feminism carries some conviction.

However, I prefer to use the term 'Moral Right' for this group and to argue that they constitute only one strand of the much more complex political constellation to which I will continue to refer in these pages as the 'New Right'. It is true that many of the key policy elements associated with this term, like monetarism, in fact were introduced prior to the election of Reagan and Thatcher. It is also the case that there is little new about the ideology of this brand of Conservative politics; it is drawn from the regular repertoire of right-wing political thought since the eighteenth-century. However, there is something new in the particular amalgam of these ideas and their integration in a populist strategy, that is, an ideology and a policy programme designed to appeal directly to the 'common sense' of the masses, by-passing the middle layers of experts and professionals which, in liberal-democracies, usually mediate ideas between governments and the lay-person. Indeed, populist politicians affect to despise experts and intellectuals and seek to establish an intimacy and an alliance with the 'man-in-the-street'. The ordinary person is raised to a symbol of common-sense and decency whose views and values ought to be the benchmark of government policy.

This populist style is linked to the overall objective which lay at the heart of the Reagan–Thatcher political vision: that is, to set the 'little man' free from the dulling paralysis of the bureaucratic regulation of the modern state, from the demoralising dependence of welfare protectionism and from the moral uncertainty of Left liberalism. This release of the creativity, initiative, enterprise and self-discipline of the individual was necessary, they claimed, to reassert their countries' economic, political and military position on the world scene, threatened not only by the military might of the USSR but also the economic might of Japan and Western Europe.

Both leaders had humble origins, experienced privation and believed in the efficacy of the Protestant ethic in delivering one from it (Reagan, 1965:1981; Young, 1989). Both declared themselves 'radicals' in that they intended to effect a fundamental change of government direction to bring about what they saw as a model society characterised by a minimal non-interventionist state, free markets, low taxation, a strong military defence, and an ethic of responsible individualism. At the same time they both came from a Protestant religious tradition which does not spurn worldy success but exacts acknowledgement of traditional moral values. In both cases. their future vision was one derived from the fantasised past: in Reagan's case it was early American society with its orderly farming communities and frontier spirit; in Mrs Thatcher's it was mid-Victorian England with its thrusting industries, its Non-Conformist Chapels and its entrepreneurial drive.

The appeal of this utopia was that it was based on the known, the tried, the proven – at least in the national collective consciousness; it was the past placed in a modern setting. Unlike Left utopias which exhort ordinary people into uncharted waters with pilots who know as little about what to expect as the traveller, that of the New Right was safe and familiar from school history books, and it appeared to offer better opportunities for doing what citizens had to do anyway, which was to look after themselves and their families. New Right strategy combined the hard-nosed rational calculation of supply and demand and what the market can support, with the romantic promise of individual freedom from the restrictions of modernity. The myths of the past were resurrected not to be replicated in modern times, but to provide the content of a political programme, based on the interests of the 'Individual' which were constructed in such a way that they appeared to respond to the lived experience and aspirations of concrete individuals located in rather different parts of the social body.

This image of the New Right parties empowered by the economic and social values of the past to take the nation into the tough competitive world of the future was played off against that of the social and liberal democrats which, ironically, was projected as old-fashioned and out-of-touch, capable only of stagnation.

The advantage of this pragmatic compromise with conservatism and classic liberalism, was that it enabled it to attract a number of different constituencies and widen its electoral base, particularly with new voters. However, the disadvantage was that it constructed a contradiction at the heart of New Right politics which was itself a major obstacle to the realisation of its objectives at least in the moral sphere.

It should be noted that much New Right thinking concentrates on political economy and political philosophy and has little to say about the family or practical morality at all. However, there are serious implications for private life and moral behaviour which derive from its philosophical underpinnings. As we shall see, in these respects there are serious ideological conflicts over the philosophical and ethical heartland of the New Right. These are often represented as a polarity between the economic liberals and the social conservatives; I believe more insight is gained from conceiving them as stretching a spectrum with the American libertarian, Robert Nozick, at one end and the British neo-conservative, Roger Scruton, at the other, with a number of variations in between. These differences go a long way in explaining the inconsistencies in the discourse and policy preferences of New Right politicians in relation to gender equality and the family.

Right libertarianism

Nozick (1974) starts out from the view that human beings have natural inviolable rights to freedom, that is, to do what they like, provided that they do not harm anyone else. Hence while he accepts the premise that the external world and its resources are not owned by anyone since they predate human beings, natural resources may be appropriated by anyone provided no other person is harmed in the process. This involves a complicated argument that resources privately owned are always more productive than those left idle and therefore will enable the proprietor to compensate for the loss of free access to the initial resources, for example, through the provision of employment, housing or other utilities or facilities. On the basis of the infinite variability of human beings in ability, aptitude, motivation and effort, Nozick is clear that extensive inequalities between individuals are unavoidable. Any attempt to equalise or redistribute resources would violate the sovereign rights of other individuals. No individual should be deprived of their freedom for the sake of some overall general good, or 'society', for since this is not a human subject, it has no rights nor can it benefit from another's sacrifice. Only a minimal state is required based on a contractual relationship with citizens: in return for taxes, it protects individuals from aggression by others and it protects private property.

When we turn to the private sphere, the implication of Nozick's position is that there is no role for the state to promote one particular morality or type of family. Individual rights and a free market in private property provide for the greatest pluralism of institutions and in life-style. In his meta-utopian framework, Nozick sees society consisting of a series of free communities with their own provision for education, health-care, welfare and family forms. Ineffective, unsatisfactory, unreliable, uncaring communities would fail because individuals, free from coercion to stay, would migrate to more successful ones. Nozick does not rule out obligations to family or community, but it would be morally indefensible for them to be enforced by the state. Thus, diversity is guaranteed and the survival of communities will depend on their capacity to meet the needs of individuals.

Nozick's Right libertarianism limited his influence on those who act in the realities of the political world, but the basic principles he states are not so far removed from the radical liberal scenarios of the more politically palatable Frederick Hayek and the populariser, Milton Friedman.

Neo-liberals

For example, while Hayek does not adopt Nozick's 'rights' paradigm, his organising concept of freedom – 'the state in which a man is not subject to coercion by the arbitrary will of another or others' (Hayek, 1960, p. 11) – is remarkably similar. Coercion is not only bad because it enslaves: it is mostly unnecessary. Individuals will voluntarily co-operate so as to best meet their own needs. Out of the 'mutual adjustment' of their choices, made in the largely unconscious context of a common cultural experience of 'habits, conventions, language and moral beliefs', a 'spontaneous social order' emerges (p. 24). The role of government is to formalise the general framework of rules for the decisions and actions of individuals which facilitates the greatest freedom and which apply equally to all. This 'rule of law' sanctions coercion only in relation to those who transgress.

Hayek is not so averse to government activity in the economic or welfare fields as Nozick, as long as any provision is available to all citizens, does not monopolise markets or the provision of services making competition over the economy as a whole ineffective, or act in such a way as to secure privileges for those who could not secure them on their own account. However, any attempts at distributive justice inevitably conflict with the freedom of the individual since they involve the coercion of some, the taxpayers, in order to benefit others, thereby undermining equality before the law. They are the first steps on 'the road to serfdom'.

The same 'voluntarism' also marks Friedman's work. The freedom from material scarcity and political coercion can best be achieved by voluntary co-operation in producing and exchanging goods. The individual produces more and better if he can see that he will personally benefit from it: 'If an exchange between two parties is voluntary, it will not take place unless both believe they will benefit from it' (Friedman and Friedman, 1980, p. 31). This incentive to individual self-improvement multiplied many times over produces a market for goods and services conducted through the exchange mechanism of prices which 'enables people living all over the world to co-operate to promote their separate interests . . . without requiring people to speak to one another or to like one another' (p. 32). This *deus ex machina* provides the multitude of exchanging individuals with all the information they need to make their own decisions in relation to producing, buying and selling, and it distributes income between them in such a way as to reward ability, initiative and effort, thereby providing the incentive for the whole worldwide operation.

Both Hayek's and Friedman's accounts of the efficacy of the market in guaranteeing freedom are based on the same radical individualistic assumptions found in Nozick. Of course, by defining the market as the aggregation of individual choices, the neo-liberals are able to ignore the effects of international corporations on the structure of financial and commodity markets and on the determination of prices. By narrowly and legalistically defining freedom, rights, justice, equality in terms of the individual and personal relations between individuals, they are able to disregard the *structural* restrictions on individual choice and the *impersonal* coercion experienced by individuals as a result of poverty, ill-health, unemployment, inadequate education, exploitative employment contracts, and unequal domestic responsibilities. For Hayek, inequalities between people are unfortunate but they are not unjust, so long as they are the anonymous consequences of the impartial operation of the market. To interfere by introducing measures of distributive justice would bring about a greater injustice, for it would involve some individuals making judgments about the relative value or worth or need of other individuals about which no consensus could ever be reached. Not only would this lead to economic inefficiency by breaking the relationship between reward and quality of service, but also it would undermine the moral framework of the market and society itself, by treating some people differently from others; that is, it would violate the universal justice of the rule of law.

Hayek's individualism is tempered by his view that there is a need for a moral framework: 'freedom has never worked without deeply ingrained moral beliefs' (Hayek, 1960, p. 62), that is, that a minimum cultural consensus is a necessary condition for social stability and voluntary restraint, without which there could be no guarantee of freedom. Social conventions and mechanisms for social censure are a basic prerequisite for the reliable knowledge of behavioural response without which social interaction would be anarchistic and unpredictable. Nevertheless, these do not require a unitary culture. On the contrary, according to Hayek, a diversity of traditions provides the best conditions for individual freedom and choice. Government intervention in private life of the kind envisaged by the moral re-armers would be likely to violate the liberty of the individual which Hayek insists must always be the overriding principle of social organisation.

Neo-conservatism

By contrast, Roger Scruton, one of the best-known spokesmen for the neo-conservative strand in the British New Right, regards 'the philosophy of liberalism with all its attendant trappings of individual autonomy and the "natural" rights of man' as the enemy of conservative thought! (Scruton, 1980, p. 16).

For Scruton, human nature is profoundly social. 'There is no autonomy that does not presuppose the sense of social order...the autonomous individual is the product of practices which designate him as social' (p. 73). In a later book, *Sexual Desire* (1986), he reiterates this concept as 'moral personhood', the product of the 'intentionality' of social interaction, and roots his belief in the ideal of marriage as part of the moral foundation of society in its capacity to elevate sexual desire to the mutuality of respect for the integrity of the human subject. Combining Kant and Hegel, Scruton insists that humans are defined by the fact that they treat each other as ends, not means. This 'human bond' is the cement of society which transcends mere contractual agreements. It is the basis of an individual's sense of identity within a social order: indeed it gives him the capacity to act as if he were an autonomous individual.

The family is important in Scruton's schema because it is the place where the 'transcendent bond' is first experienced and where an individual is presented with the fact of his public life. The family is not based on contract or consent between individuals, but on love which generates the social values of obligation and allegiance subsequently transferred to other social objects. The family is crucial to a stable sense of identity because it provides the experience of continuity in the world. Parents re-enact childhood with their children. They live the future in them after their own deaths as they live the past through their own parents. 'Past and future are made present, and therein lies the immediate and perceivable reality of the transcendent bond which unites them' (Scruton, 1986, p. 145).

Scruton argues that this produces in people a natural conservatism, for it is this sense of belonging to an institution which values one for one's own self and not as a means, which provides one with a history and a future in the present, that gives meaning in the world. Human beings will seek 'to conserve social continuity so that people may envisage generations which stretch before and after them' (p. 145). It is an attempt to find meaning in a life which inevitably leads to death and oblivion. There is little evidence of deep religious conviction in

Scruton. Rather he believes it is politically necessary to fight secular-isation because the decline in religious feeling weakens the recognition of the social bond. Religion for Scruton is not important for its truth value, but for its role in reinforcing those values generated initially in the family – allegiance, tradition, heritage. It is these which construct meaning, certainty and security in the present by linking the past with the future.

The family and other institutions which provide for this experience need to be protected, conserved in a changing world, because they provide the basis of the relationship of the individual to society and to the state, which for Scruton is the highest expression of the transcendent bond. Thus, the state is required to protect it, through law. Here again we can see Scruton's opposition to liberalism. The state and civil society are not separate, they are interdependent. 'Just as the private individual needs to find himself reflected in the social order so as to recognise externally the value of what he does, so must that order find its image in the state' (p. 81). Therein lies the state's authority. The more the state relinquishes to private conscience, the more it weakens the bond between itself and its subjects and in so doing undermines its own legitimacy. For Scruton, the law is not, as liberals would have it, a means of individual freedom, but is an expression of social conscious-ness: 'the law must cover all activity through which the bonds of trust and allegiance are cemented or broken' (p. 75). Thus, the private life of individuals may be the legitimate object of state intervention, not because the activities they may engage in are harmful to themselves, but because of the harm they inflict on the values of a nation's social consciousness.

There is a close affinity between the ideas of Scruton, academic, once editor of the conservative journal the *Salisbury Review*, regular columnist for the conservative *Daily Telegraph* and guru of contem-porary morals in media chat shows, and those of the Social Affairs Unit and the British pro-family lobby, exemplified by the contribu-tions to the National Family Trust's publication, *Families Matter* (Whitfield, 1987). He shares with them certain policy preferences: active state promotion of traditional values and traditional family life and a distaste for the predominance of the economic and consumer-ism, while still retaining a commitment to private property. Scruton achieves this by making a distinction between private property – that endowed with social meaning, self-realisation, and permanence – and consumption – the object of appetite, 'property pathologised'. His views conflict with others in the New Right on the question of the state's duties and obligations, favouring as he does something akin to the welfare state, so long as its provisions are conceived in terms of relieving want, not pursuing equality. The extent of the contradictions at the heart of the New Right are revealed in his assertion that 'conservative thinking is incompatible with any suggestion that the conservative is an advocate either of liberal ideals or of the so-called minimal state' (Scruton, 1986, p. 33).

Romantic humanism of the Right

This view, however, is directly opposed by Frederick Mount, well-known author, journalist and one-time director of Mrs Thatcher's advisory Central Policy Review Unit. His position is an eccentric mixture of anti-collectivist liberalism, anti-religious humanism and a secular defence of the family on grounds of values not that different from those of the libertarians of the radical movements, i.e. the survival of spontaneity, creativity, love and passion, adding further complexity to the ideological strands in New Right thinking pertaining to the family and personal life. Mount is highly suspicious of the contemporary Christian revival and averse to attempts to impose specific codes of conduct on the family on the grounds that, whether they take the form of the confessional, legal prohibitions or welfare interventions, their real aim is to curb the family as a rival power-base for the population's commitment.

Mount (1982) argues that the early Christian Church had little but contempt for marriage and the family, emphasising the superiority of virginity, abstinence and celibacy deriving from its founder's view that 'If any man come to me, and hate not his father, and mother, and wife, and children, and brethren, and sisters, yea, and his own life also, he cannot be my disciple' (Luke 14:26, cited p. 15). The reason for this antipathy to family life, Mount finds explicitly stated by St Paul: 'He that is unmarried careth for the things that belong to the Lord, how he may please the Lord. But he that is married careth for the things that are of this world, how he may please his wife' (I Corinthians 7:31, cited p. 17). This demand to renounce earthly pleasures was the basis for the institutionalisation of celibacy among the Catholic clergy, the establishment of monastic orders and the cloistral life. Family life, then, is seen by the Church as a rival to the control of its members' hearts and distracts them from a higher loyalty and a higher love. The family is the ultimate 'subversive' organisation because it constitutes a sphere of private resistance to the demands of the Superordinate. The Church's endorsement of marriage was no more than an historical accommodation to reality and the only way to control the sexuality of its flock.

He believes that feminists have been misled by the official ideologues of male supremacy in the Church and State, into believing that the family is the bulwark of social order. As a consequence, feminists have mistakenly identified the family as the source of all the inequalities and oppressions that they observe and experience in that order. Mount argues to the contrary that 'these inequalities themselves originally seeped through into marriage from the outside; from the public world' (p. 241).

Mount presents an impressive array of material to show that in the popular, as opposed to the orthodox, view of marriage, there has always been a commitment to the ideals of love and equality, of mutual care and affection on the basis of personal and sexual attraction. While Mount admits that the reality frequently did not live up to these ideals, he nevertheless insists that there was an alternative pattern of popular marriage, 'more realistic and tolerant of failure, more concerned with rubbing along with and physically looking after your family, less interested in spiritual purity, earthier, less ambitious' (p. 254). In this 'alternative history of love and marriage', the mute subservient Woman of the official story is replaced by women who own property, rule households, run businesses, economically support their families, and who either circumvent or confront their subordination to men. Mount's alternative history is not an attempt to argue for separate spheres, that private power is an adequate substitute for public power, but to show that it is not heterosexual love and family life that is the cause of inequality but the historical regulation of private relationships by the Church and State.

Unlike the moral conservationists, Mount does not see the current high rates of divorce as evidence of the moral decadence of our age or of the death of the family. Rather they are the result of the democratisation of divorce: it has become cheap and simple and thus available to the mass of the population for the first time. As to the criticism that such freedoms are selfish and result in human misery, Mount retorts that: 'the "psychic casualties" of the Church's teaching on marriage can certainly rival the casualties which may result from the relaxation of the divorce laws' (p. 214). He is most scathing of the pious homilies of those who would turn the clock back and reimpose traditional values: 'The comparison between a mythical past of happily married couples and a modern world of fleeting unions and abandoned children can be sustained only by historical stone-blindness or bad faith' (p. 214).

The book is really a hymn in praise of secular love which Mount sees as the source of human creativity and capacity to care for others. It is this that through the centuries, in its many forms, keeps pushing through the network of religious doctrines, legal restrictions, social conventions and cultural censorship designed to keep it under control. Heterosexual attraction, sexual love, marriage and family affection represent for Mount the formless, classless, timeless expression of the indomitable human spirit. As such, his analysis suffers from the same problems as all attempts to understand complex social phenomena in terms of a single principle: it simplifies explanation but tells us little about the phenomena.

Nevertheless, Mount offers a refreshing and provocative analysis of anti-familialism which cuts across the conventional Right–Left, religious–secular, antifeminist–feminist divides. His contribution cannot have been welcomed by the opposing forces in the politics of the family.

Rhetoric and reality: the cracks appear

Recognition of this complexity of right-wing thinking is helpful in understanding the contemporary politics of the family. It perhaps explains increasingly frequent and virulent rows between Conservative politicians. For example, in the Commons debate of the Alton Bill to reduce the time limit on abortion, a Conservative MP, Teresa Gorman, stridently declared in that abortion 'is a matter of civil rights. It is a matter of the right of a woman to decide on her own future and her own fertility' (*Daily Telegraph*, 23 January 1988), while another of her party, Terry Dicks, asserted that 'the minute that any woman takes part in any sexual act other than by force, she loses her complete rights to control over her own body' (*The Guardian*, 23 January 1988). The Bill was defeated. On another occasion, a junior education minister was strongly criticised by pro-family Tory MPs for his speech to the Girls' School Association, in which he pointed out that educational success was particularly important for girls in view of the trend in divorce and the large number of women who become sole breadwinners (*Evening Standard*, 16 November 1988). On yet another, a Conservative MP won leave to introduce a bill to give tax relief to working mothers who employ home-helps or child-minders despite the out-bursts of another who decried the bill as harmful to children and the family by assisting selfish mothers who wished to work (*The Times*, 7 March 1990).

These conflicting ideological strands may also account for why the National Campaign for the Family received the following response to their appeal to Mrs Thatcher to initiate policies to strengthen the traditional family:

> the Government agrees wholeheartedly with the Campaign that marriage and the family are two of the most important institutions on which society is based. Particularly at this time of rapid social change and accompanying stresses, marriage has never been more important in preserving a stable and responsible society... But there is a limit to what the Government in a free society can do and Government action in itself cannot change attitudes towards the family. The influence for change must come from within and be directed at society itself. The Government also believes that it would be wrong to seek to promote the interests of the family as an institution in particular situations where this conflicted with the best interests of its members as individuals. (cited in Whitfield, 1987, pp. 230–1)

Examination of Mrs Thatcher's speeches reveals the same emphasis on a belief in the family as a cornerstone of society but the same avoidance of any detail of government intervention to strengthen it. Despite the rhetoric, Mrs Thatcher remained fairly consistent. From her early statements in the Conservative Research Department Paper, *Family Policy*, in 1952, Mrs Thatcher's prior attachment to the individual prevailed.

The family became pivotal in the politics of unity in the contemporary Conservative Party. It came to symbolise what both factions within the party, the economic liberals and the moral conservatives, could agree upon: anti-collectivism and anti-egalitarianism. Restoring the power of initiative and choice to the individual by economic deregulation and privatisation, the reduction of taxation and the scale of public welfare, enabled individuals to look after their families in the way they chose. Radical liberal economic policy was thus lined up with the moral shibboleths of traditional conservatism. It is quite astounding that unity was preserved for so long, for which credit must go to the political intuition and rhetoric of Mrs Thatcher herself.

Nevertheless, no matter how successfully the rhetoric papered over the disparate elements within the party and convinced sympathisers among the electorate, the contradictions at the level of practical policy-making were not to be overcome. It is arguable that the increased volubility of British pro-family organisations in the later 1980s was not a response to encouragement derived from legislative success, but a propaganda drive by those disillusioned with the failure of the government's pro-family rhetoric to substantially materialise – with, in my view, some justification. Despite the establishment of a Family Policy Group, there very few policy initiatives out of Downing Street and a more restrained and pragmatic tone in relation to moral and family issues in the General Election Manifestos of 1983 and 1987. The morally neutral approach of Conservative Central Office with an eye on the weather-vane of public opinion, the Conservative Women's Committee and ministers like Angela Rumbold, had prevailed against the railings of the Conservative Family Campaign (Isaac, 1994).

Concern at the abandonment of pro-family policy was voiced by contributors to *Family Portraits* (Anderson and Dawson, 1986), a publication of the conservative Social Affairs Unit. For example, Hermione Parker is highly critical of the Thatcher administration's record in relation to family income support which she considers amounts to 'subversion of the traditional family' (p. 70), while in relation to the need to return the moral and financial responsibility for young people to parents, David Marsland complains that 'halfway through the second term of a Government which stresses its commitment to the family, there is little sign of any change' (p. 87).

A series of articles criticising the government in this respect appeared in the Conservative press in the run-up to the 1987 election: Paul Johnson claimed that 'the lack of a family policy is a devastating hole at the heart of modern Conservatism . . . the Government over the past decade has lamely continued policies which further erode it' (Johnson, 1987). Richard Whitfield, the Chair of the National Campaign for the Family, in launching the new pressure group, criticised Mrs Thatcher for putting too much emphasis on the individual instead of co-ordinating government action to combat 'the national crisis in family life' (Hildrew and Smith, 1987). The American press ran similar criticisms of Reagan for reneging on his commitment to strengthen the traditional family and Christian values.

It appears that no less than some of their left-liberal and feminist opponents, supporters of the conservative governments in both countries assumed an identity between political rhetoric and political practice, between intention and delivery. The public statements of prominent politicians in relation to policy were taken as expressions of instrumentality, when they may have had a different objective, for example to express a deeply held personal conviction or to appease a potentially oppositional faction within their own ranks, or again to appeal to a sentiment forcefully articulated in the public opinion polls. The importance of the family issue for this particular political constellation was its symbolic function in unifying the economic liberalism and the traditional conservatism which cohabited uneasily in these revived right-wing parties, and its metaphoric function in translating their monetarist and militaristic policies into a populist language by which to engage directly with the general public.

What the politicisation of the family has shown, however, is that it is a topic which arouses a great deal of emotion and anxiety, and which is capable of mobilising women who are slow to be brought into the arena of political debate and activity on other counts. It is ironic that where it did so, it did not tend bring them closer to the feminist movement in large numbers. Some part of the reason for that phenomenon must be attributed to the association of feminism with an anti-family ideology and practice. While the media did have considerable responsibility for that association, the examination of the feminist movement carried out in Chapter 3 suggests that it was not without foundation.

Feminists faced with dismay the 'other women's movement' and the electoral successes of the New Right. Women's votes threatened to become increasingly important to the politics of the last decades of the twentieth century and the direction in which they would be cast was not at all clear. Some felt it was time to rethink the family and reconsider the interests of women in relation to it. It is to these issues that we now turn in Chapter 7.

7

Feminists Reconsider the Family

With the emergence of the pro-family movement and the radicalisation of conservative parties on both sides of the Atlantic, feminists felt besieged. After the exhuberence of the radical moment in the 1960s, both the strength of the traditionalist reaction and the sourness of the political mood in the USA and the UK took them by surprise. Both added pressure to the existing internal divisions within the women's movement described in Chapter 3.

On one side there were those, such as Eisenstein and Dworkin, who insisted on no dilution of feminist principles and demanded of both feminist and mainstream political organisations that they should confront the reactionaries head-on, that there should be no sell-out, either theoretically or politically. This is understandable given that it was the radical feminists who had taken the brunt of the considerable anti-feminist, anti-homosexual and other sexist abuse in the war over the family. On the other side, were those equally committed feminists who had always been or had grown uneasy about the repudiation of the family as inherently oppressive to women and about the priorities of the radical separatist strand within the movement.

In this situation, many backed off and devoted their energies to pursuing less dangerous disputes within discrete areas of academic research or to working in organisations with more clearly delimited parameters. Thus we find academic feminists developing what Robert K. Merton once called theories of 'the middle range' (Merton, 1948). In the case of the family this meant exploring the economics and sociology of housework, the early socialisation of girls, reproductive issues, the history of the family, the psycho-dynamics of mother–child relationships, family violence, child abuse, the familial networks of obligations and care, family law and so on. To this work we owe the burgeoning of serious academic feminist literature, women's studies courses and the mainstreaming of a gender perspective in most academic disciplines in universities. Others became involved in independent research and policy centres, women-friendly employment policy and implementation, women's advisory centres, refuges, health units, single issue organisations and pressure groups. Feminists had families, worked on, with and for families, but on the general issue of the family, so sensitive and painful inside feminist circles, a public discretion developed.

The American Left rediscover the family

In the mid-1970s, however, a series of articles and books by prominent left-of-centre academics broke with the radical orthodoxy on the family. Eli Zaretsky, in *Capitalism, the Family and Personal Life* (1976), and Christopher Lasch, in *Haven in a Heartless World* (1977), argued that, rather than the family being a site of oppression as portrayed by feminists, it became a refuge from the fragmented, bureaucratised impersonal instrumentalism of working life under industrial capitalism. As such it formed the basis of the working-class community and a source of resistance to capitalist values. Both are concerned that in contemporary America even the family is under threat of disintegration from rampant consumer capitalism reducing all human relationships to the cash nexus.

Of the two, however, Lasch was much more controversial, imputing some blame to nineteenth century 'forces of organised virtue, led by feminists' and their twentieth-century successors in the health and welfare professions. The therapeutic interventions sanitised personal relations, denuding them of passion and spontaneity, leaving children with no deep passionate and secure attachments. In addition, a combination of the intensification of work demands or unemployment, and the 'ideology of familial equality and togetherness' had feminised the role of the father and undermined his authority, hence there is no mechanism for the internalisation of social order through the development of the superego. Conscience and self-discipline does not develop; only the rational calculation of consequences. Authority is now either obeyed or challenged on the basis of its strength, rather than on its moral legitimacy. Happiness is defined by the short-lived thrills of acquisition endlessly titillated by consumer capitalism and sexual novelty. Thus, Lasch sees the problem of modern society as the decline of Oedipus and the rise of Narcissus.

Both Zaretsky's and Lasch's accounts of family life in the past are highly romanticised and underestimate the numbers of families broken by premature death of one or both parents, desertion or destitution, and the extent of cruelty, violence, incest and neglect that existed within them. They also underestimate the extensive absences from the home of the father given the long working day, and the extent to which working-class women of all ages had to take paid work for families to survive. The question must be asked – for whom was the home a refuge?

The same oversimplification extends to the contemporary family. Lasch in particular underestimates the extent to which parents have continued to behave in an authoritative and indeed authoritarian manner in relation to children. He also overstates the diminution of paternal authority and underestimates paternal involvement with childcare. On the one hand, much research into the changing roles of men and women (Henwood, Rimmer and Wicks, 1987; Strober, 1988) shows that males still retain final authority in relation to the most important familial decisions largely because of the characteristics of male employment. On the other hand, research has also shown that the greatest change has occurred in the increase of fathers' participation with children (Acock and Demo, 1994; Ferri and Smith, 1996). The relegation of the father in intact families to a purely economic role suggested by Lasch does not seem to be borne out (McKee and O'Brien, 1982; Wheelock, 1990). He also too easily identifies expressivity and laxity with women and authority and discipline with men, rather than seeing them as a function of role which traverses the mother–father divide. For example, most of the social disciplining of the child falls to the mother, in that in the early years at least she typically spends more time with the child and hence is a figure of both omnipotence and authority to the child.

Despite grounding his analysis of the ills of modern society in Freud's theory of the inevitability of the conflict between libidinal desires and the demands of Culture and the necessity of Repression, when it comes to Lasch's own theory of the relationship between the erosion of family life and the growth of a generalised inadequate self-indulgent personality structure, he collapses into similar sociologising as the feminists he criticises. The internal weakness of Lasch's formulations lies in the fact that the referent in his scenario is not the Father of the Oedipal triad, but the real father in the American nuclear family who Lasch fears is becoming redundant. In his anxiety, Lasch has conflated the two.

The book caused a furore. The Left Establishment were appalled; the Right were gleeful. For obvious reasons, feminists were particularly hostile to Lasch's book but doubts about the radical orthodoxy on the family began to emerge within feminism itself.

American feminists rethink the family

In 1977, Alice Rossi, a well-known feminist academic, published an essay, 'A Biosocial Perspective on Parenting', in a special edition of *Daedalus*, the prestigious journal of the American Academy of Arts and Sciences. It startled feminist circles by asserting that the standard feminist position that gender roles and family forms are socially constructed was misguided and that its 'advocacy of "variant" marriage and family forms is inadequate and misleading because it neglects some fundamental human characteristics rooted in our biological heritage' (Rossi, 1977, p. 2).

Impressed by modern genetics and endocrinology which suggest a complex interaction between environmental stimuli, physiological events, psychological motivations and social behaviour, Rossi had come to the view that the biological evolution of the human species had resulted in 'differences in the ease with which the two sexes can learn certain things' (p. 4). She does not doubt that men can learn to care for young infants, but she is insistent that women have a natural predisposition derived from endocrinal changes produced in pregnancy and birth. However, it was Rossi's unsubstantiated conclusion that such maternal predispositions persist throughout the later stages of child-rearing, making pointless self-conscious attempts at androgynous socialisation and domestic reorganisation, her description of the children of communes, as 'almost uniformly neglected, deprived and tormented . . . uneducated, disorganised and disturbed', and her acerbic remarks on the self-centred, irresponsible hedonism of countercultural parents, that provoked an angry reaction from a large number of feminists (Breines, Cerullo and Stacey, 1978). But there was more to come.

In 1978, the *Socialist Review* ran a relatively mild article by the feminist Barbara Easton in which she suggested that the tendency of feminists and the Left to be associated with an anti-family stance may push women with concerns about their personal and family lives towards right-wing elements because they were providing a forum for such concerns. She warned: 'It is time for feminism and the left to address these questions' (Easton, 1978, p. 34). This was followed by support from another well-known feminist, Jessie Bernard (1981), hailed the levelling off in divorce rates and more positive attitudes towards marriage revealed by attitudinal surveys, as evidence that the 'crisis of the family' was over and suggested that it was time to 're-assemble the pieces' in more appropriate family structures.

The challenge was taken up in the same year by a series of public lectures at Stanford University, subsequently published as *Rethinking The Family* (Thorne and Yalom, 1982). A number of the contributions were fairly forceful about what was inadequate or misleading about radical and feminist positions. Zaretsky made his plea, alongside Linda Gordon and Clair Brown, for rebalancing the view of the family to emphasise its positive qualities, particularly since alternatives had not yet been developed, a veiled reference to the ephemerality of the counter-culture communes. Susan Westerberg Prager warned against the too easy assumption that individualistic principles best promote women's interests as the basis of marital property law. Nancy Chodorow and Susan Contralto were critical of feminist work which identifies the mother as the main agent in the reproduction of inequality, either via a simple conditioning theory as in Firestone (1971), or via a version of psychoanalysis as in Dinnerstein (1976), because behind both lies the assumption of the perfect mother, the very starting point of feminist critique.

However, it is true to say that while the Introduction to the volume locates it 'in the wake of controversy over the family' (p. 1), the controversy is not confronted in any of the papers. Rather each one deals overwhelmingly with academic issues which have arisen within 'family studies' in various disciplines and almost studiously avoids engaging with the political battle over the family raging outside the doors of academia.

Others were not so discreet. One uncompromising critic was Jean Bethke Elshtain, a respected feminist academic in political theory circles. Her critique, contained in a series of articles and later in her book, *Public Man, Private Woman* (1981), focuses on one of feminism's basic tenets: 'The Personal Is Political'. She claims that by collapsing the personal and the political spheres, feminists, particularly radical feminists, have both defined politics out of existence by declaring it everywhere, and infected every human relationship with its worst aspects. Relations of intimacy, desire, tenderness and mutual reliance are redrawn as stifling dependency and oppression. At the same time, the diffusion of power rules out arriving at criteria by which to judge which person or institution is more or less oppressive and thus provides no guide to concerted action. Finally, by declaring open season on the whole field of the personal, feminists have weakened further the limited protection individuals have against the exploitative inroads of market-place rationality and bureaucratic state interventions.

Elshtain argues that the abuse and neglect that exist in the family are the result of frustrations and brutality of 'relations of exchange and the values of the marketplace' displaced on to the weakest members of families. However fragile and vulnerable the emotional ties of family are, they sustain attitudes and values conducive to genuine self-esteem, intrinsic loyalties and collective support. For Elshtain, as for Zaretsky and Lasch, the family is the institution which more than any other, has the capacity to relate in ways not defined by the market place.

However, when it comes to the market economy Elshtain, like the feminists she criticises, seems guilty of 'reducing politics to crude relations of force or domination'. To see the market economy and indeed, modern public life, as simply oppressive and brutally destructive of identity, self-worth and social relationships, is just as simplistic and seems to smack of the same 'politics of displacement' with which she characterises the women's movement.

There is little doubt that capitalist economies have profound effects on the structures and cultures of the countries in which they have developed or have been inserted. However, there is a little less certainty that such effects are as universal or as entirely negative as Elshtain and others assume. First, there are considerable differences between market-based societies. Secondly, certain of the negative features attributed to the effects of capitalism – bureaucratisation, professionalisation, stratification, racism, sexism, the dominance of the impersonal, the instrumental, the rationalistic, the intervention in private life and personal behaviour – can be found in societies in which capitalist relations are non-existent or are not dominant.

Thirdly, for all its shortcomings, the market economy can and does provide people with positive identities, both individual and group, which are a source of both intrinsic satisfaction and collective value, and most certainly of resistance to the alienating and demoralising tendencies of the system itself. Indeed such features are particularly appreciated by women returners to employment, whose identities have often been submerged in those of their husbands, children, or elderly, disabled parents. The very individualistic and impersonal forms of appraisal, based as they are on competence and effort, can come as a welcome relief from those based on subjective and often unlimited definitions of need and love.

It is precisely because Elshtain polarises the private (family) and the public (capitalism), attributing all evils to the latter, that she fails to see not only what beneficial effects the closer integration of the two realms has brought to women in the form of an independent identity and alternative resource base, but also the infiltration of values of social need, solidarity and collective responsibility into the public domain which, transformed into new political demands, resulted in what has been called 'welfare capitalism'.

It is almost a truism to point out that markets are not and cannot exist in a political and social vacuum. It seems to be recognised less often that while social institutions are subject to mechanisms of the market economy they are not necessarily wholly subordinated to them. In relation to the family, while it may be true that much of its unhappiness is an effect of frustration deriving from the public realm, it is the relations of power within the family which allow these to be displaced on to its vulnerable members, and it also the public realm, either through the individual wage or the social wage, that enables those vulnerable members to escape. Like it or not, the two spheres traverse each other even if they indeed ideologically construct each other as separate. And there are benefits as well as costs in that.

A U-turn by the mother of feminism?

Elshtain's work drew the ire of many feminists but its philosophical character tended to confine its readership to other academic feminists. In terms of the politics of the family, it was the entry of the founder of post-war American feminism, Betty Friedan, into the debate that had the greatest public impact. Prompted by alarm at the numbers of women that the pro-family lobby had been able to mobilise, the National Organisation of Women Legal Defence and Education Fund decided to hold a National Assembly on the Future of the Family with Friedan as convenor.

The story, previewed by the *New York Times Magazine* the day before (Friedan, 1979), was that the feminism of the 1970s had run its course. While it had achieved many of its objectives, it now faced a bedrock problem in the conflict between the demands of the work-place and the demands of family life. For some women the very success of the women's movement in pushing open the doors of male privilege had closed the doors of marriage and children. Others, whose work outside the home had become a financial necessity, faced a double burden since nothing had been done to change the domestic arrangements inside the family. The central tenet of feminism – free to choose – had to be reaffirmed, but it had to include the freedom to choose to have a child, to choose to work and to combine them with family life without it becoming an intolerable burden. Thus, 'the second feminist agenda, the agenda for the 80s, must call for the restructuring of the institutions of home and work' (p. 92) and this required a rejection of the anti-familialist stance associated with the women's movement as much as it meant a rejection of the funda-mentalism of the pro-family position.

The article and the NOW (National Organisation for Women) Assembly which endorsed Friedan's views created a considerable stir, but it was their expansion into a much publicised and widely distributed book in 1981 that marked the beginning of the Great Debate within feminism. *The Second Stage* (Friedan, 1983) was regarded by many feminists as reneging on the ideas and the politics of Friedan's *The Feminine Mystique*, a view reinforced by the media which hailed the book as a U-turn by one of the movement's gurus. A careful reading of the two texts reveals, however, that there are more continuities between them than there are deviations. Of course, for some feminists this has no merit, since it merely confirms their view that Friedan was a conservative in the first place, and for others that Friedan should be denied the label 'feminist' altogether.

Friedan's critique of the feminine mystique and familialism never had endorsed rejection of relationships with men or the family in general. For her, the targets of feminism were unequal access of women to all areas of public life, as well as the sexist socialisation and education of girls. These were the objectives enshrined in the NOW agenda and toward which America moved much faster and more profoundly than in Britain (Wilson, 1987). She also attributed great importance to issues of sexual reproduction, without control of which other opportunities for women would be severely limited. On these issues, Friedan held faith.

The problem as she sees it is that in the struggle to compete with and do as well as men, women have adopted a mode of behaviour and values more usually associated with men. This she terms 'Alpha-style leadership' adopted from the Stanford management guru, Peter Schwartz. Friedan is concerned that feminism is now in danger of 'aping the accepted dominant Alpha mode... in its zeal for acceptance and respectability, and in its own acceptance of polarization' (Fiedan, 1983, p. 249). Polarisation refers not only to the aggressive opposition of women against men but also to the opposition of women against certain qualities within women themselves. Expressions of polarisation vary from the 'career "superwoman" hellbent on beating men at their own game' (p. 44), the repudiation of men as innately rapacious, the denigration of married women as prostitutes, to the rejection of natural childbearing in favour of test-tube technology.

Friedan says she understands such extreme responses in that they burst out of the same anger which gave vent to *The Feminine Mystique* in which she herself likened the family to a 'comfortable concentration camp'. It was a righteous anger at the denial of the right to be oneself. However, its conversion into a self-legitimating ideology and a sexual politics was an error on two grounds. First, it 'denied the profound, complex human reality of the sexual, social, psychological, economic, and yes, biological relationship between woman and man. It denied the reality of woman's own sexuality, her childbearing, her roots and life connection in the family' (Friendan, 1983, p. 51). Secondly, being confined to the bedroom, it did not threaten the fundamental economic and political interests in the way that mainstream feminist strategies did, and so it 'didn't really change anything' (ibid.). Ultimately, Friedan argues, the dominant rhetoric of sexual politics reinstated the contradiction which feminism had attempted to overcome: that between the family and equality. It has exchanged one 'half life' for another and has perpetuated the male conception of women as sex objects which it sets out to repudiate.

Friedan is also concerned about the long-term deleterious effects on women themselves. Her interviews with career women report regret about the time devoted to their work to the exclusion of a satisfying personal life, either because they have not had children or because they did not participate enough in their rearing to build deep emotional relationships with them. Others face the dilemma of the 'biological clock'; others suffer stress trying to be 'superwomen' at work and at home.

While these are concerns primarily of educated professional women, Friedan also addresses the situation of women who work out of necessity, because they are lone parents, or because one income is not enough to maintain a family. Such women are forced to carry the responsibility of a job and the housework and childcare. The position for these women, she warns, is getting worse as a result of the decline in economic growth and the cut-back in government employment and income support programmes. There are also likely to be a growing number of them in poverty as high divorce rates continue and public funds for abortion are withdrawn.

The answer to these problems of the late twentieth century, Friedan says, is not to return to the form of family prescribed by the Moral Majority. Rather it is to 'confront the American family as it actually is today' and to restructure the institutions of work and home accordingly. This requires comprehensive policy measures using a mixed economy of public, private and voluntary agencies. They include substantial and interchangeable maternity and paternity leaves and benefits; family-friendly employment practices and benefit packages; government incentives for the provision of various types of childcare services; care allowances; housing and home financing policies to facilitate the combination of privacy and communality.

So far none of these ideas and recommendations run counter to the principles that lay behind *The Feminine Mystique*, though there is a different focus on the balancing of work and family life, occasioned by the changes of the intervening 17 years. There is much play on 'freedom' and 'choice', bywords interestingly of both the feminist and the New Right 'revolutions'. Gone are the demands for the state to provide everything, but Friedan is equally clear that individuals and families should not have to fend for themselves. Hence there is a new accommodation to the voluntary sector not as a substitute for the welfare state but as a form of community involvement. The plurality of provision is geared to the plurality of need as defined by the plurality of choice. Friedan agrees with the strand of pro-family ideology which decries the crass materialism of modern times and emphasises the need for emotional ties and spiritual values found in family relationships. However, for Friedan, moral traditionalists mistake the form for the substance. This takes us to another of the continuities with Friedan's first best-seller.

The same emphasis found in *The Feminist Mystique* on the basic human right to self-fulfilment, which familialism denied women, is developed in *The Second Stage* (Friedan, 1983) into a notion of 'generative power', a metaphor that links self-realisation to childbirth and childcare, to new social movements seeking to improve the quality of life, and to the protection of the planet itself. Ultimately, it is Friedan's metaphysics of personhood and her view of women's special gifts that make the family so important to her.

This is why her greatest anger is reserved for those feminists who repudiate them as patriarchal myths. It is not the positive choice of chastity or homosexuality as the basis of personal intimacy and love that she rails against, but the angry denial of heterosexuality and motherhood as a genuine choice for others. Thus, her disclaimer that she 'does not think everyone has to be a mother to "fulfil" herself as a woman' (Friedan, 1983, p. 86) is not really in contradiction to her question, 'isn't motherhood, the profound human impulse to have children, more than a mystique?' (p. 73). The latter remark questions, perhaps unconsciously, the socialisation paradigm in which the feminine mystique is explained. It innocently gestures towards the problems as yet unresolved in feminism, as in other discourses, of explaining the desire for a child that is outwith the pressures of social expectations and indeed can be contrary to them. It is a comment on contemporary social science and indicative of the profound social changes that have occurred this century that the question 'Why do women want children?' is much more interesting than 'Why do they not?'

The family, then, for Friedan, is not a form. It is the name for the place where the need for 'love and identity, status, security and generation' is met (p. 319). It is true that for her the reciprocal relationship between mother and child is privileged in providing for that need, and so by implication the heterosexual relationship. But this is largely a symbolic identity. Friedan may be inspired by a humanist mysticism of the Life Force, but she is first and foremost a liberal, a realist and a pragmatist. She has no problem, therefore, in staunchly defending NOW's affirmation of the pluralism of family forms:

> We do not share the frequently voiced opinion that American families are in a state of hopeless collapse. People are living together in new combinations for the intimacy and support that constitute a family. (p. 102)

It is difficult for British audiences to appreciate the impact of Friedan's public statements for there is no real British equivalent. Betty Friedan is not simply one among many academic feminist activists, but the leader of a major pressure group that has been integrated into American mainstream politics and is regarded as an important force by the American Establishment. Organised feminism made headway in American society, precisely because it used to good

effect the language and institutions of liberal democracy, and in doing
so strengthened the latter's legitimacy. The political standing of feminism goes some way to explaining why it was important to right-wing
Republicans to use the Moral Right to discredit it. It was then 'Friedan's pivotal, highly public role in the founding of contemporary
feminism ... [that made her] ... an important sculptor and barometer
of mainstream feminist consciousness as well as of popular perceptions about what feminism is' (Stacey, 1983, p. 560). Her *New York
Times* article and the subsequent statements of other leading NOW
spokespersons ensured that the war over the family was no longer
simply between the pro-family movement and an alliance of feminists,
liberals and socialists but had taken hold within the ranks of the latter
coalition.

Further revisionism

By the mid-1980s the doubts within feminism about the family had
become a public debate and exploited by the media. Another text to
hit the headlines and the media chat-shows was *A Lesser Life: The
Myth of Women's Liberation in America* (1986). Its author, Sylvia
Hewlett, a director of the Economic Policy Council (EPC) of the
United Nations Association of the USA, a self-identified feminist
and one of its successes, criticised American feminism for its 'fatal
error in ignoring the importance of the family and the home in the
lives of the majority of women' (p. 160) and its absolutist position
on gender equality. As a result, American women have had to
compete in the labour market on the same terms as men, terms
rendered impossible by women's continuing domestic role, while
men have been given the excuse for abandoning their traditional
financial responsibilities. This, she claimed, had led to a deterioration
of women's position and accounted for the limited appeal of
feminism for most women, indeed to their alienation from it. Hewlett
claims that, by contrast, the British and European women's movements have achieved much more for women, because they made sure
that women's maternal and domestic responsibilities were protected.
With better maternity benefits and leave, job protection, child benefits
and childcare provision, British and European women have also been
able to make greater advances in the employment stakes, evidenced,
for example, by narrower wage differentials between men and women
than in the United States.

Hewlett's attack on the Women's Liberation Movement (WLM) drew the hostility of American feminists (Morgan, 1986; Friedan, 1986), but she is no advocate of hearth and home. The anger derives from her personal tribulations experienced in trying to combine motherhood and a professional career, and her women-friendly policy proposals, designed to deal with these obstacles, are similar to those advocated by Friedan (1983). She wants an equality between the sexes which recognises those differences deriving from maternity and children but which does not allow them to impede women's full participation in public life.

However, her analysis has some serious flaws. First, the WLM cannot be held to blame for the greater economic vulnerability of women; we have already seen that such trends were well advanced before the advent of modern feminism. Secondly, she mistakenly attributes the greater social support for children and families in Britain and Europe to the characteristics of their brand of feminism. In fact the significant factor is the greater collectivist traditions in the political cultures of these countries, a legacy of the centralised nature of imperial states with their greater interest in the bureaucratic control of their populations, and their strong socialist and labour movements also with statist inclinations. Thirdly, she overestimates the level of material support at least in Britain, where, despite the family rhetoric, government fiscal and social policy has consistently disadvantaged families with dependent children. Fourthly, there is little mention in her policy proposals of the ways in which men's working lives could be modified so that they can take a full share in child-rearing and housework. While at the present time it is women who are in most need for support, in the longer term, if such policies are confined to the category of mother, they will reinforce the current gender divisions in employment and within families, both at the structural and ideological level.

Progressive pro-family politics

One political consequence of all this angst was the launching in 1982 of a new pressure group, 'Friends of Families', with the aim of spearheading a progressive pro-family movement involving 'the trade union movement, the women's movement, the civil rights movement, the liberal wing of the religious community, environmentalists and community activists' (Lerner, 1982, p. 142). The launch elicited a considerable support. There are a number of reasons for this.

First, and probably the most immediate, was the real fear felt by considerable sections of the politically informed population about the legislative and social consequences of the Moral Right. Secondly, while the pro-family movement had been successful in mobilising very large numbers of people, it had also succeeded in antagonising constituencies of opinion in the moral domain. Many of the churches, philanthropic organisations, charity agencies, private and voluntary sector 'caring' organisations became increasingly uneasy as the right-wing dimension of the movement became prominent (Friedan, 1983; Pankhurst and Houseknecht, 1983). In particular the aggressive demonstrations and violent attacks made on abortion clinics and their staff by anti-abortionist campaigners in 'Operation Rescue' alienated many women, even those who shared their views of the right to life.

Thirdly, there was evidence of a renewed interest in parenting and the family and their beneficial or pleasurable aspects among people loosely associated with progressive politics. Mostly belonging to the college-educated middle classes, they constituted a smaller potential constituency for a progressive pro-family alliance, but with importance beyond their numbers in terms of articulacy, organisational skills, and influence. Fourthly, lone parent organisations saw the opportunity of gaining wider support. The rise in their numbers had been a major factor in triggering off the rise of family politics, and they had been much maligned in the process. The fact that most of these organisations included the word 'family' in their names is indicative of their determination to resist continued marginalisation and to be considered a legitimate family form.

The interest shown in the Friends of the Family initiative demonstrates that more than the fundamentalists had a stake in the family and that a rupture of the unspoken embargo on the subject in progressive circles was long overdue. However, it also has to be said that as the basis of a coherent package of persuasive premises and workable policies the analysis left a great deal to be desired, and it was this that its more serious critics exposed (Ehrenreich, 1982b; Epstein, 1982; Ellis, 1983).

At the level of electoral appeal, many of the proposals put forward can be found in the traditional liberal democratic kitbag, such as full employment, stability of work location, equality in employment and pay, socialised health-care and community-controlled childcare.

Desirable though these poicies might be, it is difficult to see h
were to be made any more attractive to the electorate under
label than they had been under the previous one. They h̶ ̶ ̶ᴜᴇen
already rejected as unfeasible in the economic climate of the 1980s
without massive tax increases, and they smacked too much of the New
Dealism which the New Right had persuasively identified as part of
the economic problem in the first place.

The analysis of the reasons for family breakdown suffers from
traditional Left economism and fails to come to terms with the
implications for political analysis and strategy, not only of feminist
work on relations of power within families but also of mainstream
psychological research on the internal dynamics of family life and
theories of cultural change. These discourses suggest that the causes
of distress in families cannot be entirely displaced on to external
factors, such as poverty, bad housing, poor education, ill health,
though these of course do impose sometimes intolerable strain on
families.

In trying to appeal broadly, Friends of Families gave the term
'family' a definition so elastic it is difficult to find anyone outside it.
It apparently extends beyond the nuclear family to refer to any two or
more people committed to a long-term personal relationship. In one
sense this relational ecumenicalism which breaks the monopolistic
hold that the traditional family conventionally has on love and reliance, is to be welcomed. However it does present problems for policy
specification.

In modern liberal democracies, the family 'has become an aggregate
of related individuals, each with rights that may be in conflict. Consequently, the interests of women, children and other dependants,
once assumed to be identical with those of the father, are now
demanding and receiving support... the history of the nuclear family
is a history of the partly successful struggle of these subordinate
groups' (Ellis, 1983, p. 48). For example, in Britain the debate over
the phasing-out of child tax allowance accruing to the father and the
introduction of child benefit paid to the mother exposed the conflict of
interests between husband and wife beautifully symbolised in the
media as the battle between the wallet and the purse; the Gillick
case was illustrative of the conflict between the rights of parents,
those of children and those of the medical profession; the Cleveland
case in which large numbers of children were removed from their
parents pending investigation of suspected child sexual abuse raised
the even more complex policy issues around the rights and obligations

of parents, the health authorities, social services departments and children.

It is for this reason that it is difficult to assert a simple causal relationship between family stability and specific economic problems or the general state of the economy. Whether economic measures would strengthen families or not depends on a number of variables, such as the financial situation of the family, its internal dynamics, and the impact point of additional resources in the 'career' of the family. As Ehrenreich remarks, 'While...most of the good things Lerner proposes would make families happier insofar as they might make people in general happier, they cannot be counted on to foster the family stability he values so highly' (1982b, p. 303). She points out that they may well have the opposite effect by decreasing women's financial dependence on men and therefore much of the necessity for either partner to stay in the relationship. In her book *The Hearts of Men* (1983) Ehrenreich argues that the stability and security of the traditional family was always predicated on the willingness of men to become wage-earners and to share their wages with their dependants. That assumption was built into the structure of the economy in the form of the 'family wage' and was reinforced in family law. It is this system against which men have rebelled in what she terms the masculine revolt against the ideology of the responsible male. Far from feminism or female emancipation causing family instability, it is in fact its effect.

Steiner (1981) reviewed some of the research on whether public assistance keeps families together by enhancing their material well-being or whether it encourages dissolution by reducing the dependence of the wife and the responsibility of the husband. Data from the negative income tax experiments conducted in the early 1970s by the Office of Economic Opportunity in the urban areas of New Jersey, Seattle and Denver and in rural areas in North Carolina and Iowa showed consistently higher dissolution rates among families in receipt of the additional income support. However, the problems involved in the evaluation of these experiments, and the contradictory evidence from comparisons of states which have non-experimental long-term differences in AFDC (Aid to Families with Dependent Children) provision leads Steiner to conclude that it is not possible to arrive at a conclusion one way or the other: 'Money may divide as well as cement families' (p. 96). But this was a view that was ignored in the Friends of Families policy package.

The rehabilitation of motherhood

Another development from the late 1970s related to the rethinking of the family amongst progressives was the rehabilitation of motherhood in feminist circles.

During the early period it was the right to control fertility and to reject 'compulsory' motherhood that were central issues in feminist struggles . I have already discussed one of the most forceful expressions of this position in Firestone's work, but there were others which emphasised the more practical obstacles that motherhood put in the way of women's liberation, such as the collection of essays in *Pronatalism: The Myth of Mom and Apple Pie* (Peck and Senderowitz, 1974) and *The Mystique of Motherhood* (Heron 1981). Certainly issues of mothering are largely absent in the feminist anthologies of the period, an omission which black feminists felt acutely. Apart from the political priorities of the WLM, there was another reason for this of which Snitow (1992) reminds us – most of the activists were young.

The late 1970s, by contrast, witnessed a flush of feminist publications exploring motherhood. These tend to fall into three categories: those which revisit the relationship between feminist daughters and their mothers, begun by the best-seller, *My Mother/Myself* (Friday, 1977); those which try to explain *why* women are hooked on becoming mothers, despite its repercussions for women's other talents and ambitions, and argue that only by integrating men into the mothering experience will the mould be broken (Dinnerstein, 1976; Chodorow, 1978; Ruddick, 1980; Oakley, 1980; Riley, 1983); and those which argue that mothering can be detached from the patriarchal form, motherhood, and become the basis for the creation of a female culture (Rich, 1976).

The latter approach developed into 'cultural feminism', or what Farganis (1994) describes as 'female essentialism', associated with Mary Daly (1979, 1984) and Carol Gilligan (1982) in the USA and with Dale Spender (1980, 1982) in Britain. This faction rejects equality feminism and insists on an elemental difference between the sexes. Motherhood is valorised as the source of specifically female virtues and values. Women, it is claimed, have been prevented from encoding their different experience of the world by men's lust for power which has deformed language and dominated nature. Women live imprisoned in a male linguistic universe, the only escape from which is to embrace a separate culture in which language can be strippe its phallocentrism enabling women to penetrate older meanin ancestral matriarchy and reach nature's regenerative powers. One outcome of this perspective was the feminisation of language which the media had a field-day trivialising. However, while becoming a major school of thought in academic feminism, cultural feminism on the whole did not play a major part in the politics of the family largely because of the esoteric nature of much of its output.

Much of this rethinking about motherhood took place in the relative seclusion of the universities, and certainly led to an intellectual flowering of feminist theory. But it also suffered from its relative detachment from the socio-economic realities in which mothering was experienced by the majority of women, in which co-parenting was seldom possible given employers' expectations of male workers or potentially problematic in the context of high levels of divorce, and in which most lone motherhood was either involuntary or a negative choice involving considerable reluctance and pain. While there are good grounds for recognising theorising as a distinct activity independent of political outcomes, unless the ideas are made accessible they do not seem particularly relevant to activists, in this case on the road defending the hard-earned employment and reproductive rights from the onslaughts of the pro-family and in particular the anti-abortion movement.

Some of the ambiguities within the feminist movement around motherhood were to come to a head later in the USA over the case of Baby M in 1987. The new reproductive technology which Firestone had thought would liberate women from the birthing process, was used to enable an infertile professional couple to contract with a working-class mother to carry for them a foetus fertilised by the husband's sperm for a fee. When the biological mother refused to hand over the baby, the case became a celebrated law suit in which the legal, philosophical and moral issues which the case raised became the topic of national debate. The specific ambiguity for feminists was whether the principle that women should have complete autonomy over their own bodies on which their stance on abortion was based, should override the principle that women's destiny should not be determined by their biology on which was based the long struggle to separate childbearing from child-rearing and the demand for equal opportunities outside the home.

Feminists who supported the rights of the birth mother found themselves treading in the quagmire of maternal instincts in the uncomfortable company of social conservatives and religious traditionalists, opposing many of their natural allies among single forty-plus professional women, lesbians and gays who hoped for a ruling that would not reinforce traditional conceptions of parenting. In the event the judge ruled in favour of the contracting couple, but on the grounds of the 'welfare of the child', a decision that looked suspiciously more determined by the socio-economic advantages that the couple could provide, than by the relative merits of each woman's case.

These issues revealed a much more diverse range of attitudes and positions about the family than the apparent polarisation of the politics of the family suggested.

British feminists reconsider the family

As far as the family was concerned, feminist journals in Britain over the decade ignored it as a general issue for much the same reasons of political delicacy as in the United States. The prevailing orthodoxy remained that the family was inherently oppressive to women and inimical to their interests.

Where rethinking took place it was on the margins of both feminist and socialist circles in largely theoretical journals like *m/f*, *Ideology and Consciousness* and *Politics and Power*, marked by a common concern to overcome the intellectual and political problems produced by essentialist and reductionist meta-theories. Developments in psychoanalysis, semiotics and philosophy emanating from Europe in the work of Lacan, Barthes and Foucault seemed to offer ways of breaking with this form of theorising in what came to be known as 'discourse analysis', the predominant methodology of postmodern theory. For the purposes of the present discussion, the important feature of this approach is its ability to see social phenomena as the often unintended and contradictory products of the interplay of different discourses operating at different levels, which are retained in their forms and operations. Of course it is understood that not all discourses have the same relation to power and that struggles take place for the ability to define. However, it is argued that success is never total. The representations produced are never wholly reducible to the conditions that produced them nor immune to further transformations.

In relation to the family, one text from this intellectual current, Donzelot's *The Policing of Families* (1980) was very influential. The book applies the insights of Foucault's *The History of Sexuality* (1976;1979) to a historical account of the modern family. Its importance lies not so much in the significance of any empirical findings as in the new way of thinking about the relation between the family and other social institutions and about the relations between family members. His analysis reveals the inadequacy of understanding the modern family as a mere transmitter for the implementation of certain functional necessities deriving from the economy or the Oedipal Complex or male dominance, and suggests that a more fruitful approach is to regard it as the site and target of a whole range of independent policy interventions each of which constitutes its effects (and thereby the family itself) in different ways (Hodges and Hussain, 1979; Hirst, 1981; Adams, 1982).

This is not the place to provide a full account of Donzelot's argument though it is well worth the reader's time and has informed the historical account provided in Chapter 1 of this book. It certainly exercised a number of well-known feminist academics. On the one hand they welcomed Donzelot's insistence on substituting the term 'families' for 'the family', his recognition of familial class differences and his disaggregation of the family unit consequent on the differential significance of its members for the strategies of different intervening agencies. They also admitted that his approach has the potential for making visible the power relations internal to families largely ignored by both conventional social science and Marxism. However, most could not accept his view that the various reform movements concerned with the preservation of children in the nineteenth and twentieth centuries resulted in the formal diminishing of the patriarchal powers of the father and the enhancement of the status and gradually the power of women. In as much as Donzelot neglects the fact that in the respect of the role of provider, men's status was not diminished but increased, they have a point, but this merely reinforces Donzelot's point that there was no unitary agent co-ordinating the activities of the various reforming agencies and their consequences could be unintended and contradictory. However, his critics were not convinced. Because Donzelot fails to represent familial relations as the effects of a prior oppression of females by males, they claimed the book did little more than 'take over the insights of feminist analyses of the family while stripping them of their feminist significance' (Sevenhuijsen and Withuis, 1984, p. 86) and so ends up presenting history from the male standpoint (Bennett, Campbell and Coward, 1981).

This feminist impasse on the family informs even those feminists who embraced the Foucauldian project. For example, Ros Coward's *Patriarchal Precedents* (1983) sets out to demonstrate that there has been a conflation in western social science and public discourses of quite separate aspects of the domain of the sexual – sex, sexuality, sexual identity, sexual divisions and sexual relations – such that anatomical difference has become synonymous with differences in identity, activity and location in a system of power relations. In the process, one instance – the reproductive sex act – became privileged and defined as the determinant of all others. This became inscribed in one of the central dichotomies in western philosophical thought – that constructed between 'nature' and 'culture'. The reproductive act was theorised as that most elemental, that is, most natural aspect of human beings upon which culture worked, such that it became organised into systems of relationships between individuals, systems of property relations and systems of political authority and subordination. It was in this sense that the basic biological reproductive unit became converted into the basic social unit – the family.

The body of Coward's text is a masterly investigation of how this was accomplished theoretically by the speculative histories of the origin and social development of the human race which abounded in the social sciences in the nineteenth century and how these were paradoxically reinforced by critical discourses in anthropology, sociology and Marxism which rejected the ahistoricism, ethnocentrism and reductionism of such accounts, but whose own accounts of the social organisation of sexuality assumed or inadvertently reintroduced their basic preconception of natural heterosexuality and reproduction as their starting point.

By contrast, Coward, following Foucault, rejects the notion of an essential human sexuality and demonstates how it is the play of diverse discourses that defines sexuality in specific historical and institutional contexts, in the case of the nuclear family, via the restructuring of the population by medical, educational, legal, moral interventions intended to improve the state of the nation and its human stock. Central to her account is that such a history is constructed in contradiction. In this Coward should be regarded as a major theorist of what Farganis (1994) has identified as the phase of feminism characterised by 'gender diversity and the politics of postmodernism' (p. 11).

This makes particularly puzzling her review of Donzelot (Bennett, Campbell and Coward, 1981) in that it was precisely his insistence that the policies and practices that gave birth to the modern privatised family had contradictory effects on its members that she and her co-writers rejected and her conclusion in *Patriarchal Precedents* that 'this unit works to the *absolute* disadvantage of women' (p. 285).

It is difficult to understand this continuing adherence to a view of the family as a homogeneous entity unified by its objective of the domination of women, in the face of evidence of widespread diversity of familial forms produced by various ideologies and material practices. It might be more fruitful to abandon the theory of the family as being absolutely, directly, inherently and consistently oppressive to women in favour of an analysis that identifies which aspects, which characteristics, which types of relationships, which practices and which values oppress women, which are neutral and which advantage them. This is still likely to produce disagreement between women but it would enable productive discussion to take place between a more diverse constituency, on a much wider platform of issues, and would provide the opportunity to inscribe in feminist politics the interests of those women who believe in the goal of sexual equality but choose to invest their own primary emotional commitment in their family life.

Carol Smart similarly draws back from the full implications of Foucault and discourse analysis. In *Ties That Bind* (1984) Smart criticises both Marxist and feminist conceptions of law for their con-spiratorial character. She asserts that law is not simply a superstruc-tural reflection of the economic base, but is better regarded as 'a collection of practices and discourses which do not all operate together with one purpose'; they 'cannot simply be read off from the stage of capitalist development'. She also abandons the idea that the law simply represents and serves the interests of men; indeed she even questions whether an unambiguous set of male interests can be readily identified. Smart claims to reject 'general theories of law and patri-archy in favour of less deterministic accounts of specific legislative changes in relation to family structures and dominant sexual practices' (p. 22).

Smart's substantive analysis of changes in family law in the post-war period does indeed go some way to exposing the complexities of the formulation and implementation of legislation and the ideological conditions in which it operates. In particular Smart recognises the political struggle that is involved in determining the form and sub-stance of family law. However, this goes only so far. In her accounts men and women continue to be unproblematised categories and enter stage as extra-discursive entities, the interests of which are treated as pre-given unities. As a result she finds an assumed oppression of women by men outside law, reflected and reproduced in law: 'the law can, therefore, be understood as a mode of reproduction of the existing patriarchal order, minimising social change but avoiding the problems of overt conflict' (pp. 21–2).

The overall impression is that the new patterns of family relations are no less oppressive to women than the old. The appearance of greater liberalism in personal life merely hides the continuation of state regulation of women's sexuality through the agency of marriage and the family. The liberalisation of divorce is merely an accommodation to the new demographic and economic conditions: the state recognises the crisis in marriage and so contains the disaffection by facilitating the legitimate change of partners, thus retaining the institution itself, and intensifying the state's capacity for surveillance. This view results in a number of dilemmas. For example, while wishing to redress the unequal treatment of cohabiting women in law, Smart is unhappy about extending to them the rights of the marriage contract because it would make heterosexual coupledom more attractive that other forms of intimate relationships. Similarly, the aim of ending the economic dependence of women on men leads her to prefer that the maintenance of children is passed to the community at large through taxes and National Insurance payments, removing all responsibility from the biological father. Interestingly however, this logic is not pursued when it comes to custody. Smart does not question the general practice of awarding custody to the mother, despite the fact that she makes much of the way in which it is informed by and reinforces the ideology of motherhood and traditional gender roles. There is no doubt that despite the commitment to greater theoretical and methodological sophistication, there is little revision of substance or language in her conclusion that 'the family is the primary site of women's oppression' (p. 145).

There is less ambivalence about defending the orthodoxy of the 1960s in Barrett and McIntosh's *The Anti-Social Family* (1982):

> Marriage is an oppressive institution for both the married and the unmarried, and provides the major legal support for the current family form . . . it endows the relationship with respectability and social privilege and thereby devalues all other relationships. It is the end of women's economic independence. (p. 143)

They recognise the popularity of family life and do not dismiss it as a delusion or an expression of false consciousness: 'we see investment in the family as an easily comprehended, indeed highly rational, choice'

(p. 21) . . . 'we see the opportunity for warmth and interdependency as a major factor in the appeal of marriage and family life' (p. 23). And indeed they endorse the fact that for many people the family does satisfy emotional, psychological and everyday material needs. However, they argue that such needs could be met by other social forms were these not systematically prevented by the dominance of familial ideology embedded in legal, welfare and cultural forms. It is in this sense that the family is profoundly anti-social.

The social forms which the family denies and deprives are the socialist ideals of collective forms of domestic activity and provision – communal dining halls, laundries, nurseries – and the communal forms of social intercourse – social centres, the 'revitalisation of public life', collective households. The privatised family is identified with individualism as an ethic, with a selfish concern for one's own, and with a rabid consumerism which oils the wheels of capitalist production. It is clearly the enemy of socialist collectivist ideals and forms of social organisation. It is also the enemy of feminism because it inscribes the gender relations of dominance and subordination. In an inversion of Zaretsky's and Lasch's position, Barrett and McIntosh argue that rather than the family providing warmth and comfort against a harsh external environment, it is the family that, by monopolising intimacy and security, has denuded other social relations of their humanity and left them cold, instrumental and mercenary.

The problem is that this position is simply the opposite side of the coin to the conservative view. Both reinforce the ideological distinction between the public and the private and ignore the complex ways in which needs are constructed and met in myriad forms, cutting across this artificial divide in what might be called a 'mixed economy' of need satisfaction. Families recognise through their material practices, even if it is not often articulated intellectually, that many of the needs of their members cannot be satisfied entirely within the family context.

There is a wealth of charitable, voluntary and self-help organisations of a neighbourhood, youth, ethnic, community, sporting, cultural, social, educational, spiritual, political nature which testify to the value that people of all ages, classes, races, sexual orientation and abilities place on communal and public life and the vitality of a realm intermediate between those of work, the family and the state. In Donzelotian terms, it is a sphere created out of the intersection of familial desires, individual aspirations, the broad population welfare objectives of the liberal state and the investment drive of private and public capital.

It is of course true that there are groups in society whose social marginalisation impedes access to these social satisfactions but their isolation is much more a function of their poverty and lack of financial and material independence than it is their status *vis-à-vis* the family. It is only by hypostatising the family in the so-called traditional form of breadwinning husband, housewife mother and dependent children insulated from the external world, that both conservative and socialist utopian visions can maintain the fiction that human needs are neatly divided into private and public, with the satisfaction of the former contained by familial provision. Their differences lie only in the issue of the effectivity and desirability of this state of affairs.

There is much less certainty among writers in Segal's interesting edited collection, *What Is To Be Done About The Family?* (1983) which provides autobiographical reminiscences and evaluations of the cultural, political and personal context in which radicals of the 1960s and 70s attempted to find alternatives to the family.

Mica Nava for example, while emphasising that the politicisation of the personal was a necessary and progressive step in the advancement of women, believes that:

> its effects were at the same time very contradictory. Both the confessional mode of consciousness-raising and the elevation of domestic life into an object available for scrutiny and assessment (in which good conduct could be awarded the metaphorical badge of 'good feminist') were also profoundly moralistic and ultimately inhibiting. They emerged as a transmuted form of regulation. (Nava, 1983, p. 81)

She expresses considerable discomfort with early feminist critiques of the family. In particular she believes that there was a gross underestimation of the psychic complexity of sexual and parenting relations, and the revolutionary and uncompromising character of feminist politics contributed to its failure to engage fully with family policy formulations and to have a greater influence among women generally.

In the same volume Denise Riley (1983) raises similar points in the context of questions about mothers and children. For example, she claims that where feminism had engaged with the problem of mothers it was largely in the context of the negative effects that motherhood has for women. She also warns that the interests of women and those of children cannot be assumed to exist 'in some automatic harmony' separated from the problems of the family or men. Reflecting on a growing uncertainty about feminist and socialist articles of faith, Riley wonders 'if there are general and distinct socialist and feminist object-ives in the care of children, or a quintessentially feminist set of demands to be made' (p. 141).

This volume clearly registers a different tone in feminist discussions about the family. There is less confidence in the old certainties, more willingness to consider that there might be aspects of family life which are not entirely oppressive of women and a greater toleration of those who continue who commit themselves to it. The feminist editor signals the change: 'we want neither to prescribe nor prevent tradi-tional family arrangements, but to increase the possibility for choice and equality in our domestic lives' (Segal, 1983, p. 229).

Nevertheless, this re-thinking about the value of family life remained a relatively subdued affair in private discussion and limited academic circles. The accommodation of British feminism to the persistent popularity of marriage and variants of the 'traditional' family among women happened quietly and discreetly, where it did, as part of its more general accommodation to mainstream politics.

Another feminist prophet recants

The exception to this British compromise was Germaine Greer, who with the usual attendant international media attention published *Sex and Destiny* (1984), a vigorous critique of Western population policies in the Thirld World. As always it was a highly idiosyncratic intervention.

The nuclear family comes in for the same critique as in *The Female Eunuch*, but it is no longer opposed by a unisex utopia of free heterosexual exchange and children cared for in common. Indeed, she now distances herself from the sexual and social anarchy of the 1960s and contrasts it with the emotionally rich, sexually responsible and constrained family of traditional societies. Now it is the clarity of role, position, rules of privilege, obligation and duty toward all kin associated with the extended family of the Third World that is acclaimed.

Greer argues that the penetration of western capitalism and the promotion of the western family form and family planning policies are destroying traditional family systems which had their own mechan-isms of limiting population size to what their economies could sustain.

The result is economic underdevelopment and widespread poverty and social dysfunction. Her focus for concern is that in the process the community of women which, in patriarchal familial structures, provides for the mutual support and protection of women, is undermined:

> The Family offers the paradigm for the female collectivity: it shows us women co-operating to dignify their lives, to lighten each other's labour, and growing in real love and sisterhood, a word we use constantly without any idea of what it is. (p. 241)

Greer recognises the paradox for 'a twentieth-century feminist to be among the few champions of the Family...for most Families are headed by men and men play the decisive roles in them' (ibid). However, in her view the culture of sisterhood more than compensates for women's lack of power or exclusion from the public sphere. It also appears to compensate for arranged marriages, forced separation on marriage from blood kin and subjection to the rule of mother-in-law, complete obedience to husbands, polygamy, female infanticide, clitoridectomy, enforced chastity and a whole range of other practices from which Greer does not flinch from accepting as part of the bargain. Indeed it is implicit in her discussion that such practices have a positive function in separating women from men socially and emotionally, and uniting them in a common female experience.

It is extremely difficult to see what *Sex and Destiny* offers feminists in their attempt to address the problems facing women in contemporary society: rather there is a nostalgic flight from them.

British feminism enters mainstream politics

In Britain, no such equivalent organisation as Friends of the Family emerged. As we have already seen, the battle over the family was never quite as intense or explosive as in America. This was partly because religion in Britain does not play the same part in national cultural life, but also because British feminism was so closely imbued with socialist ideology and ethics that it had eschewed mainstream politics and tended to be marginalised with other 'extreme left' groups. It thus never achieved the political influence of, nor was it taken as seriously as its American counterpart. It may well be that the very success of American feminism made negative reaction more likely when the political climate changed rightwards. One might speculate that in

Britain it was the trade union movement that took the brunt of the conservative backlash, precisely because it was conceived as a serious political force.

Indeed, it was the assault on the institutions of the Left by the Thatcher government from 1980 that galvanised feminists to abandon the movement's purist rejection of reformist politics, and consider joining other political organisations in an anti-Thatcherist coalition. The leftwards shift of the Labour Party between 1979 and 1983 facilitated feminist accommodation (Rowbotham, Segal and Wainwright, 1979; Wilson, 1980a; Coultas, 1981; *Feminist Review*, Editorial, 1982). (For a review of this strategy a decade later, see Harriss, 1989.) It also offered the added value of the wider dissemination of feminist ideas: 'Thousands of working women vote Labour but have never been actively mobilised by the Labour Party. An alliance between the women's movement and the Labour Party could broaden the popular appeal of feminism' (Coultas, 1981, p. 42).

Feminists entered mainstream politics in substantial numbers particularly at the municipal level and especially into the Labour Party and trade unionism. Considerably younger and more educated than traditional women members, they faced much suspicion at first, but conciliation was facilitated by the need to defend against the common enemy of the New Right. This was all very timely since, as has already been pointed out, it was in the early 1980s that American psephologists began noting that divergences were developing in the traditional 'gender gap' in relation to policy preferences and voting behaviour. The same voting trends among women were observed in Britain making the parties much more sensitive to women's issues and to the voices of women within their membership (Hills, 1981; Dunleavy and Husbands, 1985; Campbell, 1987; Coote and Pattullo, 1990; Lovenduski and Norris, 1996).

Women's Committees in local authorities pressured for equal opportunities policies in employment, women-focused public services, the public funding of community groups many of which were run by women, and for practical policy responses to address violence against women. Such policies in themselves increased women's participation in local politics. Ethnic minority women were particularly targeted both for council employment and as community leaders. The Greater London Council led the way: it funded over 400 women's groups of which 300 belonged to ethnic minorities. In the 1980s, at the height of Thatcherism, two large London borough councils had black women elected as Leaders, the first black women MP was elected to a London seat, and a black woman was appointed as chief executive officer of the Equal Opportunities Commission.

Through the TUC Women's Conference the support of the trade union movement was mobilised to promote women-friendly policies in public sector organisations, in educational institutions and in large private sector companies. Of course they were helped in this respect by the large numbers of women employees on the payrolls of organisations, their increasing importance to the labour force in the light of the impending demographic crisis of the dramatic fall in school-leavers, and the economic sense of capitalising on investment in training and retaining the best staff.

The Equal Opportunities Commission set up by the Labour government in the mid-1970s on the American model became more bullish under the leadership of the black feminist, Valerie Amos. Faced with the Tory government's demolition of previous industrial legislation which protected the low paid and hence many women, it turned to the European Court of Justice which forced the British government to comply with the European legislative and regulatory framework, for example in relation to equal pay for equal value requirements, the extension of invalid care allowance to married women and pro rata terms of employment for part-time workers.

If the 1970s was the period in the USA when women generally became politicised, it was the 1980s in Britain. The radicalism and strident character of Mrs Thatcher's politics cut sharp divisions across the nation. We have already noted those in the morality and family debate. In addition women were at the forefront of the protest against American Cruise missiles being based in Britian which consolidated into the famous Greenham Common Peace Camp and the involvement of many women's organisations not associated with feminism. Again, the most explosive political event of the 1980s, the long and violent miners' strike against mass pit closures, led to protest marches of women, some with as many as 50,000 participants, defending their families and communities. Women in the public services joined industrial action against privatisation, contracting out of services, and the closure of hospitals, schools and daycare centres. Women were also involved in action against the most controversial of Thatcher's policies, the Community Charge or 'poll tax'.

The increase in participation of women with a feminist agenda in mainstream British politics, coupled with the sterling work of a number of feminists in senior positions of independent research and policy insitutes, major NGOs and national pressure groups, accomplished a substantial and well overdue reorientation in relation to public language, representation and policy formulation. By the end of the decade the feminist influence in and the growing importance of the female voter for the Labour Party under its sympathetic leader, Neil Kinnock, the first major political leader with a card-carrying feminist wife, was clearly in evidence. In its 1990 policy statement, *Looking To The Future* (Labour Party, 1990), with its glossy magazine-style photograph of a woman and a young girl on its front cover, family issues are integrated into the whole policy review signalled through the topics which research had indicated as high priorities for women voters: child benefit, childcare, parental and family leave, education and training, sex discrimination, equal pay, lone mothers, abortion and assistance for informal carers. It also committed Labour to a Ministry for Women, with a Cabinet place for its Minister. This strategy allowed Labour to avoid the associations of 'the family party' label, which would give it problems with its feminist activists, while clearly appealing to the interest which many of the female electorate have in policies which will improve their family lives.

At the same time, the Party recognised the importance of the frustration of women with the obstacles for their progress within the Party itself. The Labour Women's Action Committee set up in the early 1980s to pressure for changes in the party's rules such to increase women's representation on parliamentary candidate selection short-lists, and on all policy-making bodies in the party, finally made some headway. It was not until the early 1990s that all these changes were finally made. Indeed they were taken further by the introduction in 1992 of the American-style 'Emily's List' organisation to encourage, select, train, groom and promote women for parliamentary election. In 1993 they managed to persuade the annual conference to introduce a compulsory quota by means of all-women shortlists in half the party's winnable seats. Though this measure had to be withdrawn after a successful legal challenge by two male aspiring candidates, ironically under the Sex Discrimination Act, it is regarded as the single most significant factor in changing the gender balance of Labour candidates as the party approached the 1997 General Election. Many of the 101 women Labour MPs who marched triumphantly into the House of Commons after Tony Blair's landslide victory both cut their political teeth in local politics in the 1980s, and benefited from the rule changes that feminists had worked for during that decade (Perrigo, 1996; Lovenduski, 1997).

I have argued that the policies of the New Right period were not in themselves primarily anti-feminist. However, there is no doubt that the combination of the indirect effects of industrial policies to create freer markets in labour, and the drastic slimming down of whole areas of health, welfare and community provision to cut public expenditure, brought politics into many women's work and family lives. It acted as a catalyst for greater collaboration between women of different social backgrounds, racial and ethnic identities and cultural values on specific campaigns. However, it would be misleading to claim that they all made their protest in the name of feminism.

It is not unreasonable to regard this period of feminist engagement with the pragmatics of mainstream politics and local community activism, as providing the direct experience of working with women whose priorities, values and understanding of their lives, particularly about sexuality and the family, was not only very different from their own but also carried a disturbing conviction and integrity not easily dismissed by feminist theory. This may account for an increasing distance between the feminism of academic debate and the debates of feminists engaged in politics and policy development.

8

New Struggles for the Soul of Feminism

The change of attitude towards the family by major feminist figures in the 1980s shocked, confused and angered many in the feminist movement. Initial reaction varied from total to partial repudiation. It was one thing to be confronted with a backlash against feminism amongst the morally and politically conservative; it was another to be faced with recidivism among the ranks. The revisionists were written off variously as 'neo-conservative feminists', 'conservative feminists', 'anti-feminist feminists', 'post-feminists'. These derogatory labels were countered both by denial and more recently by positive self-identified labels such as 'power feminism', 'the new feminism' and 'third-wave feminism'.

Rejection and reassertion

For Eisenstein (1984) liberal feminists simply fail to realise that the rise of the New Right is a reaction to the 'crisis of liberal America' of which they are part. The freedom of choice and equality of opportunity principles built into the liberal paradigm have crashed against the demands of the capitalism. Given the essential role of the family in sustaining capitalism economies, capitalist patriarchy cannot allow the principles of sexual equality to be realised. Further they fail to understand that this situation cannot be resolved by their individualistic strategy but only by a collective solution which destroys the very existence of capitalist patriarchy. Their back-tracking on the family is 'a reaction against feminism itself and its radical potential to transform society' (1984, p. 200). She denigrates such writers as '*neo-conservative feminists*'.

Others designated them part of a patriarchal backlash. Two best-sellers in the early 1990s, *The War Against Women* (1992) by Marilyn French, the author of the highly successful novel *The Women's Room*, and *Backlash: The Undeclared War Against Women* (1992) by Pulitzer Prize winning journalist, Susan Faludi, both claimed a worldwide misogynistic reaction to the improvement of women's lot.

French charts this unmitigated war against women through mysogynistic religious systems, work practices, law, medicine, language and culture, male violence and abuse. She claims that much of this women-hating is cloaked in euphemisms. The one most used is 'protection of the family'; in fact the family is simply a way of inhibiting women's economic independence, controlling their sexuality and fertility and intimidating them into submission by actual or fear of violence.

Faludi argues that New Right regimes in the USA and the UK used the family as a 'fruitful marketing tool' because it could 'draw more sympathy from the press and more followers from the public if they marched under the banner of traditional family values'. Such slogans actually served to conceal male anger at women's rising independence. 'Under the banner of "family rights" these spokesmen lobbied only for every man's rights to rule supreme at home' (p. 270). Faludi includes in the backlash not only political and moral conservative ideologues and organisations and the men's movement, but also feminists as varied as Paglia, Hewlett, Friedan, Greer and Gilligan who had engaged in rethinking gender issues and the family. In her view they and other revisionists among the centre-left intelligentsia are the respectable emissaries of the backlash, effectively legitimating the anti-feminism of the New Right, and hence she labels them *'feminist anti-feminists'*. Faludi seems unable to consider that there might be some substance, some genuine cause for concern about the family among the revisionists. She is conscious that their diversity forbids political, intellectual or social generalisations about their motivations so she concludes that it must be 'private yearnings and animosities and vanities that they barely recognised or understood themselves ... from professional grievances to domestic role strains' (pp. 31–2).

Faludi's book came in for considerable criticism in Britain for underestimating the many positive improvements in women's position that had been achieved even in the Reagan/Thatcher decade, and the ability of diverse women's organisations in alliance with men in political parties, the trade union movement and single issue organisations to defend the gains women had made in legal, civil, employment and reproductive rights.

Interviewed for *Socialist Review* (May 1992) Faludi denied claims that she treated women as passive victims of the backlash or that she indulged in conspiracy theory. It is true that in *Backlash* she does explicitly state in the Introduction that the backlash is not a conspiracy and in the Epilogue that women never really surrendered. However, the overall impression of the total 498 pages of *Backlash* is of an almost unmitigated rout of feminist forces by the organised forces of reaction. Part of the reason for this impression is that the standard against which she measures women's position is that of absolute equality with men, rather than where women came from, how far they got by the 1980s and an analysis of what they lost, what they managed to retain and what they won in that decade. Partly it is because Faludi chose to repudiate the ludicrous claim that men were now the disadvantaged group, promulgated by right-wing politicos and controversy-hungry journalists, by deluging the reader in page after page in the continuing miseries of women's inequality. Partly it is because the pages are packed with facts and insider stories selected to demonstrate the overwhelming hegemony of reactionary anti-feminism in high places. *Backlash* is a supremely depressing read for a feminist unless you are a complete masochist.

Further doubts and ambivalence

However, parallel to this defensive reaction, a serious, reflective and mature review of the virtues, limitations and failings of feminism of the 1960s and 70s was emerging among academics and activists, including many of the founders of the movement in America and Britain.

While Stacey (1983) labels the revisionism, '*the new conservative feminism*' and believes it represents 'a great leap backwards for feminists and other progressives' (pp. 560–1), she nevertheless admits that it does raise serious issues for feminism. One is the problem of alternatives to the family which can meet women's needs for nurturance, affection and security. Another is the tension between the androgynous objectives of feminism and the recognition of sexual difference which provides the basis of a feminist politics. Others include the failure of the movement to develop an evaluation of heterosexuality which does not denigrate it as ideologically unsound, and to face the conceptual and political difficulties of the theory of 'false consciousness' in accounting for that female subjectivity which remains indifferent to feminism. Above all, however, it is the failure of post-war feminism to seriously address women's desire for maternity and the needs of children.

This inadequacy was all the more exposed by the theoretical rehabilitation of motherhood by cultural feminist theory on the one hand and the wave of maternities among seasoned feminists on the other. It leads Rosenfelt and Stacey (1987) to admit that:

> part of feminism's overreaction to the fifties was an anti-natalist, antimaternalist moment... The reaction to the fifties' cloying cult of motherhood freed millions of women like us to consider motherhood as a choice rather than an unavoidable obligation, but it may also have encouraged many to deny, or defer dangerously long, our own desires for domesticity and maternity. One of the ironic effects of this history is the current obsession with maternity and children that seems to pervade ageing feminist circles... More serious, our assault on conventional domesticity helped to set up feminism to take the major blame for the disastrous effects on women of the rising rates of divorce and female employment that were well under way before the women's movement... Hewlett is correct that few of us have made the needs of working mothers a central focus of our theory or politics. (pp. 351–2)

The baby boom of the 1980s was not limited to 'just-in-time' feminists, but extended to a whole generation of successful Baby Boomers, that is professional women born between 1946 and 1964. The trend hit the headlines when a number of American and British media stars, such as Mia Farrow, Ursula Andress, Farrah Fawcett, Felicity Kendall, decided to beat the biological clock in their early 40s. Hollywood cashed in on the interest among the well-off 'Thirtysomethings' with the hugely successful *Baby Boom* starring Diane Keaton, followed by another four or so similar major films and a number of television series. In fact the trend had already been identified by business forecasting consultants wh(͡ responsible for the change in advertising of upmarket comr ͡ the 1980s to the softer 'caring' mood with poten/ expectant businesswomen and New Men: 'Cari babies are the new marketing tool' (*Sund* November 1989). While one must avoid e; the relationship between the marketing indus/ behaviour, it does use social science n significant social changes in its market / these back in its advertising to the attit/

with them. In doing so it may act as a catalyst in accelerating these further.

The other side of these happy late maternities were the number of feminists who found that their biology had not waited for their change of heart. Snitow (1992), for example, is alert to the irony that her work on the history of feminism and motherhood and her critique of pro-natalism, was undertaken while she was undergoing treatment for infertility. In Stacey's view (1986), infertility is also the social psychological source of Greer's rediscovery of the traditional family.

Stacey believes that 'the pain and difficulties experienced by a generation of feminists who self-consciously attempted to construct alternatives to the family are a major source of the emergence of pro-family feminism' (p. 231). The unsustainability of these alternatives was a bitter disappointment and resulted in three common sorts of personal traumas: 'involuntary singlehood' in which both heterosexual and lesbian women long for the intimacy of long-term committed relationships; 'involuntary childlessness' in which those who delayed motherhood experienced infertility, gynaecological and obstetric problems; unsupported single parenthood often as a consequence of the failures of collective households.

The doubts and contradictions which afflicted the movement in the 1980s are reflected in the perplexity of the title of *What Is Feminism?* (1986). This text, edited by two well-known British feminists, Mitchell and Oakley, but including contributions from feminists on both sides of the Atlantic, is a sequel to *The Rights and Wrongs of Women* (1976) published ten years earlier, and is strikingly different in substance and tone. The first volume was full of confidence in its project to provide the heritage for the political unity of women through constructing a conceptual and material history of women making them visible and giving them a voice denied by traditional historiography. The second volume, by contrast, is in search of feminism itself.

Several of the articles in *What Is Feminism?* admit the weaknesses of earlier conceptions. Cott and Delmar argue that feminist historiography demonstrates that the fragmentation of the women's movement, feminist theory and the meaning of feminism currently experienced is nothing new. Cott contends that the earlier feminist movement demonstrated not a feminist unity but strategic coalitions of women the pursuit of common instrumental goals. Delmar points out the of a slippage among feminists to mistake the 'women' of iscourse, that is as 'its subjects, its enunciators, the creators its practice and of its language' for women of the extra-discursive field. Hence feminists fall into the trap of believing that they speak for all women and are shocked when some of them refuse to speak the script. Gordon's paper on child neglect and child abuse demonstrates the unsustainability of the assumption of the coincidence between women and children's interests that lay at the heart of the rehabilitation of motherhood. She believes that 'the victimisation paradigm, . . . the pressure to describe and analyse the structures and methods of male domination, must be transcended' and that feminists should now look more closely at women's negotiations with, participation in, accommodation to and struggles against the manifestations of male domination' (p. 68). The book's sombre note of realism and resignation ends with the editors' rather timid hope that 'through a creative use of anxiety we can start to look forward again' (p. 7).

'Post-feminism'

Despite Faludi's claim that the anti-feminist backlash managed to 'infiltrate the thoughts of women', opinion surveys throughout the period show a consistently high support for the goals of gender equality and for the implementation of public policy to achieve these across social classes. The much-quoted 1989 Time/CNN Yankelovich poll in the USA, for example, found that 77 per cent of women surveyed thought that the women's movement had made life better; 94 per cent thought it had helped women become more independent; 82 per cent thought it was still improving women's lives (*Time*, 4 December 1989). In Britain, a major ICM poll in 1991 (*The Guardian*, 9 January 1992) showed that 57 per cent of women supported feminist goals. Similar findings were reported by a *Guardian* Women Survey (7 March 1991) and by a series of attitudinal studies throughout the 1990s commissioned by the influential British independent think-tank, Demos (Wilkinson, 1994; Siann and Wilkinson, 1995). In each case support for feminist goals increased with the youth of the respondents across all social classes. The other surprise was that support for feminist goals differed little between female Conservative and Labour voters.

However, these surveys and qualitative studies also show that a surprisingly low percentage of women were willing to identify themselves as feminists and that this was also true for the younger age groups. In the Time/CNN Yankelovich poll only 33 per cent of women called themselves feminists and this had actually decreased by about 20 per cent from the mid-1980s. An NOP survey among British women in 1988 found that only 9 per cent of women between the ages of 18 and 34 would consistently describe themselves as feminist, and 25 per cent found feminism 'alienating' (cited in Siann and Wilkinson, 1995).

Reasons given by women in these and other studies (Roberts, 1992; Wolf, 1993; Figes, 1994; Staggenborg, 1998) were that feminism was too extreme, that it was man-hating, separatist and rejected many of the 'feminine' things that women enjoy, and that it was anti-family. Wilkinson (1994) makes the interesting point that the common negative association of feminism with lesbianism may be less a literal association than a metaphor for the perception that many feminist attitudes are alien to many women's sense of female identity. This is tied up with their sexuality, from apparently superficial expressions in terms of dress codes and social etiquette to deeply internalised desires and values with regard to intimate and domestic relations with men. While caution must be taken in drawing conclusions from social attitude surveys undertaken with different populations at different times and using different questions, it is difficult not to recognise a general pattern and a general trend here. The above research indicates a gap between the strong commitment of younger women to sexual equality and their negative perception of feminism and feminists.

Possibly the earliest commentary on the phenomenon of female dissociation from feminism was an article by Susan Bolotin in *The New York Times Magazine* (17 October 1982), which became famous because its title, 'Voices from a Post-Feminist Generation', coined the term *post-feminism*, and triggered off yet another controversy within the movement. As an activist of the 1960s and 70s Bolotin was shocked to find out through her journalistic investigations that among young women, 'feminism' had become a dirty word. She began to consider whether second-wave feminists themselves may carry some responsibility for their disaffection: maybe 'we .... had been boring with our stories of how bad it was. Instead of conveying our enthusiasms, perhaps we had sunk into the trap of setting ourselves apart as gurus of liberation' (p. 31).

The counter-attack

Feminist 'revisionists' retaliated by blaming '*victim feminism*'. Its most vehement and public champion was Camille Paglia (1990, 1992). An

American cultural scholar, Paglia was to become notorious for her iconoclastic performances in text and in person. For her, the credibility gap is a result of feminists becoming an uncritical self-perpetuating elite, out of touch with what women want and how they want to see themselves portrayed. Consequently they have failed to appreciate the new self-confidence and freedoms that young women enjoy. Women do not want to be represented as victims of male oppression, nor do they want to be told what to think, how to dress, who to have sex with, what to value and what experiences to enjoy. Paglia believes feminism has become both puritanical and totalitarian.

Paglia feels herself to be innately a child of the rebellious 1960s and celebrates the fact that feminism broke the suffocating infantilisation and overprotection of girls. It gave them the freedom to experiment, to dare, to adventure, to exploit their sexual power over men. But with that freedom came risk and potential danger. Paglia's position is that adults must accept and live with the consequences if they choose the life of adventure. On the one hand, Paglia believes that human life needs the spontaneity, creativity and excitement of the wild spirit of nature; on the other, she insists passions must be kept in control by the forces of reason or they become destructive. This is the source of the apparent contradiction between her libertarianism and her belief in the need for the discipline of a strong state, laws, religion, schooling, marriage and the family: 'Conventional marriage, despite its inequities, kept the chaos of libido in check. When the prestige of marriage is low, all the nasty daemonism of sexual instinct pops out' (1992a, p. 14).

It is this position that led her into the 'date rape' controversy. She insists that 'rape is an outrage that cannot be tolerated in a civilised society' (1992, p. 49), but refuses to apply the term to sexual intercourse that occurs as a result of too much alcohol, drugs or heavy petting getting out of hand, even if the woman does not feel that she actively consented to it. She roundly condemns the behaviour in the men but believes that categorising it as rape undermines the seriousness and criminality of cases of 'real rape'. She does not absolve males of their responsibility, but nor does she absolve women. To treat them as victims, or allow them to rationalise their own bad feelings about it by acting the victim, is patronising and infantilising, the equivalent of pleading 'diminished responsibility'. For Paglia, 'victim feminism' is a return to the patriarchal protectionism of the 1950s.

Paglia has rightly picked up some of the contradictions of feminism in that by trying to shock the public out of their complacency into recognising the continuing inequalities and injustices between men and women, it has sensationalised and presented women as archetypically victims, reinforcing a stereotype of passivity and lack of autonomy that undermines legitimate claims for independence for women and against which feminism rebelled in the first place. It is a view of women profoundly out of kilter with the way that young women want to see themselves and women in general. In this, Paglia is more in tune with the rhythms, interests, values, ambitions and fantasies of young women, despite being of the same generation as many of the founders of the feminist movement. It is her refreshingly tough, sensual, playful, erotic vision of female sexuality embodied in Madonna and the Spice Girls that they admire.

She has also astutely pinpointed another major contradiction in feminism that it shares with liberalism: 'it exalts individualism and freedom and, on its radical wing, condemns social order as oppressive. On the other hand, it expects governments to provide materially for all, a feat manageable only by an expansion of authority and a swollen bureaucracy. In other words, liberalism (and hence feminism) defines government as a tyrant father but demands it behaves as nurturant mother' (1992, p. 3).

Paglia antagonised liberal and socialist feminists by her attack on social constructionist accounts of gender differences and her embrace of the doctrine of sexual bipolarity. Her approach, however, was no more attractive to cultural feminists, for while she agrees that women are inherently different from men, closer to nature, her concept of nature has none of the benevolent, nurturant and pacific qualities that they attribute to it. In her cosmology the female is the deadlier of the species. Her outrageousness in style and substance united all the disparate warring strands of feminism in opposition against her, though in doing so she became, like Greer, one of the few academics to achieve the status of a media personality.

Rene Denfeld in *The New Victorians* (1995) also blames feminism itself for failing to engage with young women. Denfeld points out that the younger generation have no direct memory of the restricting conditions of women's lives against which second-wave feminism pitted itself. Its direct experience is of campus feminism in the 1980s and 90s which was dominated by radical feminism. This appears to offer two life-worlds for women, both equally unattractive to young women.

One is characterised by an aggressively anti-male and anti-heterosexual ideology in which women are seen almost entirely as the potential and actual victims of male misogyny and violence. Its policy agenda appears overwhelmingly dominated by anti-pornography and anti-rape legislative proposals on the one hand, and by protective political, social and sexual separatism on the other. Its main proponents are of course Dworkin and MacKinnon. The other life-world is described by Denfeld as a form of New Age spiritualism, a separate women's world characterised by what are claimed as female virtues, ways of thinking, feeling and acting fundamentally different from masculine modes. This female nature is sometimes derived from the (hypothesised) existence of egalitarian, non-violent, vegetarian, nurturing, compassionate matriarchies of prehistory. Even Gloria Steinem, the erstwhile glamorous warrior of 1960s equal rights feminism and Friedan's successor as President of NOW, moved on to prioritise questions of inner health and spirituality for feminism in *Revolution From Within: A Book of Self-Esteem* (1992).

Denfeld is struck by the similarities with nineteenth-century social purity feminists: the same repugnance of sex; the same characterisation of men as inherently lustful, violent and predatory; the same escape into spirituality, 'the angel in the house' on the one hand, and into victimhood, the abused woman, on the other; the same concentration of repressed energy into moral crusades. She claims that nineteenth-century feminism started by being a radical movement committed to political, legal and economic reforms to benefit women, but ended up compromising its potential by pursuing policies that protected women only by reinforcing their difference from and hence their dependence on men. In the process, Denfeld says they lost the support of the younger generation and the movement died. She believes the same thing is happening to twentieth-century feminism, and labels the contemporary activists 'the new Victorians'.

While I agree with Denfeld that there is an unfortunate continuity of the self-righteous moralising associated with the Victorian period in dominant strands of contemporary feminism, I think she is wrong to write off sexual politics as 'a series of moral crusades that have little to do with most women's lives' (1995, p. 216). While one might not agree with the theoretical framework, much of the political action associated with moral issues has had positive repercussions for aspects of life about which women care a great deal, such as rape, domestic violence, sexual harassment and child abuse.

What Denfeld underplays is that the great difference between most feminists of the nineteenth century and radical feminists of the twentieth-century is that the former sought to improve women's conditions *within* the family while the latter seek to create a 'virtual' place of safety *outside* the family. The problem is that the latter goal does not resonate with many contemporary women since they constitute half of the 90 per cent of the population that rate family life as very important in quality of life surveys and declare consistently high levels of satisfaction with their families, well above other aspects of life (Hardyment, 1998). Nor does it seem to be consistent with one of the most attractive principles of the post-war feminist movement – freedom of choice – when heterosexuality and family life (a choice of many women) appears to be disparaged.

Wolf (1993) summarises those features of contemporary feminism which a number of self-identified feminists believe have alienated women: the failure to recognise the shift away from purism in political and social beliefs towards greater pragmatism; the related tendency to prefer a position on the margins, preaching to the converted; a theoretical and policy agenda which had little practical relevance for mainstream women; the reluctance to genuinely engage with views different from the predominant orthodoxy; the withdrawal of feminist debate into the academic press and the university campus with a resultant tendency for linguistic obscurantism impenetrable to outsider women and fertile ground for distortion and caricature by the popular press. As Kaminer (1993) succinctly puts it: 'the feminist movement today may suffer less from a mere image problem than from a major identity crisis' (p. 53).

'Power feminism'

The 1990s witnessed an attempt by a number of feminists to address that crisis by asserting a new positive identity and a new assertive image for women encapsulated in the media soundbite '*power feminism*'.

The young, dynamic and photogenic American, Naomi Wolf, caused a furore with her best-seller, *Fire With Fire* (1993), partly because of the volte-face it accomplishes from her position in her previous best-seller, *The Beauty Myth*, published only two years before at the tender age of 25. In it, Wolf, in the best traditions of 'victim feminism', had exposed the omnipotent role of the fashion and beauty industry in the patriarchal backlash against feminism. In *Fire With Fire*, Wolf asserts that 'victim feminism' disempowers women. Young women today, she says, have benefited from the successes of second wave feminism both materially and in self-confidence. They are doing well at school; the occupational structure has shifted their way; they are beginning to penetrate even the most resistant of male bastions of power, prestige and privilege. All around them are cultural symbols of 'girl power'. They neither see themselves nor wish others to see them as helpless and hapless victims. They are starting to use the system to exert their power. What they need now is 'power feminism', a pluralistic movement that consists of different networks of women which work by creating mutual trust, support and benefit through sharing women's strengths and pleasures. This calls for 'alliances based on economic self-interest and economic giving back rather than on a sentimental and unworkable fantasy of cosmic sisterhood' (p. 58).

A similar view is echoed by a new generation of British feminists. Natasha Walter (1998) asserts:

> Young women today are unlikely to want lectures from feminists about their private lives...However young women dress, however they make love, however they flirt, they can be feminists. They do not want to learn a set of personal attitudes before being admitted into the club. The search for political equality today must go on alongside the acceptance of personal freedom. (p. 5)

She too regrets the moralising tone and behavioural prescriptions which are mostly about sex and its representations in contemporary life. Young women today are much more knowledgeable about sex, much more confident of themselves, much more exposed to ideas of gender equality and equal rights than were those who grew up in the 1960s. To them, the disapproval of sexual display and frivolousness in popular culture, the fear of men, and the promotion of chastity associated with feminism seem little different from the puritanism of the moral Right and no more attractive. Both patronise and infantilise them. Almost paraphrasing Wolf, and Denfeld, Walter regrets the transformation of feminism from an engine of reform (some would say gender revolution) to a religion for saving women's souls.

What comes over again and again in the words of these feminist dissidents is that while adherence to 'the personal is political' in the 1970s made feminism meaningful to millions of women in America and Britain and radicalised the feminist tradition inherited from the nineteenth-century movement, it has become too literally and too tightly interpreted. This sentiment is not confined to the younger generation. For 1970s veteran, Lynne Segal, 'an apocalyptic feminism has appeared which portrays a Manichean struggle between female virtue and male vice, with ensuing catastrophe and doom unless "female" morality and values prevail' (1987, p. ix). The journalist Yvonne Roberts, a 'second wave' campaigner, is more down to earth: 'Feminism is not about mystical bonds that I may or may not share with other women.... feminism is not about the creation of a new society of women. The notion that women have "special" qualities that bring peace and greenery to the world seems to me as sexist as the idea that they are all blonde bimbos or baby machines' (Roberts, 1992, p. xii). For both, feminism has become narrow dogma, a source of moral approbation of others, and a mantra to ward off the evil spirits of the enemy, both external and internal, instead of an inspirational slogan and a guideline for practical action.

There is a general view among the post-war revisionists and the new generation of feminists that feminism should move on from anger and resentment at the wrongs of women to positively acknowledge what has been achieved and celebrate the fact that young women of the millennium take for granted rights that it took feminism 200 years to achieve (Walter, 1999). If they seem ungrateful, they are no different from all new generations which tend to see themselves as the change agents, the future, and the previous generation as out-of-touch and out-of-step. In one way or another, the new writers concur with Walter's observation that 'everywhere you go, you see women flexing their muscles and demanding equality' (p. 6).

Some see it in the dramatic increase of women in politics. Margaret Thatcher, once reviled as anti-feminist, is reclaimed not as a feminist, but as an icon of female power dominant in a man's world (Burchill, 1992; Walter, 1998; Benn, 1998; Wilkinson, 1999). Traditionally feminine in her outward appearance and mannerisms and a proud mother of twins, she made no secret of her lack of traditional home-making skills and her employment of a full-time nanny from the birth of her babies. Unrepentantly ambitious, she provided living proof that the female character is equally capable of single-minded ruthlessness as of polymorphous nurturance. While retrogressive in public policy in many ways, the individualistic ethic which Thatcher embodied did foster a new populist aspirationalism. Melissa Benn (1998) believes that 'some psychological rubicon was crossed, some new attitude was forged, that has proved crucial to how women think about themselves... The new attitude transformed... the values of earlier generations of strong women... into a new constellation; these celebrated... the virtues of power, success and the importance of self' (p. 38).

In the US the feminist herald of the new female power was Paglia; in Britain an equally bright, provocative iconoclastic journalist of popular culture, Julie Burchill. For Burchill the icons of the age, Thatcher, Navratilova, Madonna, the Spice Girls, represent 'Bourgeois Feminist Triumphalism' of which she herself is a specimen – strong, independently minded, ambitious women who despite inauspicious social backgrounds and the prejudices of the system made it big-time on their own terms. These women have fascinated feminists and non-feminists alike because they created a new model for a female public life, as Benn says of Thatcher: 'a model...of the will to power, of triumph over circumstance, of stepping over and above her sex rather than identifying with it' (Benn, 1998, p. 42).

It may be that these icons of female power have such a grip on the female psyche because they do embody both the feminine and the feminist, both different from men and equal to them. They embody not a consensual androgeny but a tantalising ambiguity. And maybe too they have been cathartic for women in offering a vicarious delight in the heroine's transgression of the norms of feminine virtue *and*, unlike the vamps of old, getting rewarded handsomely for it!

It must be said that while all these writers emphasise women's new-found will-to-power, they are not sanguine about the reality. All discuss at length the continuing inequalities between men and women: the disproportionately small number of women in senior positions in politics, in the judiciary, in finance, business, industry and commerce, in the professions, in universities, in the media, in the armed forces, in the trade union movement; the concentration of women in part-time work, in particular types of employment and at the lower levels; the differential earnings of men and women; the smaller investment in training and development for women and differential rates of promotion. They also note that these inequalities in paid work are matched by the inequalities of work in the home. They acknowledge the persistence of prejudice and discrimination, sexist assumptions, sexual harassment and violence against women. They note that in the growing polarisation of the population into the work-rich and the work-poor, women with children are the fastest-growing group in poverty.

Nevertheless, these writers do not let these continuing inequalities get out of proportion with the advances that have been made. They are anxious that the self-confidence and aspirations of the girls and young women who are the subject of their investigations, should not founder in disillusionment and demoralisation when they confront the realities of gender inequality. And this, they say, will happen in force if and when they become mothers because the workplace remains fundamentally unfriendly towards the demands of family life. Numerous polls, surveys and qualitative research reinforce that view. The key concern for women today is how to balance work and family life.

We have already noted the greater aspirations of young women in relation to work as a source of identity and independence and its impact on their educational success and employability. In any case, paid work is now as much a necessity for them as it is for young men. With the proportion of women as a percentage of the total labour force expected to rise to 51 per cent by 2002 (Wilkinson and Howard, 1997; Blau and Ehrenberg, 1998), the dependence on women's wages to maintain family living standards, and the breakdown of 40 per cent of marriages in Britain and 50 per cent in the USA, the option of the life-time full-time homemaker is not one available to most women. Macro-economic trends, educational upgrading and upskilling (Pryor and Schaffer, 1999) as well as changes in cultural expectations thus are working together to produce the conditions for gender equality in the public sphere and the 'post-modern family' (Stacey, 1996) in the private sphere. However, we have also noted that the family still features high in women's priorities and that parenthood provides a majority of women with their main source of identity (Wilkinson and Howard, 1997; Duncan and Edwards, 1999). Since neither employers as a whole nor the government in the USA and the UK have developed a framework which accommodates women's two roles, the family continues to be at odds with the realisation of equality tantalisingly offered by women's mass entry into public life and the icons of female power in the media (Blau and Ehrenberg 1998). It is this contradiction at the heart of contemporary women's lives that feminists of both the older and new generations alike seek to address (Hewitt, 1993; Roiphe, 1996; Friedan 1997; Hochschild, 1997; Lister, 1997, 1999; Benn, 1998; Buxton, 1998; Walter, 1998, 1999; Franks, 1999; Segal 1999).

New feminism?

Taking as their philosophy, pragmatism rather than purity, these writers concentrate on motherhood as both a source of satisfaction and joy and as an obstacle to equality at work. This approach enables them to avoid the clash of political absolutes over the nature of the family as an institution. However, there are good substantive reasons for this focus as well.

A MORI poll for the *Mail on Sunday* (25 June 1995) reported that 60 per cent of British women identified having children as the main reason why women did not succeed as well as men at work, double the number who identified male discrimination. And this is borne out by data on women's wages. Whereas women on average are paid 20 per cent less than men, the pay of young graduate professional women is 92 per cent or more of that of their male counterparts (*The Independent*, 3 December 1996). This reflects the decrease of the 'attribute gap', i.e. the differential levels of qualification between men and women, which by 1997 had reversed, with females outperforming males at almost all stages of assessed educational achievement (Ofsted/Equal Opportunities Commission, 1996). Women typically lose more than half the earnings they would have made throughout their working lifetime when they have children, the so-called 'family gap'. The least likely to suffer wage discrepancies are those women who remain childless or who take protected maternity leave and return to work within the time scale (Joshi *et al.*, 1996). Motherhood also has a detrimental effect on promotional prospects. It plays a substantial role in the fact that women constitute under 25 per cent of secondary-school head-teachers, about 33 per cent of barristers, 18 per cent of hospital consultants, 7 per cent of university chairs, 4.5 per cent of company directors, 4 out of the 106 top executives on ITV boards and 21 of 120 at the BBC. At corporate senior management level, only 30 per cent of women have children compared with 75 per cent of men (Walter, 1998). Of Britain's top fifty women featured in a three-part serial on successful women, half of them were childless (*The Guardian*, May 1997). Despite the greater strength in the USA of the women's equal rights lobby, and the greater proportion of women in senior posts in the high earner sector like the large corporations and the higher professions, the same pattern prevails for women with children (*The Economist*, 18 July 1998). At the other end of the earning scale, it is having children that is the single most significant factor in female poverty in both Britain and America.

Whatever their relationship to work in terms of self-esteem, self-identity and sociability, women of every class have registered the economic need for employment under contemporary conditions. But they are also reluctant to give up the psychological gratifications that they derive from family life, in particular from children. Women draw on a number of strands in weaving together their ideal and material lives, amongst which feature: a legitimate and valued role beyond the home, financial independence, self-respect and the respect of others, recreational sex and some fun. Yet for 80 per cent of women born since the 1960s a stable heterosexual relationship and children continue to be part of that ideal and reality. For these women, therefore, the major priority in their lives is not dispensing with marriage and family life but balancing them with work. In this particular sense, it is true that women want to 'have it all'. Hence in both America and in Britain, their prime concern is childcare and family-friendly employment policies.

This concern provides a practical empathy between the 'new feminists' and non-aligned women, and an opportunity to change the public image of feminism. The overwhelming view of 'third wave feminists' is that while women have accommodated the economic and social transformations of the second half of the twentieth-century, men have changed little, even where personally overtaken by their effects. Until they do, women will continue to meet obstacles to their full participation in public life, and children will be short-changed in parental time and attention. Of these writers, Jayne Buxton, in *Ending the Mother War: Starting the Workplace Revolution* (1998), is most explicit in addressing the feminist debate and in her policy proposals.

Buxton sets out to distance the new feminism from what she regards as the sterile debate between Earthmothers and Superwomen. She deals with the Earthmother myths fairly perfunctorily, dismissing any claim that mothers staying at home *per se* will secure a happy family and secure, well-adjusted children, or that working mothers are the cause of family breakdown, emasculated, demoralised fathers and delinquent children. She insists with the support of research findings that the mother working or not working is not the issue: 'but the question of how much she works, how long are the separations, and whether these separations prevent her from being sensitive to her children's needs' (p. 146).

She gives considerably more attention to the myths of Superwoman, partly I think because she believes that they are increasingly influential. For Buxton, the maternal feelings that Superwoman reduces to induced guilt are in fact more complex and generated from within. They include positively missing children and yearning to be with them. This maternal love is so frequently reported by mothers as an intensely felt physical link, that Buxton finds it 'difficult not to be persuaded that the mother–child bond has elements that are primal and deeply rooted' (p. 39). While Buxton is strongly in favour for fuller involvement of fathers with their children, she does not *feel* that the relationship is of the same fundamental order. This reflection on the nature of mothers' feelings about their babies and young children in particular and their intuitive sense of its difference from even the most loving fathers, is common to those feminist authors whose writings are woven with interior explorations of their personal experiences as new mothers.

It is the same conception of mother love which lies behind Buxton's view that childcare is not amenable to the management techniques of the organisation of time and the co-ordination of demand and supply. Children's time-scales of need are infinitely varied and do not fit into the systematic timetable of adult work. They need presence, not a defined short period of concentrated attention. Mothers become disconnected from the everyday experiences of their children; children feel marginalised.

For this reason she does not support the traditional feminist demand for full-time daycare as the solution to women's inequality at work. Nowadays, employers see it as the answer to their increasing need for a female labour force, educationalists as the means to improve the intellectual development of children, particularly from disadvantaged families, and social workers as a way to help women and children out of poverty. To politicians it provides a means to reduce the welfare costs of poor families and lone mothers, meet the demands of contemporary women who are increasingly important in the voting stakes, and improve the human capital of the next generation on which the long-term health of the national economy depends.

Buxton sounds like a lone voice against this groundswell of opinion. So deafening is the pro-care lobby that she has to call upon the support of Patricia Morgan, a prolific writer for the right-wing think-tank, the Institute of Economic Affairs, and a central figure of the moral conservative movement in Britain. Much of Buxton's array of evidence of the detrimental effects of day-care on children are drawn from Morgan's *Who Needs Parents?: The Effect of Childcare and Early Education on Children in Britain and the USA* (1996). To be fair to Buxton, she rejects Morgan's solution that women should stay at home with their children. Nor is she opposed to day-care in itself. What she is against is pre-school children and particularly the under-twos being in the care of non-parents and particularly in the care of professional care workers, for the full adult working day, for the full working week. She is for maximising the quality of day-care provision by comprehensive government regulations, and minimising the time in care which she believes should be limited to 20 hours a week at the most. Her concern is not limited to public and private nurseries for low and average income families but applies to care by nannies and au pairs in wealthy households.

Buxton's critique of current policies is that they entail women having to accommodate the other parts of their lives to workplace cultures and traditions, putting intolerable pressure on women coping with the 'double-burden' and the 'double-shift'. The effects of this are not confined to the difficulties and unhappiness experienced by individual family members but are being felt in the aggregate in levels of social cohesion. A management consultant herself, Buxton draws upon the work of the management guru, Charles Handy (1997), who has been foremost in warning business that the survival of the market economy in the twenty-first century will depend on its role in sustaining a democratic, economically and socially inclusive society. His is only one contribution to what has been a wide-ranging debate over the last decade about the roots of 'social capital' and the role of public policy in its regeneration (Etzioni, 1993, 1995; Fukuyama, 1995, 1997, 1999).

This debate profoundly influenced the Clinton/Blair administrations and the development of a 'third way' philosophy and policy agenda (Giddens, 1998). Their interest in shifting the culture from a socially irresponsible radical individualism let loose by their predecessors to a 'communitarian individualism', has kept the family high on their political agendas as a working example of mutual interdependence, care and responsibility. However, there is the making of a policy contradiction here. On the one hand, paid work is regarded as the best means of supporting the material and moral wellbeing life of families. Hence, they have promoted employment, taxation and childcare policies for those in work which are family-friendly and welfare policies for those not in work which will encourage and facilitate them into employment, most controversially for lone parents. On the other hand, both governments increased the expectations of parental responsibility with regard to financial support for children, children's conduct and educational achievement. Yet all recognise that a fundamental element of the creation of social capital is time, but with both parents in the labour force this means that there is less time for family life. Those in employment in the USA and the UK are working increasingly longer hours, consequently children are deprived of time with their parents. One reason for this is that the organisation of work is still based on the anachronistic model of the male breadwinner/female homemaker family.

Some communitarians propose traditional solutions. Buxton's are rather more radical, entailing the wholescale reconceptualisation and reorganisation of the workplace to accommodate the consolidation of women's employment as part of the restructuring of the economy on a global scale.

Buxton draws heavily on work-life research and consultancy organisations such as the Families and Work Institute, the work-life consultancy WFD, and the Ford Foundation in America and New Ways to Work and The National Work-Life Forum in Britain which insist that few careers really require life-time continuity and that few jobs cannot be re-engineered to suit some form of flexible working. But it does require that whole functional areas of companies are redesigned in this way so to ensure that the overall performance and output is the same and can be co-ordinated and managed effectively. For example, the 'projectisation' of work enables individuals to work on however many discrete projects fit their time-frame, with the project teams themselves responsible for the dovetailing of individuals' schedules. 'Deputisation' allows some tasks to be allocated to a more junior employee who gains experience as a by-product. Some roles can be structured as 'job-splits' rather than 'job shares'. The 'concentrated week' allows for fewer but longer working days. The concept of 'career sequencing', that is professional development pursued over an extended period and in concentrated peaks and plateaus without loss of status or promotion, replaces the linear, front-loaded and continuous tradition. These quality-of-life, professional and personal development policies provide the framework for other more familiar family-friendly policies, such as maternity and parental leave, workplace nurseries and childcare vouchers, flexitime, job-sharing, working from home, and routine part-time jobs.

Such a holistic approach to work organisation would legitimate a new philosophy of work-life balance which would benefit both men and women not only for greater involvement in their families, but for other valuable activities that require time out, like sports, the arts, politics or voluntary service. This would unblock considerable creativity and enterprise in the workforce and mainstream forms of working which while targeted only at women as at present, locks them into the 'mommy track' and engenders resentment from the male and childless female workforce. While few organisations have achieved this level of what the Families and Work Institute calls the fourth stage in the development of work-life agendas, Buxton provides sufficient evidence from cutting-edge organisations from both the private and the public sector, for example IBM, Xerox, Lloyds TSB, Granada, Oxfordshire County Council, and Barking and Havering Health Authority (where the Chief Executive post was job-shared by two powerful professional women), to convince one that this is not just another feminist or New Age management utopia. It is certainly the practical message promoted by other feminists keen to close the reality gap with 'I'm not a feminist but...' women.

Roberts puts it in a nutshell: 'the issue for feminism, then, in a work-oriented society, is to negotiate the best possible deal – one which makes the workplace more humane, the work ethic less dictatorial, the rewards fairer, the personal sacrifices less damaging, and the neglect of children, minimal' (1992, p. 188).

It is true that Buxton's *Ending the Mother War* focuses on highly qualified women in management, the professions or the media and that it rarely touches on the majority of women who have different problems: poor pay, insecurity of employment and social security inflexibilities. Nevertheless, from a feminist perspective all gender inequalities are unacceptable, even if they affect well-paid, privileged women. And it does the cause of women's equality no good at all when the media can pounce on stories of high-achieving women who resign from executive positions in international corporations to immerse themselves in motherhood, like Penny Hughes, the 35-year-old president of Coca-Cola UK, because 'they can't hack it'. In fact like she and many others in her position (well documented by Buxton) exchange the unrelenting rigidities of corporate culture for 'portfolio careers' tailored to their needs to work, to earn and to enjoy their children. In the case of Hughes it brings in well over £100,000 a year for about 10 days' work a month (*The Sunday Times*, 12 July 1998). At a more modest level, workplace rigidities drive increasing numbers of women into self-employment: 25 per cent in the UK and 32 per cent in the USA (Wilkinson, 1994). It may be that if the influence and actions of those women who have made it through the glass ceiling and into motherhood (along with other imperatives of the global economy and the gradual 'feminisation' of cultural values) motivate senior management of corporations to shift their workplace cultures away from the linear pattern and rhythms of traditional male employment, the general stigma of part-time working and discontinuous service will diminish and benefit working women throughout organisations whatever their level.

The American and British 'new feminism' publications are not strictly academic texts; they are largely journalistic, aimed at a more popular audience. Hence they often lack depth and rigour resulting in internal theoretical and empirical contradictions. Their presentations of theoretical approaches are sometimes thin and superficial. Like many of those they oppose, they are highly selective of material which supports their case and they ignore that which does not. Like other public discourses, they 'flatten complexity' and exclude 'any elements – such as ambiguity, conflict and contradiction – which threaten that coherence' (DiQuinzio and Young, 1997). In other words, these books are polemics in an ideological battle for the soul of feminism in relation to the general public and particularly a new generation of women. Having said that, however, they are dynamic, bursting with life, enthusiasm, hope and determination, and from that point of view are a breath of fresh air. And their optimism is fairly realistic because their goals are well grounded, though if achieved would amount almost to a revolution in the lives of millions of women.

Ambivalence and vacillation

Most of the texts, for the reasons given above, emphasise the external factors which continue to create tensions and contradictions in women's attitude to and role in the family and neglect internal psycho-social ones. Having established broadly common policy ground between feminists and non-aligned women they are eager to get on with the battle for practical results, especially while the political climate is auspicious. Any conflict of interest between women as individuals and women as mothers is externalised in the incompatibility between the composition of the labour force and the organisation of work.

Buxton, for example, says that *Ending the Mother War* 'is primarily for and about mothers ... it is they who are trapped within a debate which offers them just two choices, one of which often involves sacrificing their own needs and ambitions, the other of which can lead to the sacrifice of their children's and families' wellbeing' (p. xiv). Yet the genuine conflict of interest which this pinpoints receives little attention in the book and this is because at root Buxton conflates the interests of women as women with that of women as mothers. And in this construction, the interests of women–mothers and those of their children coincide. However sensible this conception is for the purposes of practical politics, it is not intellectually sustainable. Women have gained sufficient ground to combat continuing male prejudice and discrimination. What they have much less control over is their desire for children and the dramatic effects which children have on their lives, with or without New Men. Children introduce another dimension into the male–female equation. They constitute the real constraint on women's equality with men. One of the central principles on which American abortion law is based is that the ability of women to control their reproductive lives is essential to their ability to participate equally in economic and social life, a recognition in law that 'in important respects, the interests of women as individuals and the interests of children are at odds' (Fox-Genovese, 1995, p. 506). The feminists we have been examining will argue that the source of this conflict is in the failure of society and, in particular, work organisations to adapt to the genderquake. However, there is sufficient evidence from women's reflections on their relationship to their children, their partners and their work, that there are also other powerful forces at work.

Buxton concentrates on women and children, though her arguments apply equally to the similar incompatibility between the traditional regime of the workplace and the needs for care of the elderly, an issue which will increasingly require attention in the twenty-first century as it feels the full implications of the demographic changes of the twentieth. This underlines the warnings of the new feminists that governments and employers must recognise the value of care work both in its own right and for its economic contribution to total social welfare, and adjust both welfare and employment regimes to accommodate it for both sexes. It is certainly the case as Lister (1999) points out, that if the ethics of care are predicated on female aptitudes and virtues (Sevenhuijsen, 1998) divorced from the ethics of justice, the current exploitation of women's 'gendered moral rationality' (Duncan and Edwards, 1999) or 'compulsory altruism' (Land and Rose, 1985) will simply be reinforced.

The feminist ethics of care literature tends to assume a relatively conflict-free psychological attitude to caring among women. Though not directly engaged with this literature, Rosalind Coward's *Our Treacherous Hearts* (1992) provides an account of the internal psychodynamic environment in which female moral rationality develops, that suggests an altogether more complex situation.

The book was provoked partly by the fact that 'in the last ten years women have appeared not just willing but positively eager to assume double responsibilities in the home: they have felt uneasy if their own achievements began to outstrip those of their male partners and they have been almost frantic to retain male sexual approval' (p. 12), and partly by the media attention paid to the numbers of 'having it all' career women who having reached the top gave it all up for their children. The explanation they gave for the abandonment of their work life was not because they could not hack it, but simply the pull of maternal love. However, what is interesting is that most of the women in Coward's interview sample in this position revealed that in fact they had not been fully happy at work before they got pregnant: 'some of the conditions which lead to women putting their family first are at play long before the family arrives and predate any falling in love with their babies (p. 20). Coward found in these cases that the women had a deep-set ambivalence about their careers.

All the women reported that family and children represent a more 'real' priority than work which was much less vital to their sense of self than it was to their partners. Explanations varied from not being single-minded enough to become a 'company man' or motivated enough by the drive for money, to a dislike of the competition, aggression and envy in work environment. However, pressed further, the interviewees admitted that envy and competitiveness was not absent from relationships between mothers, and that their children's aggressive behaviour provoked anxieties derived from their own repressed anger. In both cases the problems they experienced in the workplace had been merely deflected into family relationships.

Drawing on Freudian and Kleinian psychoanalytic ideas, Coward believes woman have their fair share of individualistic, egoistic and aggressive impulses, but they find these feelings more difficult to handle than most men. This stems from childhood feelings of envy, rivalry and hostility which children fear because of the maternal retribution that may follow. While boys are constructed i ᵗʰᵉⁱʳ separ- ateness from the mother and hence have more escaɟ hostile envious love for their mothers, girls identify with and hence repress their hostile feelings. In later life,/ which are highly competitive and envious trigger o anxieties and create discomfort in women.

The home in this context may seem very appealing because it represents an altruistic world which is the antithesis of work life. The family rears children as moral beings, requires of its members individual sacrifices to serve the good of the collective, inculcates the ethical standards of the community and reconciles these with those of society at large. Women are still seen to be more central to these processes than men. Girls today continue to grow up internalising their role in this moral work and develop a stronger sense of altruism and guilt than boys. Yet at the same time they are encouraged to do well at school, developing the drive to achieve and compete in preparation for getting a good job and being financially independent. Thus, 'what is particularly difficult is that the moral altruistic notion of motherhood is completely at odds with the requirements for the professional world' (Coward, p. 45).

It is also the case that while the full-time housewife may have suffered considerable loss of status in this post-feminist world, pregnancy and motherhood has not. It is part of having it all, and for many women imparts a very intimate sense of the power of their own bodies (dramatised perfectly by the image of the very pregnant nakedness of the Hollywood actress, Demi Moore, on the cover of *Vanity Fair*). For women whose lives do not provide financial independence or social esteem, babies confer social status and provide them with someone, albeit a dependent infant, who will think they are somebody worthwhile and of value. Research reveals that this is one of the main dimensions of teenage pregnancies.

However, this need for unconditional love is not confined to young deprived girls. While many women believe that their love for their children springs from the unselfish and altruistic need to care, often it is a need on the mother's part to be loved above all others and to the exclusion of others. This is rarely attainable from partners, and, maybe even unconsciously, disappointment in men's love leads women into making themselves the centre of their children's lives, often excluding their partners hence reinforcing the traditional division of emotional and domestic labour. Some women become so obsessive about their children that they create a dependency in them which is unhealthy for both in the longer term. The children's dependency turns into the mother's dependency on her children, who will at some point 'abandon' her. As Coward puts it: 'Burying yourself in the neediness of others is not quite the same as an altruistic concern for them. Our culture has difficulty in separating the two, and mothering an activity which hovers above the narrow dividing line' (p. 52).

Possibly Coward's most controversial view is that 'feminism is almost invariably seen as a struggle . . . with men. But the truth is that the deep struggle of feminism was with the previous generation of women. Feminism could be called the daughters' revolt' (p. 91). In Chapter 3 we saw some evidence for this in the writings of the 1970s feminists. The women in Coward's sample display ambivalent and contradictory feelings towards their mothers which Coward sees as a reflection of their mothers' feelings towards them. On the one hand the mothers in the 1950s mothers invested a great deal in their children and derive intense pride in their achievements. With daughters, however, this was tinged with resentment because their success implied a devaluation a life of housework and mothering. Yet most women still long for their mother's approval. It may be that the apparently inexplicable drive to nest and bear children is part of the continuing identification with the mother. It also provides mothers with the potential for a renewed importance in a daughter's life and a sense of expert authority. Yet that too is often a further source of tension between the generations of women, because the ideals of motherhood have changed and the childcare practices of daughters is often felt by their mothers as, and indeed is, a criticism of the way they had been brought up. These manifest tensions and the inner conflicts to which they relate express themselves in feelings of guilt which often, says Coward, lead to women's decisions about their work and family life.

It is these internal psychological patterns that are at the core of women's continued attraction to family life, but on the whole women do not confront them. Rather they prefer to live with the illusions of innate biological differences in which women are kinder, more caring and altruistic than men, or of the misogyny of the system. In doing so they simply project their ambitions on to their men and their children, expecting them to satisfy them. This complicity lets men off the hook, allows their work to continue to take precedence and justifies their lesser involvement with childcare and domestic organisation.

While Coward describes the home as providing an escape from conflictual feelings about work, Arlie Hochschild (1997) believes that for many women work provides a refuge from home: 'In this new model of family and work life, a tired parent flees a world of unresolved quarrels and unwashed laundry for the reliable orderliness, harmony and managed cheer of work' (p. 44).

In fact both may be correct in that they describe two contradictory but interconnected tendencies at the heart of the contemporary family: a centrifugal force drawing individuals to the protection of the family from the exposure to and demands of the anonymous external world, and a centripetal force propelling them to the exterior as an escape from the intensity of familial relationships. The modern family is 'an unstable compound that is threatened at any moment from the defection by its members, owing to that relational feverishness which exposes them to the temptations of the outside, as well as to that overvaluing of the inside which makes escape all the more necessary' (Donzelot, 1980, p. 228). The tensions generated are both managed by and play themselves out in the person of the mother as both the organisational and emotional heart of the family. It is hardly surprising that it spawns so many casualties.

Third-wave feminism: reconciling feminism with family life

This chapter has reviewed the shifts in the thinking about the family and its relationship with feminism that have taken place in the last decade or so of the twentieth-century, as the personal circumstances of second-wave feminists have changed under the pressure of the biological clock and as it has become apparent that women generally have resolutely and vocally resisted the feminist claim that the family oppresses them. If these revisionist feminists are to be labelled 'post-feminist', it clearly does not mean that they think feminism is passé or redundant to the position of women today. Certainly some of what was revolutionary about the fundamental claims of second-wave feminism, they take for granted, though they have no doubt that it made impressive and lasting gains for women. However to different degrees they all believe that somewhere along the line it got detached from how mainstream women conceived their desires, interests and priorities and became overly preoccupied with issues of cultural representation and violence.

Without open declarations – and it is interesting that even amongst these writers, the visible 'white spaces on the page persist where careful thinking on families is needed' (Lindemann, 1997, p. 2) – most are in effect reconciled to a reformed nuclear-type family characterised by dual-earner status and egalitarian relationships between the adult partners, and the joint parenting of children, even where their own personal circumstances differ. For most this is not a reconciliation with traditional morality but with their own psychological, emotional and social desires. Nor is it one which denigrates other forms of families, such as lone parent or lesbian and gay families, which in their view have the same capacity for unconditional love and support. What is beyond the pale to certain strands within feminism is the relative rehabilitation of men and heterosexual even romantic love, of which Coward's *Sacred Cows* (1999) is possibly the most outspoken example. It criticises feminism for clinging to tenets which have been overtaken by the shift in power between the sexes toward which feminism itself contributed:

> Claiming the moral righteousness of the oppressed to assert dubious rights is a refusal to face up to the possibility both of men's vulnerability and of women's potency. It [womanism] refuses to accept women's role in constructing objectionable aspects of masculinity and it justifies everything done in the name of woman, often at the same time denying men the right to do or express themselves in the same way. (p. 124)

Male fragility and vulnerability may seem an unlikely theme for the author of *Backlash*, but it appears even Faludi has sensed the new balance in gender politics. *Stiffed: The Betrayal of the Modern Man* (1999), published with much media fanfare, claims that the male backlash against women is only a symptom of a profound crisis of manhood afflicting contemporary men. It is caused by the loss of the material and psychological conditions which provided meaning and purpose to men's lives and the substitution of a celebrity culture and 'virtual' reality. Brought up to expect that their status as adult men would come from their useful contribution in productive employment, in their community and as a breadwinner, contemporary men are confused and demoralised.

Such views are seen as betrayals and surrenders and guarantee the continued categorisation by some as part of the anti-feminist backlash.

Indeed it was all too much for Germaine Greer and forced her to write a sequel to *The Female Eunuch*. The book she 'vowed' she would never write, *The Whole Woman* (1999), exhibits the same bombast, passion, wit, raunchy rhetorical ire and cavalier disregard for the protocols of validity of reason and evidence as its precursor. This is Greer the celebrity, demonstrating that she can still outperform anyone for outrageousness and draw the crowds and the media. She was courted on radio; the BBC ran a documentary on her life; she played to packed audiences on her UK promotional lecture tour.

The book was inspired by her anger that feminist revisionists of her own generation and the younger lifestyle feminists had gone off the

rails, become complacent and were misleading women into believing
the battle had been won:

> We were settling for equality. Liberation struggles are not about assimila-
> tion but about asserting difference with dignity and prestige, and insisting
> on it as a condition of self-definition and self-determination. (p. 1)

While she gestures occasionally toward some gains in the last 30 years,
it is very hard to identify these in a landscape thick with every con-
ceivable slight, injustice, injury and crime against women. Women's
increased participation in the labour force and the inroads that the
most educated have made in the higher occupations are written off:
'Women always did the shit work; now that the only work there is is
shit work men are unemployed' (p. 13). Recent successes of women in
parliamentary elections are ridiculed. Every achievement Greer turns
into a cost because, she claims, women deny their own identity and
become the clones and the dupes of men who continue to openly or
covertly hate them: 'Some men hate all women all of the time; all men
hate some women some of the time' (p. 14). In the pursuit of spurious
equality and spurious sexual freedom women are not being liberated
but indeed further enchained to patriarchy.

Real liberation means asserting difference from men and this for
women resides in the body in its natural state. It is because men wish
to phase real women out and create those in the image of their desires
that the female body becomes the true battleground between the
sexes:

> If state-of-the art gestation cabinets could manufacture children and vir-
> tual female fetishes could furnish sexual services, men would not regret the
> passing of real, smelly, bloody, noisy, hairy women. (p. 84)

Until then, men try to control women by defining sex as penetration
by the penis and constructing the perfect model of female desirability
through their control of the beauty and fashion industries, marketing
and the media. They control female fertility through medical practice
and reproductive technology. Otherwise they escape from real women
into pornography, into anal sex and even into transsexual surgery.

It is clear that there is only one solution. Women must be made to
realise that there is a fundamental mismatch between the sexes, that
while women want love, a relationship and commitment, men are
terrrified and incapable of them or at best indifferent. With greater
financial independence, women can survive without men and must

learn not to need them. Greer recommends female segregated communities and sees in the multi-generational matrifocal families consequent on divorce and other failed heterosexual unions the prototype for a new women-centred world. Rediscovering traditional womanly crafts and substituting chastity, masturbation or same-sex love-making for the unreliable penis may in the end be more rewarding.

Greer rails against the lifestyle feminists for abandoning poor women in their unseemly haste to become one of the boys: the lipstick, briefcase and city suits of the professional women and the sexually aggressive language and behaviour of 'lairy-girls' are a complete sell-out of feminism. However, it is difficult, as ever, to see what effective public policy can be derived from Greer's own position. Possibly it is that the state should support mothers, though since governments are the embodiment of misogyny and male privilege and women politicians are their puppets, it is difficult to see why that should be an appropriate strategy for 'real' feminists? Greer has nothing to say on the New Deal for lone parents, the national childcare strategy, the minimum wage, the new tax credits, family-friendly employment measures and increased child benefit which assist average income and poor women for which many of the so-called revisionists of Greer's generation and the new (generation) feminists have fought. Perhaps even more surprising, she makes no comment about the Department for International Development's (with a woman Minister) prioritisation of women and poverty in UK government aid policy. Greer calls women to arms to re-claim the feminist movement, but even if they were aroused by her bellicose prose, where would it lead them? Like her other books in this genre, the success of *The Whole Woman* is 'as much a triumph of style as substance' (Tillyard, 1999).

Those Greer castigates recognise the persisting tensions and unequal burdens within the family, but they tend to see this as more a consequence of the incompatibilities of work and family under the current structure of employment than of incompatibilities inherent in male–female relationships or power relations in the family. All agree that considerable material inequalities persist between men and women but believe these derive primarily from anachronistic gender assumptions of the workplace and the exploitation of women's continuing sense of responsibility for children. They believe that there is a need for a feminist movement to give the lead on these issues. All agree that at present feminism is failing to give that lead and needs re-directing and re-invigorating.

In criticising what they regard as the errors or limitations of second-wave feminism, third-wave feminism nevertheless takes many of the philosophical assumptions and material achievements of second-wave feminism for granted, and is reacting against both the conservative backlash which would put them back in the family, and against the hegemony within feminism which would keep them out of the family, or at least out of families that involve men. Ann Oakley's (1997) assertion that 'the essence of the backlash lies in the contention that the nuclear family has been unreasonably attacked' (p. 37) invites the question of what is unreasonable in this context.

9

Feminism and the Family: Still at Odds?

Women are so closely identified with family in popular and scholarly thought that reconceptualising gender necessarily requires rethinking kinship, household, and domesticity. The substantive reason is that the family is the primary institution for organising gender relations in society. It is where the sexual division of labour, the regulation of sexuality and the social construction and reproduction of gender are rooted. Gender hierarchy is created, reproduced and maintained on a day-to-day basis through interaction among members of a household. In a real sense, then, the debate about women's place in the family is actually a debate about women's place in society. (Glenn, 1987, cited in Andersen, 1991, p. 238)

The story of the relationship between feminism and the family told in this book demonstrates a historical contradiction between the equality of women and the family. American and British feminists of the eighteenth and nineteenth-centuries challenged prevailing notions of women's capacities, status and place in society from within the traditional parameters of women's place in the family. The heady and unstable mix of Enlightenment egalitarian rationalism and non-Conformist spiritual egalitarianism which fired them nevertheless rested on unquestioned assumptions about a domestic division of labour so profoundly unequal as to appear 'natural'. The tendency for the resultant tensions to be articulated in moralistic terms, therefore, were present from the beginning. Feminism's very success in establishing the case for women's equality in the public sphere exposed the limits of that equality to lie in the fundamental inequality in the private sphere. Possibly one of the most important contributions of twentieth-century feminist scholarship has been to explode the myth of separate spheres itself.

229

By the 1960s feminist theory and politics had exhausted its tolerance of collusion in women's familial role and began a revolutionary attack on its basic premises. As we have seen, this meant an assault across the board, from macro-level analyses, for example, of the relationship between women's subordination in the nuclear family and the maintenance of the capitalist economy, to micro-level examination of, for example, discrimination in the workplace, abuse in families and cultural stereotyping. While feminist theory exposed the unacceptable face of marriage and family life, feminist politics took it on in a comprehensive if not always coherent range of campaigns and activities. The family was the cornerstone of patriarchy both as an ideology and as economic and political system. It was not simply an obstacle to women's equality, it was antithetical to it.

The period of the most intensive activity of the women's liberation movement in the late 1960s and early 1970s coincided with the convergence of a number of trends which were to mark out the decade as a distinctive watershed in the politics and culture of Britain and America. For many, these far-reaching cultural changes were manifestations of a profound moral malaise and the collapse of the 'traditional family'. The feminist movement became associated with these changes and indeed was seen by some as the prime causal factor.

Economic transformation and women's labour market participation

While it is true as Stacey says that 'the history and fate of feminism are intimately tied to the history of the family' (1986, p. 237), they are equally affected by changes external to both. Critical here are changes in the global and national economy and patterns of employment. The cultural changes of the 1960s were facilitated by unprecedented economic growth based on mass consumption and a demand for labour that could not be satisfied by traditional sources. Employers turned to dormant supplies of married women of all social classes and to immigrant labour to meet their needs. The increase in female employment itself fanned the consumer boom, expanded the tax base for government welfare spending and hence contributed to economic growth and the spread of affluence.

Underlying this age of prosperity, however, were economic trends which were to lead to the transformation of western economies and to the return of major world recessions, high unemployment, and income polarisation. Foremost among these trends was the shift in the developed economies from heavy industry and manufacturing to the service sector and the accompanying decrease of blue-collar jobs, largely male, and the growth of white-collar employment, largely female. This became fully apparent only when the full employment of the 1960s gave way to the redundancies and industrial strife of the late 1970s and early 1980s, and the new 'flexible' employment patterns of the 1980s and 90s (Walby, 1997; Creighton 1999; O'Connor *et al* 1999).

These trends were responsible for the dramatic increase of female labour participation, and in particular that of married women. Such trends took place in the context of the traditional structure and culture of labour markets, characterised by vertical and horizontal gender segregation in which women tended to be employed on a part-time or temporary basis, on lower wages and with less job security and occupational benefits than men. While the last report from the UK Equal Opportunities Commission before the millennium indicated a narrowing of the pay and promotion gender gap, especially among young professionals (EOC, October 1998), in fact only 13 per cent of women earn more than their partners, 25 per cent earn the same and 62 per cent earn less. A far larger proportion of women are at the lower end of the pay range than men.

The real impact of the restructuring of western labour markets has been on the family unit. While in the majority of American and British homes the male continues to be the primary wage earner, the combination of job insecurity, wage stagnation, and cuts in public expenditure has seriously undermined his capacity to financially support his family without the additional income earned by his female partner. It is ironic that no sooner had the industrial working classes achieved the male family wage and breadwinner status of the middle classes, than the very economic forces that welded them into the political power able to achieve that status, undid the conditions for its survival. (Horrell and Humphries 1997; Creighton 1999). However, the cold winds of economic change have chilled middle-class families as well, perhaps for the first time: corporate mergers, downsizing, outsourcing combined with an over-supply of graduates and professionals resulted in middle-class insecurity and indeed male under- and unemployment. Increasingly two incomes have become necessary to maintain a middle-class life-style.

The impact of women's employment on changes in family life, together with control over fertility, can scarcely be underestimated.

It is directly linked to decisions about childbearing, the timing and the number of children. It reduces the time available for childcare, house-work and partner. It provides for a wider range of interests, friends and social networks, but reduces the time for the maintenance of kinship ties and community involvement. It has implications for tradi-tional networks of familial obligations and care. It unsettles traditional male authority within the family, shifts the balance of power within households and raises questions of equity and co-operation. It can provide the basis for truer partnership between men and women, but also for personal and domestic conflict. Western countries with the highest levels of female employment also have the highest levels of divorce (Becker, 1991).

As we have seen, a number of commentators regard these changes as in effect the cause of the breakdown of the nuclear family and a range of negative social and economic consequences. The most recent of these are those associated with social capital theory of whom the best known are Etzioni (1995) and Fukuyama (1995). This school advances the view that the progressive development of the 'contract' society which began with the Enlightenment project, has led to an increasing individualisation of social relations and a decline of social cohesion. The latter relies on the commitment of groups to sets of informal values and norms that facilitate co-operation, trust and reci-procity of responsibility, obligations and duties. The main source for the generation, reproduction and circulation of social capital is the family; 'its prime purpose [is] to lay the basic foundations for the moral education of the next generation' (Etzioni, 1993). The break-down of the family and the individuation of its members, therefore, undermines the capacity for society to maintain the levels of collective solidarity necessary to counterbalance the negative social effects of large-scale self-interest and to be effective in the new organisational and technological frameworks of the twenty-first century.

The social capital school rejects both the standard explanation of the Left, that family breakdown is caused by poverty, and the standard views of the Right that it is caused by the perverse incentives created by the welfare state or by the cultural revolution of the 1960s, in favour of a more complex interaction between a number of factors. Prime among them, however, are women's employment outside the home, control over fertility and the impact of both on the traditional sexual contract between men and women, defined by Fukuyama as 'a tacit trade of fertility for economic resources' (1997, p. 44). The decrease in women's economic dependence on men and the decline in their need to invest in chastity, he believes, has resulted in the breakdown of the single most important co-operative social norm that sustains social capital, that is the norm of male responsibility for women and children. This in turn reinforces women's need to be able to do without a male partner.

Social capital theorists do not deny the capacity of non-nuclear family forms to provide loving, secure and ethical environments for children; indeed they compare such families positively with conflict-ridden two-parent families or two-career absentee parents. Their point is that the socialisation of children is a heavy duty which requires the energies, time and the long-term and sustained emotional invest-ment of more than one person. They are also well aware that there is no turning back the clock. Leaving aside women's increased taste for greater independence, female employment is essential for contempor-ary economies.

Since they believe social capital to be a public good, their solutions, therefore, are directed toward government action. Since Fukuyama identifies men as the problem – 'there is no deficit of mothers and motherhood; there is, however, a severe deficit of fathers and father-hood' (1997, p. 116) – he favours targeting policies at them, such as those to improve their employability skills through training and job creation so that they would have more to offer women. (It does not seem to occur to Fukuyama that they might equally spend the extra money on themselves.) Etzioni has a few more ideas: family-friendly employment practices enabling mothers and fathers to work from home, share jobs, work flexitime and have recognised time off for children's needs; statutory maternal and paternal rights; generous child allowances; pre-nuptial counselling; practical training in perso-nal relations and parenting in schools; pre-nuptial arrangements about property and finance; marital counselling; 'cooling-off periods' for divorcing couples; financial incentives for coupledom through tax and benefits. These ideas have clearly influenced both Clinton's and Blair's pragmatic policy attempts to strengthen families.

While not writing in the social capital paradigm, Ulrich Beck (1986:1992) shares the view that the contemporary family is in profound trouble and that its source is in the growing independence of women, though he constructs the problem slightly differently. He identifies the crisis as the inevitable outcome of the contradiction at the heart of industrial society between the forces of modernisation, that is the individuation, commercialisation and mobilisation of human labour, which he locates in the labour market, and the forces of feudalism, that is, the traditional ascription by birth of social status and opportunity, which he locates in the family. Beck rejects the common view that the traditional ascriptive elements of the family are remnants from a feudal past. Rather he argues, the modern bourgeois form of the family was created in the nineteenth century in the same moment as the industrial revolution. At that point, economic development needed separate spheres for men and woman so that a class of paid workers would have the incentive to seek work, to support a class of unpaid home-workers who in turn would provide for their physical and psychological needs:

> Production work is mediated through the labour market and performed in return for money. Taking it on makes people into self-providers . . . Unpaid family work is imposed as a natural dowry through marriage . . . taking it on means dependence for support. . . . The distribution of these jobs – and here lies the feudal foundation of industrial society – remains outside of decision. They are ascribed by birth and gender. (Beck, 1992 p. 107)

The inequalities endemic to the relationship between productive and reproductive work are obscured by romantic love between the sexes. The dynamism, innovation and competitive expansion of the market economy was sustained because the whole was held intact by the feudal character of gender relations.

Beck explains the ongoing war between the sexes as the external expression of the unfolding of the contradiction between the principles of modernity – individual freedom and equality – and those of its complementary neo-feudalism – ascribed status and inequality, between the practice of modernity in the contractual nature of labour market relations and practice of feudal relations in the collective communality of marriage and the family. Inevitably modernity will win as the universal logic of the market extends beyond its gender boundaries and draws women into its processes and values.

Taken to its logical conclusion, the market economy implies a society of mobile, achievement-oriented individuals, unhindered by intimate personal relationships, the needs of children or obligations to kin. In Beck's view, the increase of marital and relationship conflict is the breaking out in the private sphere of the endemic conflicts of late modernity and is not the personal responsibility of couples though they experience it as a uniquely personal problem. It cannot, therefore, be solved by personal endeavour within the family, even with the help of the growing army of counsellors and psychotherapists which relationship problems have called into being.

He poses three future scenarios. First, it is possible that there may be a return to the traditional form of the family urged by a political lobby of moral traditionalists, but Beck thinks this would lead only to more marital conflict and divorce because younger women may not tolerate the disappointments and inequalities of marriage when the basis for the male breadwinner model no longer exists for a large number of men. Secondly, he envisages the possibilities of gender equalisation along the lines of the male model in conformity with the market economy – a model he attributes to large parts of the women's movement. This leads to a life alone, the negation of deep-rooted social ties which bind, and the erosion of the capacity to develop intimate relationships: 'the designs of independence become the prison bars of loneliness' (p. 123).

The third possibility is new forms of living beyond male and female roles which would require the 'limiting and cushioning of market relationships' and the 'reunification of work and life' (p. 124). However, his particular proposals for this promising third way do not inspire much confidence. For example he seems oblivious to the rank unfairness of his proposal to move from individual occupational mobility to co-operative forms whereby employers would adopt the principle that 'if you want him or her, you have to find a career opportunity for his or her spouse' (p. 124), or to the rank sexism of his solution to the problem of childcare in 'the legal recognition of a new speciality – day mothers'! (p. 125)

In fact it is pretty clear that given the global nature of Beck's explanation of marital breakdown, nothing short of the entire restructuring of the institutional structure of advanced industrial society will make any difference. In the meantime what is really happening is 'the sensitive practice of all sorts of communal life, an attempt at renovating the relationship between the sexes . . . and a reawakening solidarity based on shared and admitted oppression' (p. 125).

This may be what Stacey (1996) seeks to illustrate by her description of a Christian pentecostal wedding ceremony in California at which the participants and the guests all seem to belong to the same four-generational divorce-extended family, and by her account of the bride's collaboration with her first husband's live-in Jewish lover 'to build a remarkably harmonious and inclusive divorce-extended kin network whose constituent households swapped resources, labour and lodgers in response to shifting family circumstances and needs' (p. 24). This is not a new model family; simply an idiosyncratic, creative attempt by individuals, kin, friends and communities to remake family life out of the remnants of the modern and the pre-modern family, like a pathwork quilt: 'Americans today have crafted a multiplicity of family and household arrangements that we inhabit uneasily and reconstitute frequently in response to changing personal and occupational circumstances' (Stacey, 1990, p. 17). It is 'post-modern' because it follows a period, somewhat briefer than generally thought, of a single dominant family form, but has not yet settled into an alternative pattern and indeed may not do so. She uses the term to signal 'the contested, ambivalent and undecided character of contemporary gender and kinship arrangements' (p. 17).

Stacey, like the social capital theorists and Beck, however, makes too much of contemporary discontinuities in family life from previous periods. Despite these changes, there are, in fact, centrifocal forces which reinforce women's greater investment in the family. Among these we have noted the frustration of the 'glass ceiling' among professional women; the double shift of work and domestic responsibilities; the continuing wage/salary gap between men and women making it a rational choice for most women to mother; the continuing expectations of employers that males will put their work first; the repetitive, dead-end, part-time and short-term nature of many women's jobs; the lack of good-quality affordable childcare; the work/welfare trap; the demands of caring for elderly and disabled relatives; the continuing high expectations of good mothering; the continuing reluctance of men to take full share in familial and domestic responsibilities.

Nevertheless there is no doubt that there have been profound changes in gender relations and family life and it is clear that feminism was as much an outcome and reflection of these changes as it was the cause. However, it certainly exposed the cracks in the domestic edifice, supported mechanisms to undermine it and celebrated evidence of its demise.

The clash of principles: women's empowerment vs maternal altruism

The feminist deconstruction of the conventional family and its reconstruction as the site of women's oppression was much publicised and popularised both by feminists themselves and by the media. While the beneficiaries of the feminist battles for equality, at least initially, were mainly white, well-educated, middle-class women, the attack on the family and male privilege within it 'placed housewives on the defensive just when sizeable numbers of working class women were attaining this long-denied status' (Stacey, 1990, p. 12).

Stacey's participant-observer research (1990) into two families and their extended networks in 'Silicon Valley', Santa Clare County, California in the 1980s throws light on the strength of working-class women's opposition to feminist-supported family reforms, and is a corrective against the dismissal by many feminists of the pro-family movement as blue-rinsed, well-off right-wingers. The research also reveals the attraction of fundamentalist evangelical religion for women in providing comfort and certainty in a confusingly uncertain and insecure post-modern world. However, as we have seen, the religious values of most women active or sympathetic to the pro-family movement, predated the impact of the economic and moral crises of the 1970s and 80s, and was not restricted to the full-time housewife. Indeed it was that very ability to appeal to women across social, ethnic and geographical boundaries that was a source of the credibility and the political strength of pro-family women.

Whereas the nineteenth-century counter-movement in the USA and the UK against the women's franchise movement had been contained by the discourse of female moral superiority which provided the rationale for votes for women and did not fundamentally challenge the existing sexual division of labour in society or disparage the role of housewife–mother in the family, in the case of the post-war feminist movement no such accommodation could be made. Indeed it might be said that pro-family organisations were able to represent themselves as the moderate voice of women by exploiting some of the more strident anti-family declamations by major feminist 'prophets' and hence to define the negative public image of feminism. Internal divisions within feminism prevented a coherent well-considered strategic response and the public reaction of some of the more purist sisters forced feminism into an increasingly politically marginal position. Pro-family groups even began to appropriate the feminist discourse of 'choice', for example in promoting women's choice to be a full-time mother, or to work part-time, or to 'say no to sex'.

This counter-movement has been described as an anti-feminist backlash. I have argued that while this is probably accurate about those highly politicised, professionally organised groups within it who are committed to a very coherent, articulated conservative ideology, it is much less so about the grassroots women of the movement whose involvement is largely derived from more diffuse religiously-oriented moral values. Studies have repeatedly demonstrated that they are not unsympathetic to a range of feminist values and goals which relate to equality of opportunity or to the protection of women. However, such female equality and employment are endowed with a different set of meanings. Degler (1980) gets to the nub of it: 'the family's existence assumes that a woman will subordinate her individual interests to those of others – the members of her family. Feminism . . . calls that assumption into question and . . . seeks its ultimate elimination' (p. vii). It is this priority of feminism that traditional women oppose. Self-identity, self-esteem and hence self-interest are closely tied up with ethical self-sacrifice to the greater good of their families. Contemporary economic and cultural trends are eroding their capacity to fulfil that emotional, moral and material function. Hence, they see the breakdown of traditional gender identities, gender relations and gender roles in private life and domestic settings as undermining of families and destabilising of society itself.

The epitome of such changes is the growing consolidation of gay and lesbian lifestyles and communities as a legitimate part of the diverse and pluralistic mainstream of contemporary western societies. It might be thought that the decline of the most promiscuous and libertarian strand of the gay movement, partly in the wake of the AIDS crisis, and the growth of stable, long-term same-sex couples demanding their legal recognition by the state and sanctification from the church, would have reassured the morally conservative. However, to those whose value systems are closely linked to traditional religious dogma, such demands are even more frightening and evidence of a world turned upside down.

Homosexuality, for moral conservatives, represents the opposite of the gender identities, roles and intimacies based on reproductive sexuality which is the only ground on which religion sanctifies carnal knowledge. Hence it is ungodly. Homosexuality and heterosexuality define each other. So long as homosexuality remains in the role of the 'Other', the religious heresy, the social deviance, it can be contained, even tolerated though reviled and marginalised. When it attempts, however, to assert its commonality with heterosexuality along a humanitarian and ethical continuum, it threatens the whole life-world of traditionalists. As does the development and commercialisation of the new reproductive technologies such as *in vitro* fertilisation, artificial insemination by donor, prenatal diagnostic testing, embryo transfers and genetic cloning. The doctrine and material conditions of choice begin to penetrate the last certainties in an uncertain world.

And in a particular respect traditionalists are right. The consolidation and stabilisation into 'pretend families' and social communities of sexual relationships previously clandestine, transient, and stigmatised, and the creation of biological 'families' previously unknown to nature, both relativise marriage and the conjugal family form statistically, and offer alternatives to the young, the disappointed, the dissatisfied and the disaffected.

The fears of the religiously oriented are not unrealistic. Western societies both in principle and for pragmatic reasons uphold a liberal tolerance of differences in religion, ethical values and ways of living. Education in such countries is expected to be open-minded, and encouraging of intellectual curiosity and debate. In the context of a fair degree of freedom from censorship, the media feeds on the unusual, the bizarre, the sensational, the 'forbidden', often under the guise of disapproval. Television, film and video allow us all to transgress, to taste the forbidden fruit of illicit sex, violence, sadism, the perverse, the erotic, without indulging, without the guilt and without the cost. To many, such secular liberalism is devoid of morality. To parents such license is morally offensive and exposes children to negative influences which are external to and not under their control.

It is understandable if the distaste and repulsion is tinged with subliminal envy. Those who have worked hard, saved for the rainy day, played by the rules, kept their lusts in check, observed familial obligations, endured infertility and sexual dysfunctions, see what they have missed. They see fun, pleasure, carefree sex, self-indulgence and irresponsibility. And when such life-styles have serious negative consequences, they see the hedonists bailed out either by wealthy families or by the state. It is understandable if the politics of morality are also the politics of resentment and envy.

The costs of choice

What is indisputable at the end of the millennium, is the increase in choice for women. The discourse of choice is so hegemonised by consumer capitalism that it is often forgotten that choices in ways of living are an outcome of the lifting of the material and cultural conditions of non-choice. This is liberating and empowering but choice also involves making decisions and that brings into play the interests of and the consequences for others, and hence the costs of choice. It is not the array of alternatives that makes choice difficult, it is the pɪocess of decision-making that brings us face to face with the costs of choice. Most of us have experienced or will experience the personal costs in the emotional anxiety and sometimes distress involved in making such choices or in having them inflicted on us by the choices of others. These are retained forever in guilty mental images of, perhaps, the tearful child pressed to the nursery door, the brave tremble of the farewell hand of a frail elderly parent or the disbelieving, stunned pain of a partner informed of an infidelity.

There are also the costs borne by those generations – most immediately children and grandparents – who are not participants of choice but who have to live with the consequences. The growing interest in children as social actors rather than passive dependents among sociologists, social statisticians, family lawyers and social policy specialists has revealed new and disturbing insights into the impact of adults' decisions on children's emotional lives and sense of identity as well as their social and economic welfare (Church and Summerfield, 1994; Mayall, 1994; Qvortrup *et al.*, 1994; Hernandez, 1995; Brannen and O'Brien, 1996). In the conflicts between mothers and fathers, stepmothers and step-fathers, 'children with their naturally intense bonding ability become the only partners who do not leave' (Beck, German Edition 1986:1992, p. 109). Support organisations for lone and stepfamilies, specialist relational and child welfare professionals, and academic researchers agree that while some children experience only relief at the leaving of an abusing parent, or reduction of stress at the end of a conflict-stricken family situation, most experience a sense of loss: there is no replacement for a parent. And while the divorce-extended family of half- and step-siblings, additional grandparents and a whole array of other relatives may enrich the lives of many children, for others it brings the attenuation and sometimes the loss of one whole branch of their original family. Whatever the longer-term outcome, almost all children experience intense difficulties during family breakdown and the transition to either lone family or family reconstitution, foremost among which are the multiplication and intensification of conflicting loyalties and the renegotiation of previously unquestioned intimate and domestic relationships.

It has become almost commonplace that boy children bear a disproportionate amount of the cost of choice. While young boys and youths have always been associated with trouble, their behaviour has been thrown into greater relief by the notable educational successes and growing competence and confidence of girls. Parental choices, it is claimed, have left boys without decent male role models and hence prey to the anti-social tendencies of the peer group (Dennis and Erdos 1992). This growing worry about boys is conceived as part of a crisis of masculinity occasioned by the way in which 'the combination of feminism and changes in the economy have undermined the assumption that masculinity entitled men to a superior position' (Coward, 1999; Faludi 1999; Phillips, M. 1999).

Not only have men slowly lost the material comforts of the willing slave at home, but also the social status and self-esteem of a masculinity tied up with the capacity to be a breadwinner and afford a full-time housewife-mother. When the dual-earner mode was chosen voluntarily by couples, it enabled an incremental modification of gender roles and a quiet renegotiation of masculinity and femininity. When it became an economic necessity in situations where it was often easier for women to get and keep jobs than it was for men, it presented a stark challenge to the self-esteem and sense of identity of both partners and the relationship between them. It is no accident that there has been a clutch of hugely popular films around these themes, of which probably *Brassed Off* and *The Full Monty* are the best examples from the UK.

The impact of these changes on the capacity and willingness of the next generation of young men, particularly those without marketable skills, to become responsible partners and fathers is a matter of some concern. Some find the answer to the lack of money and status in the informal and illegal economy, but often with the consequence of acculturation into the local criminal milieu and getting caught. Women, in the same blighted environments, on the whole have another identity and set of responsibilities in relation to children wherefrom they derive a sense of purpose and authority. Less set adrift by the employment situation, more embedded in interpersonal support networks, they remain more in control of their lives for their kids' sake. Hence they become less dependent on men, and less willing to tolerate their bad behaviour. In turn, the men feel less obliged to stay when the mother and children are able to manage.

These changes in work and family life have led to the growing polarisation of the population into the work-rich and the work-poor, and together with the reductions in welfare spending in the 1980s and 90s have resulted in the economic stratification of and increase of poverty among children in the UK and the USA, with the children of lone mothers faring worst of all (Rainwater and Smeeding, 1995; Ditch *et al.*, 1997; Ely *et al.*, 1999). The decrease of labour market activity by lone mothers is a particular worrying feature in the light of

Kiernan's (1996) research using a British national longitudinal survey, which demonstrated that the educational attainment, economic position, family formation and dissolution behaviour of children from lone mother households positively correlated with maternal employment. Indeed outcomes for daughters were similar to those from intact dual-earner families.

However, the issue which equally affects the majority of children given the normalisation of the working mother is the reduction of access they have to their mothers' time. We have seen that despite the impression sometimes conveyed by purveyors of the globalisation thesis, the majority of fathers continue to work full-time, the majority of women part-time. Nevertheless, given women's 'double-shift', the time left for undivided attention to children is very limited. Children of professional/managerial couples may get even less since both parents tend to be employed full-time and work on average about 15 hours a week longer than other two-earner families. An industry of professional and informal child-carers has mushroomed in both the US and the UK to fill the gap left by working parents. Etzioni (1993) does not think such substitutes can invest the time, energy and commitment to children that parents do, and predicts an ensuing crisis in both countries brought about by this 'parenting deficit':

> Between 1960 and 1990 American and British society allowed children to be devalued, while the golden call of 'making it' was put on a high pedestal . . . few people who advocated equal rights for women favoured a society in which sexual equality would mean a society in which all adults would act like men, who in the past were relatively inattentive to children. (pp. 18–19)

Etzioni has been criticised for his failure to relate the parenting deficit to the radical individualism of the market economy and its failure to provide adequately for families without requiring long absences of parents from the home (Derber, 1993). In addition, although he pointedly denies that he is advocating returning women to the home, and always emphasises the need for fathers to be directly involved with child-rearing, it is disingenuous of him to ignore the gendered structure and culture of employment. It is neither rational in instrumental terms nor culturally acceptable for most men to work shorter hours and take off time for child-care. Nevertheless, we have seen in Chapter 8 that there are a number of feminist professional women who echo Etzioni's concerns and have braved being castigated as part of the anti-feminist backlash, to write about why women, including many feminists, remain committed to children and family life. However, their analysis of work organisations is more realistic than his and their proposals certainly more radical.

Governments in the USA and the UK have come under increased pressure from across the political spectrum to provide a public policy framework to respond to the costs of choice. It is not surprising that such policy responses reflect the complexity and the contradictions endemic to contemporary family life. On the one hand, governments recognise that the current pluralism in family forms is an outcome of long-term socio-economic trends, has many positive features and should not be negatively measured against a golden age of the family which did not exist. On the other, a central justification for increased intervention in family life is that families are under stress, indicators of which are child poverty, domestic violence, poor health, school-age pregnancy, educational underachievement, rising crime and drug abuse, a syndrome of symptoms strongly associated with family break-down. The Clinton and Blair Governments strain not to be judgmental about different types of personal relationships and family forms, yet continue to stress that according to the same indicators, the ideal of marriage offers the best option for satisfying the human need for intimacy, love, affection and companionship, and the two-parent family the optimum support system for children.

While policy development in America is more diverse than in Britain because of the significant autonomy of the individual states, one can find commonality of policy responses. On the one hand there is little evidence that taxation is being used as carrot or stick to get couples to the altar, and divorce legislation is increasingly based on the 'no-fault, clean-break' principle. On the other, divorce proceedings have been slowed down with the introduction of marital counselling and conciliation options and there has been a tightening up on men's financial familial responsibility through enforcement of child maintenance and 'pension splitting' on divorce or at the point of retirement. Family-friendly employment practices have been promoted, and packages of parental rights, and working families tax credits introduced. Other policies include holistic programmes of child support for disadvantaged families, help-lines for parents, and programmes that target fathers' greater involvement with children, as well as a range of other initiatives for dealing more effectively with serious family problems such as truanting and disruption in school, youth offending, teenage parenthood and domestic violence, which involve grandparents, schools, voluntary organisations as well as related public sector professionals. Of course this policy agenda has not satisfied everyone and has further antagonised many feminists as well as moral conservatives and economic liberals. However, whatever the practical weaknesses, pious earnestness and financial underfunding of these measures, they certainly demonstrate public recognition of the fiction of the public–private divide.

'Family' as a unifying symbol in a fragmented world

We have seen the interest and passion that the question of 'the family' can generate among the very disparate populations in the UK and the USA. Despite the very different economic, social and cultural contexts, people think they are talking about the same thing. This is because the term 'the family' operates at another register. It is not a distillation of the lived experience of discrete family life, but an abstraction which has significance in religious, moral, medical, biological, psychological, sociological, legal discourses. Since the family occupies a different place in these different discourses, no one consistent meaning adheres to it. Rather, through them it circulates and constructs an ideological world of familial terms, values, relationships, connotations. It is through participation in this ideological universe of meaning that people derive their aspirations, expectations of, respect for and commitments to family life in the abstract, which survives experiences of disappointment and even brutality. It is not divorced from their experience – indeed it would not have the pull on their sentiments if it was. However, inasmuch as the formulation for family form and intimacy is constructed by the practices of the professional practitioners of such discourses, and others with power in the material framework of family life, such as employers, their experience approximates to it.

This may be one reason for the gap often noted between the positive responses of public opinion in survey questions about the family and the apparently contradictory behaviour of large numbers of them, and indeed the ease with which people can live in this contradiction. This has little to do with hypocrisy. Nor can it be explained by 'false consciousness', by which a very large majority of the population are consigned to imbecility. 'The family' is a symbolic signifier, rather like democracy or justice, which image calls up a whole range of emotional and moral responses to which people feel allegiance. It exceeds the dominant familial form with which it is often discursively associated, such that commitment is not dependent on it. Indeed, I have argued that central to progressive politics since the early 1980s has been the attempt to appropriate those symbolic connotations of 'the family' and attach them to other forms of personal relationships and domestic organisation. This strategy has been relatively successful in relation to the lone parent with dependent children which has become normalised as 'the Lone Parent Family'. Gays and lesbians have been less successful in their campaigns for equivalent status for their 'family' form, exemplified by the continued refusal by the courts to change the categories of biological persons who are allowed to marry, and the difficulties incurred in cases of the custody of children.

Most people live a pragmatic relationship with 'the family', as they do with other normative ideals in relation to behaviour. It provides the means of voluntary regulation of modes of intimacy and care, it indicates a moral and emotional economy of desire; and it sets the parameters for social tolerance and the points of external intervention. People's practical knowledge provides them with a recognition that their own family lives and those of their neighbours vary within these boundaries and only ever approximate to the ideals which the term 'family' connote. Both the ideals and their approximation in behaviour 'float', to borrow a term from Donzelot, in relation to each other and in relation to changes in discursive constructions and practices in which they are inscribed. Contrary to the claims of feminists and the wishes of the moral crusaders, it is successful precisely because it *does not impose* a particular form by which these norms are to be achieved. Clearly one form – marriage and the two-parent family – is privileged ideologically, though increasingly not unconditionally, and certainly not uniformly in practice, as we have seen. The primary policy focus, quite sensibly in an age of diverse family situations, is increasingly on children and parenthood. It would be politically, economically, ideologically and organisationally impossible to successfully impose a particular family form in the conditions of contemporary western societies. However, if the costs of increasing individualism and choice in personal life are not addressed, attempts to restrict the parameters and inflict punitive consequences for non-conformity cannot be ruled out, as the contemporary history of the politics of the family outlined in this book has demonstrated.

Conclusion

A question of interests

If, as I have argued, there is no discursive unity to the term, the family, and the experience of familial relationships merely approximates in different ways to the family ideal, there can be no unambiguous set of interests which can be derived from it. Yet, it was precisely the feminist construction of the interests of the family as inimical to those of women that engendered the moral outrage and fear that was given organisational form in pro-life, anti-Equal Rights Amendment (ERA), pro-family and censorship campaigns and formulated women's interests very differently. However, both feminists and pro-family groups claimed that theory and practice was based on women's interests *as grounded in women's experience*. Both anti-familialist and pro-familialist forces regarded themselves as simply organisational expressions of the reality of women's lived experience of marriage and the family.

That experience, however, is diverse and differentiated, cut across by class, cultural, racial, ethnic, regional and educational differences. What is more, it does not present itself directly to the actors as the grounds for identity or for shared interests. How the experience of family life is understood crucially depends on the different access to and engagement with discourses through which meanings are constructed about the nature of the individual and social relations, of sexuality and sexual difference, of personal identity and social responsibility, of the sacred and the profane. It is these which make sense of lived experience and create vulnerabilities to specific moral and political ideologies.

As we have seen, it is the ideologies of feminism, liberalism, socialism, Christianity and conservatism, and the organisational forces which promote them that construct the interests of the family and those of women. They provide accounts of the situation of the contemporary family and women and suggest how these would change by, for example, liberalisation of abortion, equal pay, easier divorce, ERA, positive discrimination in education and employment, free accessible contraception, and so on. All of these are subject to different assessments by the contending individuals and organisations and it is the clash of these assessments which constitute the disputes in the public arena and define the issues in the politics of the family. Such calculations are conducted within and influenced by national traditions. It was during the process of the struggle between feminist and moral conservationist organisations and the movements they generated that the interests of women became formulated and re-formulated and indeed became the subject of intense public interest. It is ironic that as a consequence, more people in Britain and America became aware of the issues at stake and their complexities than the combatants could have imagined. As a consequence neither the progressive nor the conservative side have managed to hegemonise the discourse of interests, precisely because of the variety of constructions of interests – women, children, the family, men, the tax-payer, employers, social stability – to which the general public became exposed.

It is against this stalemate that recent writings and activities of women who identify themselves with the feminist label indicate a determination to move the debate on and connect the cause of women's equality with non-aligned women, and especially the 'I'm not a feminist but . . . ' younger generation.

There is a question to be posed: does it matter if the majority of women do not identify with feminism, if their well-recorded support for equal rights, equal pay, equal opportunities and equal treatment is actually an expression of the values of equality and equity more generally. This may be the case *but* in the context of fairly widespread recognition that substantive inequalities and unfairness in relation to women persist, it is in effect an expression of a belief that women *ought* to be equal to men. And that for me is the essence of feminism.

How far is the achievement of that goal in the twenty-first century obstructed by the persistence of the family? For many feminists, the obstacle to women's equality lies in the power differential between women and men rooted in the family which will persist so long as the family does. Men's power over women's confidence, self-esteem, material resources, time, priorities and behaviour within the family is paralleled by their control over women's opportunities and advancement in the workplace and in the public sphere more generally. However, reflection on the changes in the power balance between men and women as a result of the economic, social and cultural transformations that have occurred in western societies since the mid 20th century, but which began two centuries ago, suggests a revision of that position is now due. The increasing capacity for a pro-family movement largely composed of women to claim the middle ground on the question of women's interests and the family, and marginalise feminism, adds urgency to the task of feminists to rethink the family.

A review of this feminist revision and independent research certainly suggests that the feminist aim of women's equality and the realities of family life are still at odds. But it also raises the question of whether it is men or children that are now the main cause of the continuing conflict. Given the decreasing gap in indicators of inequality between men and women in their twenties of the same educational and occupational status, and between older professional and managerial women without children and their male counterparts, it does not appear a rational economic choice for women to have children in terms of their own individual advancement. There may be some grounds for regarding children as a source of a flow of resources to poor, unqualified and unskilled women, through a male earner and/or welfare services and benefits. If there are such advantages they are relatively short term, leading to long-term poverty for the women, a life of disadvantage for their children and, for the state, a significant aspect of the looming crisis of pension provision.

However, if we consider that many women do not consider work a life-time continuous process, or inherently interesting and rewarding, or of primary importance to their sense of identity, we may come to the view that having children is a rational choice for them. In this respect, they have greater choice than do men, many of whom likewise have routine jobs with little autonomy or satisfaction and poor remuneration. The difference is that the decision to leave work to rear children is a legitimate one in our culture for women, though increasingly hedged with conditions, but not generally for men. There is an underlying, often unconscious optionality about work for women deriving from their role in biological reproduction and the associated mothering function, which there is not for men.

Beck (1986:1992), makes the following insightful remark about the importance of this choice for female behaviour:

> As long as women bear children, nurse them, feel responsible for them, and see them as an essential part of their lives, children remain wished-for 'obstacles' in the occupational competition, as well as temptations to a conscious decision *against* economic autonomy and a career. In this way, the lives of women are pulled back and forth by this contradiction between liberation from and reconnection to the old ascribed roles. This is also reflected in their consciousness and behaviour. They flee from housework to a career and back again, and attempt in different phases of their lives to hold together the diverging conditions of their life 'somehow' through contradictory decisions. (p.112)

The personal reflections of the 'third wave feminists' outlined in Chapter 8 bear out these observations. Their additional insight is that it is through this process that women collude with men in 'letting men get their way' (Coward, 1992).

But the voices of these women speak of more than ambivalence about work and the role that motherhood plays in accommodating it. They speak of falling in love with their babies and describe an emotional and physical attachment to them that can best be described by what Winnicott (1965) called 'primary maternal pre-occupation'. As we saw, some of these feminists rather sheepishly attribute this maternal sensitivity to biology. However, this seems to persevere long after the stage described by Winnicott and there may be grounds for linking it to the broader changes between men and women and in family relationships. Is romantic heterosexual love being replaced for women by a romantic love for children, in the Giddens (1992) sense of seeking in the other that which will fill the lack in ourselves?

We have noted in Chapter 1 that the historical development of the privatised, child-centred 'bourgeois' family was a slow and uneven process, and that it was not until the end of the Second World War that it became general across all social classes when the view of the necessity of a close one-to-one relationship between mother and child became orthodoxy. There were those who already in the 1950s were expressing doubts about the wisdom of this intense concentration on the child:

> Society is in the process of making parenthood a highly self-conscious, self-regarding affair. In doing so it is adding heavily to the sense of personal responsibility among parents. Their tasks are much harder and involve more risks of failure when children have to be brought up as individual

successes in a supposedly mobile, individualistic society rather than in a traditional and repetitious society...More decisions have to be made because there is so much more to be decided; and as the margins of felt responsibility extend so does the scope for anxiety about one's children. (Titmuss, 1954, p.9)

Of course most of these pressures fall on mothers. These high expectations of intensive mothering have not diminished in the last 30 years. To them have been added the normal expectation of female employment, the increased educational success and aspirations of women. In the context of increased insecurity in the lives of men it is not surprising that differences between men and women's expectations of each other are intensified and marriage is under considerable stress.

Whereas before it was men who traversed the public–private divide, who derived an independent life through their work and related activities, the pub, the football match, the golf course or the political meeting, increasingly women too are claiming a life outside the family and are coming face-to-face with the inequalities of the conventional assumptions and arrangements, particularly in relation to childcare. In the new consciousness, which feminism has helped to raise, and in the new role of joint provider, women have become aware that the taken-for-granted domestic and childcare activities are sacrifices they make on behalf of the collective enterprise of the family but which are not reciprocated by the other party. Fatherhood has been compatible with work and an extra-familial life in a way that motherhood has not. There have not been the structural forces to propel men out of their traditional identity and roles; hence new men are thin on the ground. To a large extent women have done the adapting to and accommodating of the economic, social and cultural forces that have changed the British and American social landscape since the 1950s and they have become more aware of it.

Central to much family conflict are issues about equity and commitment in relation to the nurturing and caring that lies at the heart of family functions. Some modern men are voluntarily committed to sharing in these routine necessities of family survival, or they can be persuaded, cajoled, guilt-tripped or bullied. For those who cannot, the door is the ultimate answer. Women's greater independence enables them to flex their muscle with regard to what they will tolerate in male behaviour. Of course, it is often the case that the male has been lining up a new feathered bed as an insurance against just such an eventuality.

In the disappointment, anger and grief at the disintegration of what for the most part had been intended as a life-time commitment it may be that women increasingly seek in their children, their anchor, the stability, consistency and unconditionality of love which they first seek in the romantic relationship with men:

> The child is the source of the last remaining, irrevocable, unexchangeable primary relationship. Partners come and go. The child stays. Everything that is desired, but not realisable in the relationship, is directed to the child... It is the private type of re-enchantment, which arises with, and derives its meaning from disenchantment. (Beck, 1986:1992, p.118)

This disenchantment is not only with men, but also with the impersonal, fragmented and instrumental nature of most contemporary employment. Time and again the women subjects as well as the feminist writers in Chapter 8 report that there is something missing from the satisfaction they get from work, which they seek in the wholeness and completely absorbing relationship with their babies. Certainly it would seem that it is a feeling and a desire which is shared by many economically independent professional women who have children in their 30s or later. Their delay is only partly because of career imperatives; they are also increasingly discriminating about with whom they wish to parent, to the extent that many choose to have children without live-in partners. These women will not be slaves to men, but they may become slaves to their children partly as a result of investing all their emotional needs in infants whose demands are inherently elastic and dictatorial, and partly through their internalisation of the professionalisation of amateur motherhood and the philosophy of maternal altruism.

On the other hand, the high figures for re-marriage suggest that children are not adequate substitutes for adult relationships of intimacy and companionship for most women. Some commentators explain this need for bonding with another human being as a fundamental social need reinforced by the particular psycho-dynamics of mothering in western societies (Chodorow, 1978; 1989). Others hold that the increasing individualism, together with the fragmentation and superficiality of social relationships and the loss of overarching belief systems in post-modern life, lead to a search for another person who can fill up the emptiness and disperse the loneliness of contemporary existence (Lasch, 1977; Beck, 1986:92) Others suggest more down-to-earth incentives, such as the improvement in the family's standard of living that follows re-marriage.

None mention desire – that psychical and sexual energising interest in the Other – which defies being tailored to the logic of equality and common sense. Combine that desire with the other factors above, and it is likely that marriage and the two-parent family with offspring will continue to attract the majority of people at some time in their lives. It is becoming the desired mode for many gay and lesbian couples. However, the conflicts endemic to the current inequalities in hetero-sexual unions will continue to result in the dissolutions of a substantial minority, periods of non-familial living, alone or cohabiting, followed for the majority by further renewed attempts at a permanent commit-ment to partnership, involving ever more complex familial networks of relationships, responsibilities and residences. While Stacey (1990; 1996) has a point in celebrating the ingenuity, personal choice, diver-sity and potential for democracy in the intimate relationships of post-modernity, she does not convey the sheer physical and psychological exhaustion incurred in sustaining them.

Back to the future: feminism, women's equality and the family in the twenty-first century

There is a crisis in family life and it does stem from the contradiction between the partial achievement of feminist ideals for women's greater equality and the institutional framework of their lives which assumes their inequality. Women are angry, resentful, but above all disap-pointed in men. Men are largely confused. Children are anxious. Grandparents are uncomprehending. Governments are muddled and largely paralysed.

Yet, clichéd though the phrase is, there *is* no turning back the clock. The taste of freedom is not to be forgotten, no matter how bitter-sweet it might be. The assumptions underlying the gender relations of the 1950s have been de-legitimated, as testified by divorce court revela-tions of the combination of trivial squabbles and full-scale domestic conflict that go toward the ground for 'irretrievable breakdown of marriage'. The case for women's equality has been won in the hearts and minds of most of the British and American population even if there is a lack of awareness and some outright resistance to what it means to operationalise this principle in practice. Certainly, the further development of gender equality is obstructed as much by the substantive inequalities in practice in institutions which provide the formal opportunities for equality, as it is by personal prejudice, lack of will or insufficient ambition or determination. The source of these intended and unintended inequalities in today's world is less the conflict of interests between men and women, than that between women as individuals and children.

A gender equality, therefore, which is compatible with family life, with or without men, cannot be achieved until governments and businesses realise that the erosion of trust, commitment, emotional welfare and sense of social responsibility that accompanies the erosion of personal and family life, is undermining the social and cultural conditions for an effective economy and a stable society. This requires the re-integration and reconciliation of work and family for both sexes since it is the orientation of work organisations to the outmoded male breadwinner model that is the main external source of the inequalities and conflict within families and the increasing poverty of children's lives. The proposals outlined by 'third wave feminists' suggest the scale of the re-engineering of organisations this will require.

Such an organisational transformation will not happen unless there is a strong demand for it, and that demand has to mobilised and organised. Despite their apparent weak position in the labour market as individuals, on aggregate women are in a strong position. The female labour force is now an integral part of western economies. In intimate relations, despite remaining inequalities and abuse of power in some families, women have a new self-confidence, which comes partly from the shift in public opinion that recognises the failure of many men to adjust to the new economic realities and cultural climate. Feminism was a formidable political force for a short period in the 1960s and 1970s. For external and internal reasons it retreated largely to the academy where it has continued to be a powerful intellectual force in both America and Britain, but where it has lost its connection and appeal as a movement with the majority of their female populations. However, were sufficiently substantial strands of feminism to re-engage fully with the issues which the majority of women identify as their priorities, it could be a vital factor in achieving those goals and at the same time counter the negative image which many women have of it. A renegotiation of the contract between men and women and between them and the social and political institutions which regulate it, is well overdue, as is the redefinition of the family to bring it into line with contemporary realities without undermining the ideals which inspire our dreams and guide our conduct. A revitalised feminism characterised by a principled pragmatism could be a major force in carrying such an agenda forward in the twenty-first century.

References

AABY, P. (1977) 'Engels and Women', *Critique of Anthropology*, vol. 3, nos 9 and 10.

ABBOTT, P. and WALLACE, C. (1992) *The Family and the New Right*. Pluto Press, London.

ABEL-SMITH, B. and TOWNSEND, P. (1965) *The Poor and the Poorest*. Bell, London.

ABRAMOVITZ, M. (1982) 'The Conservative Program is a Woman's Issue', *Journal of Sociology and Social Welfare*, vix (Sept.).

ACOCK, A. A. and DEMO, D. H. (1994) *Family Diversity and Well-Being*. Sage, Thousand Oaks, California.

ADAMS, P. (1982) 'Family Affairs', *m/f*, no. 7.

AGLIETTA, M. (1979) *A Theory of Capitalist Regulation: The US Experience*. New Left Books, London.

ALLEN, S. (1982) 'Political Lerbianism and Feminism: Space for a Sexual Politics.' m/f, no. 7.

ALSTON, J. P. and TUCKER, F. (1983) 'The Myth of Sexual Permissiveness', *Journal of Sex Research*, vol. 9, no. 1 (February).

ALTHUSSER, L. (1969) *For Marx*. Penguin, Harmondsworth.

ALTHUSSER, L. (1971) 'Ideology and Ideological State Apparatuses', in *Lenin and Philosophy and Other Essays*. New Left Books, London.

ANDERSON, D. and DAWSON, G. (1986) *Family Portraits*. The Social Affairs Unit, London.

ANDERSON, M. (1980) *Approaches to the History of the Western Family 1500–1914*. Macmillan, Basingstoke.

ANDERSEN, M. L. (1991) 'Feminism and the American Family Ideal', *Journal of Comparative Family Studies*, vol. 22, no. 2.

ARENDALL, T. (1986) *Mother and Divorce: Legal, Economic and Social Dilemmas*. University of California Press, Berkeley.

ARIES, P. (1960) *Centuries of Childhood*. Penguin, Harmondsworth.

ATKINS, S. R. E. and HOGGETT, B. (1984) *Women and the Law*. Basil Blackwell, Oxford.

BANKS, O. (1981) *Faces of Feminism: A Study of Feminism as a Social Movement*. Martin Robertson, Oxford.

BANKS, O. (1986) *Becoming a Feminist: The Social Origins of 'First Wave' Feminism*. Wheatsheaf, Brighton.

BARRETT, M. and McINTOSH, M. (1982) *The Anti-Social Family*. Verso, London.

BECK, U. (German edition 1986; 1992) *Risk Society: Towards a New Modernity*. Sage, London.

BECKER, G. S. (1991) *A Treatise on the Family*. Harvard University Press, Cambridge, Mass.

BENN, M. (1998) *Madonna and Child: Towards a New Politics of Motherhood*. Jonathan Cape, London.

BENNETT, F., CAMPBELL, B. and COWARD, R. (1980) 'Feminists – Degenerates of the Social?', in *Politics and Power 3*. Routledge & Kegan Paul, London.

BERGER, B. and BERGER, P. (1984) *The War Over The Family: Capturing the Middle Ground*. Penguin, Harmondsworth.

BERNARD, J. (1981) 'Facing the Future', *Society*, no. 18 (Jan./Feb.).

BERRY, M. F. (1986) *Why the ERA Failed: Politics, Women's Rights and the Amending Process of the Constitution*. Indiana University Press, Bloomington, Indiana.

BEVERIDGE, SIR W. (1942) *Social Insurance and Allied Services (the Beveridge Report)*. HMSO, Cmnd 6404, London.

BIANCHI, S. (1991) *Family Disruptions and Economic Hardship: Survey of Income and Programme Participation*. US Bureau of the Census. March 1991, Series P-70, no. 23.

BLAND, L. (1978) 'Sex and Morals: Rearming the Left', *Marxism Today*, September.

BLAND, L. (1995) *Banishing the Beast: English Feminism and Sexual Morality 1885–1914*. Penguin, Harmondsworth.

BLAU, F. D. and EHRENBERG, R. G. (eds) (1998) *Gender and Family Issues in the Workplace*. Russell Sage, New York.

BOLCE, L., DE MAIO, G. and MUZZIO, D. (1982) 'ERA and the Abortion Controversy: A Case of Dissonance Reduction', *Social Science Quarterly*, vol. 67, part 2.

BOLES, J. (1979) *The Politics of the Equal Rights Amendment: Conflict and the Decision Process*. Longmans, New York.

BOLES, J. (ed.) (1991) *American Feminism: New Issues for a Mature Movement*. Sage, Newbury Park, CA.

BOLOTIN, S. (1982) 'Voices from a Post-Feminist Generation', *New York Times Magazine*, 17th October.

BOSANQUET, N. (1983) *After the New Right*. Heinemann, London.

BOTT, E. (1957) *Family and Social Network: Roles, Norms and Relationships in Ordinary Urban Families*. Tavistock, London.

BOUCHIER, D. (1978) *Idealism and Revolution: New Ideologies of Liberation in Britain and the US*. Edward Arnold, London.

BOUCHIER, D. (1983) *The Feminist Challenge: The Movement for Women's Liberation in Britain and the United States*. Macmillan, London.

BOWLBY, J. (1953) *Child Care and the Growth of Love*. Penguin, Harmondsworth.

BOWLES, S. and GINTIS, H. (1986) *Democracy and Capitalism: Property, Community and the Contradictions of Modern Social Thought.* Routledge & Kegan Paul, London.

BRADSHAW, J. and MILLAR, J. (1991) *Lone Parents in the UK. DSS Research Report no. 6.* HMSO, London.

BRADSHAW, J. et al. (1996) *The Employment of Lone Parents: A Comparison of Policy in 20 Countries.* Family Policy Studies Centre, London.

BRADY, D. W. and TEDIN, K. L. (1976) 'Ladies in Pink: Religion and Political Ideology in the Anti-ERA Movement', *Social Science Quarterly*, vol. 56 (March).

BRANNEN, J. and O'BRIEN, M. (eds) (1996) *Children in Families: Research and Policy.* The Falmer Press, London.

BRASS, W. (1989) 'Is Britain Facing the Twilight of Parenthood?', in Joshi, H. (ed.), *The Changing Population of Britain.* Basil Blackwell, Oxford.

BREINES, W., CERULLO, M. and STACEY, J. (1978) 'Social Biology, Family Studies and Antifeminist Backlash', *Feminist Studies*, vol. 4, no. 1 (February).

BRENNER, J. (1993) 'The Best of Times, The Worst of Times: US Feminism Today', *New Left Review*, no. 200 (July/August).

BROWN, B. (1978) 'Natural and Social Division of Labour – Engels and the Domestic Labour Debate', *m/f*, no. 1.

BROWN, G. (1987) 'Sustaining Families and the Legal System', in Whitfield (1987).

BROWN, L. (1979) 'The Family and its Genealogies – a Discussion of Engel's Origin of the Family', *m/f* no. 3.

BROWNMILLER, S. (1975) *Against Our Will.* Bantam Books, NY.

BURCHILL, J. (1992) *Sex and Sensibility.* Grafton, London.

BURGHES, L., CLARKE, L. and CRONIN, N. (1997) *Fathers and Fatherhood in Britain.* Family Policy Studies Centre, London.

BURRIS, V. (1983) 'Who Opposed the ERA? An Analysis of the Social Bases of Antifeminism', *Social Science Quarterly*, vol. 64, part 2.

BUXTON, J. (1998) *Ending the Mother War: Starting the Workplace Revolution.* Macmillan, London

CAMPBELL, B. (1987) *The Iron Ladies: Why Do Women Vote Tory?*, Virago, London.

CASPER, L. M., COHEN, P. N. and SIMMONS, T. (1999) *How Does POSSLQ Measure Up? Historical Estimates of Cohabitation.* US Census Bureau, Washington, DC.

CASTELLS, M. (1977) *The Urban Question: A Marxist Approach.* Edward Arnold, London.

CHODOROW, N. (1978) *The Reproduction of Mothering: Psychoanalysis and the Sociology of Gender.* University of California Press, Berkeley.

CASTELLS, M. (1977) *The Urban Question: A Marxist Approach.* Edward Arnold, London.

CHODOROW, N. (1989) *Feminism and Psychoanalytic Theory.* Polity Press, Cambridge.

CHURCH, J. and SUMMERFIELD, C. (1994) *Social Focus on Children.* HMSO, London.

CHURCH, J. and SUMMERFIELD, C. (1995) *Social Focus on Women*. HMSO, London.

CLARK, D. (ed.) (1991) *Marriage, Domestic Life and Social Change*. Routledge, London.

CLARKE, P. (1996) *Hope and Glory: Britain 1900–1990*, Penguin, Harmondsworth.

CLIFF, D. (1979) 'Religion, Morality and the Middle Class', in King, R. and Nugent, N. (eds), *Respectable Rebels: Middle Class Campaigns in Britain in the 1970s*. Hodder & Stoughton, London.

COCKETT, R. (1994) *Thinking the Unthinkable: Think-Tanks and the Economic Counter-Revolution, 1931–1983*. HarperCollins, London.

Conservative Digest (1979) 'Mobilising the Moral Majority', vol. 5, no. 8, (August).

Conservative Digest (1980) 'The Pro-Family Movement: Interview with Paul Weyrich'. vol. 6, no 5/6 (May/June).

COONTZ, S. (1988) *The Social Origins of Private Life: A History of American Families 1600–1900*. Verso, London.

COOPER, D. (1971) *The Death of the Family*. Penguin, Harmondsworth.

COOTE, A. and PATTULLO, P. (1990) *Power and Prejudice: Women and Politics*. Weidenfeld & Nicolson, London.

COSTAIN, A. N. (1980) 'The Struggle for a National Women's Lobby: Organising A Diffuse Interest', *Western Political Quarterly*, vol. 33.

COSTAIN, A. N. (1981) 'Representing Women: The Transition from Social Movement to Interest Group', *Western Political Quarterly*, vol. 34.

COULTAS, V. (1981) 'Feminists Must Face The Future', *Feminist Review*, no. 7 (Spring).

COWARD, R. (1983) *Patriarchal Precedents: Sexuality and Social Relations*. Routledge & Kegan Paul, London.

COWARD, R. (1992) *Our Treacherous Hearts: Why Women Let Men Get Their Way*. Faber & Faber, London.

COWARD, R. (1999) *Sacred Cows: Is Feminism Relevant to the New Millennium?* HarperCollins, London.

CRAWFORD, A. (1980) *Thunder on the Right: The 'New Right' and the Politics of Resentment*. Pantheon, New York.

CREIGHTON, C. (1999) 'The Rise and Decline of the "Male Breadwinner" Family in Britain', *Cambridge Journal of Economics*, vol. 23, no. 5, September.

CROMPTON, R. (1996) 'Paid Employment and the Changing System of Gender Relations', *Sociology*, vol. 30, no. 3.

CROMPTON, R. and MANN, M. (eds) (1986) *Gender and Stratification*. Polity Press, Cambridge.

DALLA COSTA, M. and JAMES, S. (1975) *The Power of Women and the Subversion of the Community*. Falling Wall Press, Bristol.

DALLY, A. (1982) *Inventing Motherhood: The Consquences of an Ideal*. Burnett Books, London.

DALY, M. (1979) *Gyn/Ecology*. The Women's Press, London.

DALY, M. (1984) *Pure Lust*. The Women's Press, London.

DAVID, M. (1983) 'The New Right in the USA and Britain: A New Anti-feminist Moral Economy', *Critical Social Policy*, vol. 2, no. 3 (Spring).

DAVID, M. (1986) 'Moral and Maternal: The Family in the Right', in Levitas, R. (ed.), *The Ideology of the New Right*. Polity Press, London.

DAVIDOFF, L. and HALL, C. (1987) *Family Fortunes: Men and Women of the English Middle Classes 1780–1850*. Hutchinson, London.

DAVIES, C. (1980) 'Moralists, Causalists, Sex, Law and Morality', in Armitage, W. H. G., Chester, K. and Peel, J. (eds), *Changing Patterns of Sexual Behaviour*. Martin Robertson, London.

DECTER, M. (1973) *The New Chastity and Other Arguments Against Women's Liberation*. Wildwood House, London.

DEGLER, C. N. (1980) *At Odds: Women and the Family in America from the Revolution to the Present*. Oxford University Press, NY.

DELMAR, R. (1976) 'Looking Again at Engel's Origin of the Family, Private Property and the State', in Mitchell, J. and Oakley, A. (eds), *The Rights and Wrongs of Women*. Penguin, Harmondsworth.

DENFELD, R. (1995) *The New Victorians: A Young Women's Challenge to the Old Feminist Order*. Warner Books, NY.

DENNIS, N. and ERDOS, G. (1992) *Families Without Fatherhood*. Institute of Economic Affairs, London.

Department of Social Security (1991) *Social Security Statistics 1990*. HMSO, London.

DERBER, C. (1993) 'Coming Glued: Communitarianism to the Rescue', *Tikkun*, vol. 8, no. 4.

DEWAR, J. (1992) *Law and the Family*. Butterworths, London.

DEX, S. and JOSHI, H. (1999) 'Careers and Motherhood: Policies for Compatibility', *Cambridge Journal of Economics*, vol. 23, no. 5, September.

DIAMOND, I. and CLARKE, S. (1989) 'Demographic Patterns among Britain's Ethnic Groups', in Joshi, H. (ed.), *The Changing Population of Britain*. Basil Blackwell, Oxford.

DIAMOND, I. and HARTSOCK, N. (1981) 'Beyond Interests in Politics: A Comment on Virginia Sapiro's "When are Interests Interesting? The Problem of Political Representation of Women"', *American Political Science Review*, 75.

DICKERSON, B. J. (1995) *African American Single Mothers*. Sage, Thousand Oaks, California.

DINNERSTEIN, D. (1976) *The Mermaid and the Minotaur* (also published as *The Rocking of the Cradle and the Ruling of the World*). Harper & Row Inc, New York; The Women's Press, London, 1987.

DIQUINZIO, P. and YOUNG, I. M. (eds) (1997) *Feminist Ethics and Social Policy*. Indiana University Press, Bloomington and Indianapolis.

DITCH, J., BARNES, H. and BRADSHAW, J. (eds) (1997) *Developments in National Family Policies 1996*. Commission of the European Communities, York.

DOANE, J. and HODGES, D. (1987) *Nostalgia and Sexual Difference: Resistance to Contemporary Feminism*. Methuen, New York; London.

DONZELOT, J. (1980) *The Policing of Families: Welfare Versus the State*. Hutchinson, London.

DORNBUSCH, S. A. and GRAY, K. D. (1988) 'Single-Parent Families', in Dornbush and Strober (1988).

DORNBUSCH, S. A. and STROBER, M. H. (eds). (1988) *Feminism, Children and the New Families*. The Guilford Press, New York.

DOUGLAS, J. W. B. (1964) *The Home and the School*. MacGibbon & Kee, London.

DUBY, G. (1994) *Love and Marriage in the Middle Ages*. Polity Press/Blackwell Publishers, Oxford.

DUNCAN, G. J. and HOFFMAN, S. D. (1988) 'What are the Economic Consequences of Divorce?', *Demography* 25, no. 4 (November).

DUNCAN, S. and EDWARDS, R. (1999) *Lone Mothers, Paid Work and Gendered Moral Rationalities*. Macmillan, Basingstoke.

DUNLEAVY, P. and HUSBANDS, C. T. (1985) *British Democracy at the Crossroads*. Allen & Unwin, London.

DURHAM, M. (1985) 'Family, Morality and the New Right', *Parliamentary Affairs: A Journal of Comparative Politics*, vol. 38, no. 2.

DURHAM, M. (1986) 'Class, Conservatism and the Anti-Abortion Movement: A Review Essay', *Berkeley Journal of Sociology*, no. 31.

DURHAM, M. (1989) 'The Thatcher Government and the "Moral Right"', *Parliamentary Affairs: A Journal of Comparative Politics*, vol. 42, no. 1.

DURHAM, M. (1991) *Sex and Politics: The Family and Morality in the Thatcher Years*. Macmillan, London.

DURHAM, M. (1993) 'The New Right, Moral Crusades and the Politics of the Family', *Economy and Society*, vol. 22, no. 2.

DWORKIN, A. (1981) *Pornography: Men Possessing Women*. Perigee Press, NY.

DWORKIN, A. (1983) *Right-Wing Women: The Politics of Domesticated Females*. The Women's Press, London.

EASTON, B. (1978) 'Feminism and the Contemporary Family', *Socialist Review*, 39, vol. 8, part 3.

EHRENREICH, B. (1981) 'The Women's Movements: Feminist and Anti-feminist', *Radical America*, vol. 15, nos 1–2 (Spring).

EHRENREICH, B. (1982a) 'Defeating the ERA: A Right-Wing Mobilization of Women', *Journal of Sociology and Social Welfare*, vol. 9, no. 2 (Sept).

EHRENREICH, B. (1982b) 'Family Feud on the Left', *The Nation*, 13th March.

EHRENREICH, B. (1983) *The Hearts of Men: American Dreams and the Flight from Commitment*. Pluto Press, London.

EISENSTEIN, Z. (1981) 'Anti-Feminism in the Politics and Election of 1980', *Feminist Studies*, vol. 7, no. 2 (Summer).

EISENSTEIN, Z. (1982) 'Some Thoughts on the Patriarchal State and the Defeat of the ERA', *Journal of Sociology and Social Welfare*, vol. 9, no. 2 (Sept.).

EISENSTEIN, Z. R. (1984) *Feminism and Sexual Equality: Crisis in Liberal America*. Monthly Review Press, New York.

ELLIOTT, B. JANE (1991) 'Demographic Trends in Domestic Life, 1945–87', in Clark, D. (ed.), *Marriage, Domestic Life and Social Change*. Routledge, London.

ELLIS, K. (1983) 'Can the Left Defend a Fantasised Family?', *Feminist Review*, no. 14; expanded version of article in *In These Times*, December 9–15, 1981.

ELSHTAIN, J. B. (1979) 'Feminists Against The Family', *The Nation*, 17 November.

ELSHTAIN, J. B. (1981) *Public Man, Private Woman: Women in Social and Political Thought*. Princeton University Press, Princeton.

ELY, M., RICHARDS, M. P. M., WADSWORTH, M. E. J. and ELLIOTT, B. J. (1999) 'Secular Changes in the Association of Parental Divorce and Children's Educational Attainment – Evidence from Three British Birth Cohorts', *Journal of Social Policy*, vol. 28, part 3, July.

ENGELS, F. (1884) *The Origin of the Family, Private Property and the State*, in *Marx-Engels: Selected Works*. Lawrence & Wishart, London, 1970.

ENGELS, F. (1892) *The Condition of the Working Class in England*. Penguin, Harmondsworth, 1987.

EPSTEIN, B. (1982) 'Family Politics and the New Left', *Socialist Review*, nos 63–64, vol. 12, nos 3–4 (May–August).

Equal, Opportunities Commission (1998) *a Brief Guide to Gender Statistics*. EOC London.

ERMISCH, J. (1989) 'Divorce: Economic Antecedents and Aftermath', in Joshi, H. (ed.) *The Changing Population of Britain*. Basil Blackwell, Oxford.

ETZIONI, A. (1993) *The Parenting Deficit*. Demos, London.

ETZIONI, A. (1995) *The Spirit of Community*. Fontana, London.

EVANS, S. (1979) *Personal Politics: The Roots of Women's Liberation in the Civil Rights Movement and the New Left*. Alfred A Knopf, New York.

FALUDI, S. (1992) *Backlash: The Undeclared War against Women*. Vintage, London.

FALUDI, S. (1999) *Stiffed: The Betrayal of Modern Man*. Chatto & Windus, London.

Family and Youth Concern (1987) *Family Bulletin*, no. 51 (Autumn).

FARGANIS, S. (1994) *Situating Feminism: From Thought To Action*. Sage, Thousand Oaks, California.

Feminist, Anthology Collective (1981) *No Turning Back: Writings from the Women Liberation Movement 1975–80*. Women's Press, London.

Feminist Review, Editorial (1982) 'Feminism and the Political Crisis of the Eighties', *Feminist Review*, no. 12 (Autumn).

FERRI, E. and SMITH, K. (1996) *Parenting in the 1990s*. Family Policy Studies Centre, London.

FIELD, F. (1976) 'Killing a Commitment: The Cabinet v the Children', *New Society*, 17 June.

FIELD, F. (1977) 'A Lobby For All Children', *New Society*, 29 September.

FIGES, K. (1994) *Because Of Her Sex: The Myth of Equality for Women in Britain*. Macmillan, London.

FINCH, J. (1989) *Family Obligations and Social Change*. Polity Press & Basil Blackwell, Oxford.

FINCH, J. (1990) 'The Politics of Community Care in Britain', in Ungerson, C., *Gender and Caring: Work and Welfare in Britain and Scandinavia*. Harvester Wheatsheaf, Hemel Hempstead.

FINCH, J. and SUMMERFIELD, P. (1991) 'Social Reconstruction and Companionate Marriage 1945–59', in Clark (1991).

FINCH, J. and MASON, J. (1993) *Negotiating Family Responsibilities*. Tavistock/Routledge, London.

FINER, SIR MAURICE (1974) *Report of the Committee on One-Parent Families (The Finer Report)*. HMSO, Cmnd 5629, 5629–1.

FIRESTONE, S. (1971) *The Dialectic of Sex: The Case for Feminist Revolution.* Jonathan Cape, London.

FISK, T. (1970) 'The Nature and Causes of Student Unrest', in Robson, W. B. and Crick, B. (eds), *Protest and Discontent.* Penguin, Harmondsworth.

FITZGERALD, T. (1983) 'The New Right and the Family', in Loney, M. *et al.* (eds), *Social Policy and Social Welfare.* Open University Press, Milton Keynes.

FLANDRIN, J-L. (1979) *Families in Former Times: Kinship, Household and Society.* Cambridge University Press, Cambridge.

FLANNERY, K. and ROELOF, S. (1984) 'Local Government Women's Committees', in Holland, J. (ed.), *Feminist Action, vol. 1.* Battle Axe Books, London.

FLETCHER, R. (1962) *Britain in the Sixties: The Family and Marriage.* Penguin, Harmondsworth.

FLETCHER, R. (1988) *The Abolitionists: The Family and Marriage Under Attack.* Routledge, London.

FOUCAULT, M. (1976; 1979) *The History of Sexuality vol. 1: An Introduction.* Allen Lane, Penguin, London.

FOX-GENOVESE, E. (1995) 'Feminism, Children and the Family', *Harvard Journal of Law and Public Policy,* vol. 18, no. 2.

FRANKS, S. (1999) *Having None of It: Women, Men and the Future of Work.* Granta Books, London.

FREDMAN, S. (1997) *Women and the Law.* Clarendon Press, Oxford.

FREEMAN, J. (1975) *The Politics of Women's Liberation.* David McKay, New York.

FRENCH, M. (1992) *The War Against Women.* Penguin, Harmondsworth.

FREUD, S. (1900) *The Interpretation of Dreams,* Pelican Freud Library, vol. 4. Penguin, Harmondsworth, 1976.

FREUD, S. (1923) *The Ego and the Id,* Pelican Freud Library, vol. 11. Penguin, Harmondsworth, 1984.

FREUD, S. (1925) 'Some Psychical Consequences of the Anatomical Distinction Between the Sexes', Pelican Freud Library, vol. 7: *On Sexuality.* Penguin, Harmondsworth, 1977.

FREUD, S. (1931) 'Female Sexuality', Pelican Freud Library, vol. 7: *On Sexuality.* Penguin, Harmondsworth, 1977.

FREUD, S. (1933) 'Femininity', Pelican Freud Library, vol. 2: *New Introductory Lectures.* Penguin, Harmondsworth, 1973.

FREUD, S. (1940) *An Outline of Psychoanalysis.* Hogarth Press, London, 1973.

FRIDAY, N. (1977) *My Mother/Myself.* Delacorte Press, NY.

FRIEDAN, B. (1963) *The Feminine Mystique.* Penguin, Harmondsworth.

FRIEDAN, B. (1979) 'Feminism Takes a New Turn', *New York Times Magazine,* 18th November.

FRIEDAN, B. (1983) *The Second Stage.* Abacus, London.

FRIEDAN, B. (1986) 'Review of "A Lesser Life"', *Time Magazine,* March.

FRIEDAN, B. (1997) *Beyond Gender: The New Politics of Work and Family.* Woodrow Wilson Center Press, Washington D.C.

FRIEDMAN, M. and FRIEDMAN, R. (1980) *Free to Choose.* Penguin, Harmondsworth.

FUKUYAMA, F. (1995) *Trust: The Social Virtues and the Creation of Prosperity.* Free Press, NY.

FUKUYAMA, F. (1997) *The End of Order.* The Social Market Foundation, London.

FUKUYAMA, F. (1999) *The Great Disruption: Human Nature and the Reconstitution of Social Order.* Profile Books, London.

GALBRAITH, J. K. (1958) *The Affluent Society.* Hamish Hamilton, London.

GALBRAITH, J. K. (1992) *The Culture of Contentment.* Sinclair-Stevenson, London.

GALLOP, G. and CASTELLI, J. (1989) *The People's Religion: American Faith in the 90s.* Macmillan, London.

GARDINER, J. (1983) 'Women, Recession and the Tories', in Hall, S. and Jacques, M. (eds), *The Politics of Thatcherism.* Lawrence & Wishart, London.

GATLIN, R. (1987) *American Women Since 1945.* Macmillan, London.

GAVRON, H. (1966) *The Captive Wife: Conflicts of Housebound Mothers.* Routledge & Kegan Paul, London.

GELB, J. (1990) 'Feminism and Social Action', in Dalton, R. J. and Kuchler, M. (eds), *Challenging the Political Order.* Polity Press, Cambridge.

GELB, J. and PALLEY, M. L. (1987) *Women and Public Policies.* Princeton University Press, Princeton.

GELLES, R. J. (1995) *Contemporary Families: A Sociological View.* Sage, London.

GIDDENS, A. (1987) *Sociology: A Brief But Critical Introduction*, 2nd edn. Macmillan, Basingstoke.

GIDDENS, A. (1992) *The Transformation of Intimacy: Sexuality, Love and Eroticism in Modern Societies.* Polity Press, Cambridge.

GIDDENS, A. (1998) *The Third Way.* Polity Press, London.

GILDER, G. (1973) *Sexual Suicide.* Quadrangle, New York Times Book Company, NY.

GILLIGAN, C. (1982) *In A Different Voice: Psychological Theory and Women's Development.* Harvard University Press, Cambridge, MA.

GITTENS, D. (1982) *Fair Sex: Family Size and Structure 1900–39.* Hutchinson, London.

GLAZER, N. (1978) 'The Rediscovery of the Family', *Commentary*, March.

GLEADLE, K. (1995) *The Early Feminists: Radical Unitarians and the Emergence of the Women's Rights Movement, 1831–51.* Macmillan, Basingstoke.

GLENDINNING, C. and MILLAR, J. (eds) (1992) *Women and Poverty in Britain – the 1990s.* Harvester Wheatsheaf, Hemel Hempstead.

GOLDBERG, S. (1973) *The Inevitability of Patriarchy.* Morow, New York.

GOLDTHORPE, J. H. (1983) 'Women and Class Analysis: In Defence of the Conventional View', *Sociology*, vol. 17, no. 4.

GOLDTHORPE, J. H. (1984) 'Women and Class Analysis: A Reply to the Replies', *Sociology*, vol. 18, no. 4.

GOODE, W. J. (1964) *The Family.* Prentice-Hall Englewood Cliffs, New Jersey.

GORDON, L. (1982) 'Why Nineteenth Century Feminists Did Not Support "Birth Control" and Twentieth Century Feminists Do', in Thorne, B. and

Yalom, M. (eds), *Rethinking the Family: Some Feminist Questions*. Longman, London and New York.

GORDON, L. and HUNTER, A. (1977/8) 'Sex, Family and the New Right: Anti-Feminism as a Political Force', *Radical America*, vols 11 & 12 part 6 & 1, Nov/Feb combined issue.

GORHAM, D. (1982) *The Victorian Girl and the Feminine Ideal*. Croom Helm, London.

GOSS, S. (1984) 'Women's Initiatives in Local Government', in Boddy, D. and Fudge, C. (eds), *Local Socialism*. Macmillan, London.

GOTTSCHALK, P. (1988) 'Retrenchment in Antipoverty Programs in the United States: Lessons for the future', in Kymlicka, B. B. and Matthews, J. V. (eds), *The Reagan Revolution?*. The Dorsey Press, Chicago.

GOULDNER, A. (1971) *The Coming Crisis of Western Sociology*. Heinemann, London.

GRANBERG, D. (1978) 'Pro-Life or Reflection of Conservative Ideology? An Analysis of Opposition to Legalised Abortion', *Sociology and Social Research*, vol. no. 62, 3.

GRANBERG, D. (1981) 'The Abortion Activists', *Family Planning Perspectives*, vol. 13, no. 4 (July–August).

GRANBERG, D. and GRANBERG, B. (1980) 'Abortion Attitudes, 1965–1980: Trends and Determinants', *Family Planning Perspectives*, vol. 12, no. 5.

GREEN, D. (1987) *The New Right*. Wheatsheaf, London.

GREER, G. (1970) *The Female Eunuch*. MacGibbon & Kee, London.

GREER, G. (1984) *Sex and Destiny: The Politics of Human Fertility*. Pan Books Ltd, London.

GREER, G. (1990) *Daddy We Hardly Knew You*. Penguin, Harmondsworth.

GREER, G. (1999) *The Whole Woman*. Doubleday, London.

GRIFFIN, S. (1971) *Pornography and Silence*. The Women's Press, London.

GURIN, P. (1985) 'Women's Gender Consciousness', *Public Opinion Quarterly*, vol. 49.

GUSFIELD, J. R. (1963) *Symbolic Crusade: Status, Politics and the American Temperance Movement*. University of Illinois Press, Urbana.

HAKIM, C. (1991) 'Grateful Slaves and Self-Made Women: Fact and Fantasy in Women's Work Orientations', *European Sociological Review*, no. 8.

HAKIM, C. (1992) 'Explaining Trends in Occupational Segregation: The Measurement, Causes and Consequences of the Sexual Division of Labour', *European Sociological Review*, no. 8.

HAKIM, C. (1995) 'Five Feminist Myths About Women's Employment', *British Journal of Sociology*, vol. 46, no. 3 (September).

HALL, S. and JACQUES, M. (eds) (1983) *The Politics of Thatcherism*. Lawrence & Wishart / Marxism Today, London.

HAMILL, L. (1978) *Wives as Sole and Joint Breadwinners*, Government Economic Service Working Paper, no. 15, HMSO, London.

HANDLER, J. (1995) *The Poverty of Welfare Reform*. Yale University Press, New Haven.

HANDY, C. (1997) *The Hungry Spirit: Beyond Capitalism – a Quest for Purpose in the Modern World*. Hutchinson, London.

HARDING, S. (1981) 'Family Reform Movements: Recent Feminism and its Opposition', *Feminist Studies*, vol. 7, no. 1 (Spring).

HARDYMENT, C. (1988) 'We Are Family', *Prospect*, June.

HARRINGTON, M. (1963) *The Other America*. Penguin, Harmondsworth.

HARRISON, F. (1977) *The Dark Angel: Aspects of Victorian Sexuality*. Fontana/Collins, Glasgow.

HARRISON, J. (1973) 'The Political Economy of Housework', *Bulletin of the Conference of Socialist Economists*, vol. 4.

HARRISS, K. (1989) 'New Alliances: Socialist-Feminism on the Eighties', *Feminist Review*, no. 31 (Spring).

HAYEK, F. A. (1960) *The Constitution of Liberty*. Routledge & Kegan Paul, London.

HEATH, A. and BRITTEN, N. (1984) 'Women's Jobs Do Make a Difference', *Sociology*, vol. 18, no. 4.

HENWOOD, M., RIMMER, L. and WICKS, M. (1987) *Inside the Family: The Changing Roles of Men and Women*. Family Policy Studies Centre, London.

HERNANDEZ, D. (1995) *America's Children: Resources from Family, Government and the Economy*. Russel Sage Foundation, NY.

HERON, L. (1981) 'The Mystique of Motherhood', in Feminist Anthology Collective (ed.), *Writings from the Women's Liberation Movement 1975–80*. The Women's Press, London.

HEWITT, P. (1993) *About Time: The Revolution in Work and Family Life*. Institute of Public Policy Research, London.

HEWLETT, S. A. (1986) *A Lesser Life: The Myth of Women's Liberation in America*. Sphere Books, Suffolk, 1988.

HILDREW, P. and SMITH, S. (1987) 'New Campaign Urges Thatcher to Tackle Crisis in Family Life', *The Guardian*, 2nd October.

HILLS, J. (1981) 'Britain', in Lovenduski, J. and Hills, J. (eds), *The Politics of the Second Electorate: Women and Public Participation*. Routledge & Kegan Paul, London.

HIMMELSTEIN, J. L. (1986) 'The Social Basis of Anti-Feminism: Religious Networks and Culture', *Journal for the Scientific Study of Religion*. vol. 25, no. 1 (March).

HINDESS, B. (1987) *Politics and Class Analysis*. Basil Blackwell, Oxford.

HIRST, P. Q. (1981) 'The Genesis of the Social', *Politics and Power*, no. 3. Routledge & Kegan Paul.

HIRST, P. Q. and WOOLLEY, P. (1982) *Social Relations and Human Attributes*. Tavistock, London.

HMSO (1984) *Employment Gazette*, September.

HMSO (1985) *Reform of Social Security*, vol. 3. HMSO, Cmnd 9519, London.

HMSO (1990) *Children Come First*. HMSO, London.

HMSO (1996) *Social Trends*. The Stationery Office, London.

HOBBES, T. (1651) *Leviathan*.

HOBSBAWM, E. J. (1977) 'May 1968', in Hobsbawm, E. J. (ed.), *Revolutionaries*. Quartet Books, London.

HOCHSCHILD, A. (1997) *The Time Bind: When Work Becomes Home and Home Becomes Work*. Metropolitan Books, New York.

HODGES, J. and HUSSAIN, A. (1979) 'La Police des Familles', *Ideology and Consciousness*, no. 5 (Spring).

HOFFERTH, S. L. and PHILLIPS, D. A. (1991) 'Child Care Policy Research Issue', *Journal of Social Issues*, vol. 47, no. 2.

HOGGETT, B. M. and PEARL, D. S. (1991) *The Family, Law and Society: Cases and Materials*. Butterworths, London.

HOLES, J. and LEVINE, E. (1971) *Rebirth of Feminism*. Quadrangle Books, New York.

HOLMAN, R. (1976) *Inequalities in Child Care*. CPAG Poverty Pamphlet 26.

HOOKS, B. (1982) *Ain't I a Woman? Black Women and Feminism*. Pluto Press, London.

HOOVER, K. and PLANT, R. (1989) *Conservative Capitalism in Britain and the United States: A Critical Appraisal*. Routledge, London.

HOULBROOKE, R. A. (1984) *The English Family 1450–1700*. Longman, Harlow.

HUBBACK, J. (1957) *Wives Who Went To College*. Heinemann, London.

HUBER, J., REXROAT, C. and GLENNA, S. (1978) 'A Crucible of Opinion on Women's Status: ERA in Illinois', *Social Forces*, vol. 57, no. 2 (December).

HUNTER, J. D. (1991) *Culture Wars: the Struggle to Define America*. Basic Books, NY.

ISAAC, J. (1994) 'The Politics of Morality in the UK', *Parliamentary Affairs*, vol. 47, pp. 175–89.

JACKSON, M. (1994) *The 'Real' Facts of Life: Feminism and the Politics of Sexuality c1850–1940*. Taylor Francis, London.

JACOBS, E. and KELLNER, P. (1976) 'Purse or Wallet?: How the Cabinet Did a Stitch-Sell', *The Sunday Times* 20th June 1976.

JAMESON, F. (1984) 'Postmoderism or the Cultural Logic of Capitalism', *New Left Review*, no. 146 (July/August).

JEFFREYS, S. (1985) *The Spinster and her Enemies: Feminism and Sexuality 1890–1930*. Pandora, London.

JEFFREYS, S. (1995) 'Women and Sexuality', in Purvis (1995).

JENKIN, P. (1977) Speech to the Conservative Party Conference.

JEPHCOTT, P., SEAR, N. and SMITH, J. H. (1962) *Married Women Workers*. Allen & Unwin, London.

JESSOP, B., BONNETT, K., BROMLEY, S. and LING, T. (1984) 'Authoritarian Populism, Two Nations and Thatcherism', *New Left Review* no. 147 (September/October).

JOHNSON, P. (1987) 'Families Under Fire', *Sunday Telegraph*, 5th January.

JONASDOTTIR, A. G. (1988) 'On the Concept of Interest, Women's Interests and the Limitations of Interest Theory', in Jones, K. and Jonasdottir, A. G. (eds), *The Political Interests of Gender: Developing Theory and Research With a Feminist Face*. Sage, Newbury Park, California.

JORDAN, B. (1995) 'Are New Right Policies Sustainable? "Back to Basics" and Public Choice', *Journal of Social Policy*, vol. 24, part 3, pp. 363–84.

JOSHI, H., DAVIES, H. and LAND, H. (1996) *The Tale of Mrs Typical*. Family Policy Studies Centre, London.

JOWELL, R., WITHERSPOON, S. and BROOK, L. (eds) (1990) *British Social Attitudes Survey Reports*. Dartmonth, Aldershot.

JOWELL, R., BROOK, L. and DOWDS, L. (eds) (1993) *International Social Attitudes*, Dartmouth, Aldershot.

JUPP, J. (1970) 'The Discontents of Youth', in Robson, W. B. and Crick, B. (eds), *Protest and Discontent*. Penguin, Harmondsworth.

KAMINER, K. (1993) 'Feminism's Identity Crisis', *Atlantic Monthly*, October.

KAVANAGH, D. and SELDON, A. (eds) (1994) *The Major Effect*. Macmillan, Basingstoke.

KIERNAN, K. (1989) 'The Family: Formation and Fissure', in Joshi, H. (ed.) *The Changing Population of Britain*. Basil Blackwell, Oxford.

KIERNAN, K. (1992) 'Men and Women at Work and at Home', in Jowell *et al. British Social Attitudes 9th Report*. Dartmouth Publishing Company, Aldershot, Hants.

KIERNAN, K. (1996) 'Lone Motherhood, Employment and Outcomes for Children', *International Journal of Law, Policy and the Family*. vol. 10.

KING, D. S. (1987) *The New Right: Politics, Markets and Citizenship*. Macmillan, London.

KRIEGER, J. (1987) 'Social Policy in the Age of Reagan and Thatcher', in Miliband, R., Panitch, L. and Saville, J. (eds), *Socialist Register 1987: Conservatism in Britain and America: Rhetoric and Reality*. Merlin Press, London.

KYMLICKA, B. B. and MATTHEWS, J. V. (1988) *The Reagan Revolution?*. The Dorsey Press, Chicago.

LABOUR PARTY (1983) 'Labour Cares About Families', in *Talking Points*, no. 32 (May).

LABOUR PARTY (1990) *Looking to the Future*. The Labour Party, London.

LAING, R. D. (1965) *The Divided Self*. Penguin, Harmondsworth.

LAING, R. D. (1971) *The Politics of the Family and Other Essays*. Penguin, Harmondsworth.

LAND, H. (1977) 'The Child Benefit Fiasco', in *The Year Book of Social Policy in Britain 1976*, (ed.) Jones, K. Routledge & Kegan Paul, London.

LAND, H. (1990) 'Eleanor Rathbone and the Economy of the Family', in Smith, H. L. (ed.), *British Feminism in the 20th Century*. Edward Elgar, Aldershot.

LAND, H. and ROSE, H. (1985) 'Compulsory Altruism for Some or an Altruistic Society for All?', in Bean, P., Ferris, J. and Whynes, D. (eds), *In Defence of Welfare*. Tavistock, London.

LASCH, C. (1977) *Haven in a Heartless World: The Family Besieged*. Basic Books, New York.

LASCH, C. (1997) *Women and the Common Life: Love, Marriage and Feminism* (ed. Lasch-Quinn, E.). W. W. Norton, NY.

LASLETT, P. (1971) *The World We Have Lost*. Methuen, London.

Law Commission (1990) *Family Law: The Grounds for Divorce*. Law Commission Report no. 192. HMSO, London.

LEBERGOTT, S. (1964) *Manpower in Economic Growth: The American Record Since 1800*. McGraw-Hill, NY.

LEE, D. J. and TURNER, B. S. (eds) (1996) *Conflicts about Class: Debating Inequality in Late Industrialism*. Longman, London.

LERNER, M. (1982) 'Recapturing the Family Issue', *The Nation*, February 6th.

LEWIS, J. (1984) *Women in England 1870–1950: Sexual Divisions and Social Change*. Wheatsheaf Books, Brighton.

LEWIS, J. (ed.) (1986) *Labour and Love: Women's Experience of Home and Family 1850–1940*. Blackwell, Oxford.

LEWIS, J. (1991) *Women and Social Action in Victorian and Edwardian England*. Edward Elgar, Aldershot.

LINDEMANN, NELSON H. (1997) *Feminism and Families*. Routledge, NY.

LIPSET, S. M. (1963) 'Fascism, Left, Right and Centre', in Lipset, S. M. (ed.), *Political Man*. Mercury Books, London.

LISTER, R. (1997) *Citizenship: Feminist Perspectives*. Macmillan, Basingstoke.

LISTER, R. (1999) 'Reforming Welfare and the Work Ethic: New Gendered and Ethical Perspectives on Work and Care', *Policy and Politics*, vol. 27, no. 2.

LOCKE, J. (1690) *Two Treatises of Government*.

LOVENDUSKI, J. (1986) *Women and European Politics: Contemporary Feminism and Public Policy*. Wheatsheaf Books, Brighton, Sussex.

LOVENDUSKI, J. (1997) 'Gender Politics: A Breakthrough for Women?', in Norris, P. and Gavin, N. T. (eds), *Britain Votes 1997*. Oxford University Press, Oxford.

LOVENDUSKI, J. and NORRIS, P. (1996) *Women in Politics*. Oxford University Press, Oxford.

LOVENDUSKI, J. and RANDALL, V. (1993) *Contemporary Feminist Politics: Women and Power in Britain*. Oxford University Press, Oxford.

LOWN, J. (1990) *Women and Industrialisation: Gender at Work in 19th Century England*. Polity Press, Cambridge.

LUKER, K. (1984) *Abortion and the Politics of Motherhood*. University of California Press, Berkeley.

LYNDON, N. (1992) *No More Sex War: The Failures of Feminism*. Sinclair-Stevenson, London.

MACFARLANE, A. (1986) *Marriage and Love in England 1300–1840*. Basil Blackwell, Oxford.

MACKINNON, C. (1989) 'Pornography: Not a Moral Issue', in Klein, R. D. and Steinberg, D. L. (eds), *Radical Voices: A Decade of Feminist Resistance*. Pergamon Press, NY.

MANSBRIDGE, J. (1986) *Why We Lost the ERA*. University of Chicago Press, Chicago.

MARSH, D. and CHAMBERS, J. (1981) *Abortion Politics*. Junction Books, London.

MARSH, D. and RHODES, R. A. W. (eds) (1992) *Implementing Thatcherite Policies: Audit of an Era*. Open University Press, Milton Keynes.

MARSHALL, K. (1985) *Moral Panics and Victorian Values: Women and the Family in Thatcher's Britain*. Junius, London.

MARSHALL, S. E. (1991) 'Who Speaks for Women? The Future of Anti-Feminism', in Boles, J. K. (ed.), *American Feminism: New Issues for a Mature Movement*. The Annals of the American Academy of Political and Social Science, May.

MARTIN, J. and ROBERTS, C. (1984) *Women and Employment: A Lifetime Perspective*. DE/OPCS, HMSO, London.

MASON, K. O. and BUMPASS, L. L. (1975) 'US Sex-Role Ideology', *American Journal of Sociology*, vol. 80. part 5.

MATHEWS, D. G. and DE HART, J. S. (1990) *Sex, Gender and the Politics of the ERA*. Oxford University Press, New York.

MAYALL, B. (ed.) (1994) *Children's Childhoods: Observed and Experienced.* The Falmer Press, London.

McCARTHY, J. D. and ZALD, M. N. (1973) *The Trend of Social Movements in America: Professionalism and Resource Mobilisation.* General Learning Press, Morristown, New Jersey.

McKEE, L. and O'BRIEN, M. (1982) *The Father Figure.* Tavistock, London.

McKEEGAN, M. (1992) *Abortion Politics: Mutiny in the Ranks of the Right.* Free Press, NY.

McLAREN, A. (1978) *Birth Control in 19th Century England.* Croom Helm, London.

McLEOD, J. (1999) 'Still Rising', in Walters, N. (ed.), *On the Move: Feminism for a New Generation.* Virago Press, London.

MELUCCI, A. (1980) 'The New Social Movements: A Theoretical Approach', *Social Science Information,* vol. 19, no. 2.

MERTON, R. K. (1948) *Social Theory and Social Structure.* Free Press of Glencoe, New York.

MILL, H. TAYLOR (1851) *Enfranchisement of Women.* Virago, London.

MILL, J. S. (1869) *The Subjection of Women.* Virago, London, 1983.

MILLAR, J. (1989) *Poverty and the Lone Parent Family.* Avebury/Gower, Aldershot.

MILLER, A. H., HILDRETH, A. and SIMMONS, G. L. (1988) 'The Mobilisation of Gender Group Consciousness', in Jones, K. B. and Jonasdottir, A. G. (eds), *The Political Interests of Gender.* Sage, London.

MILLETT, K. (1971) *Sexual Politics.* Rupert Hart-Davis, London.

MINDEL, C. H. *et al.* (1988) *Ethnic Families in America: Patterns and Variations.* Elsevier, NY.

Mintel Report (1994) *Men 2000.*

MITCHELL, J. (1966) 'Women: The Longest Revolution', *New Left Review,* November-December.

MITCHELL, J. (1975) *Psychoanalysis and Feminism.* Penguin, Harmondsworth.

MITCHELL, J. (1984) *Women: the Longest Revolution – Essays in Feminism, Literature, and Psychoanalysis.* Virago, London.

MITCHELL, J. and OAKLEY, A. (eds) (1976) *The Rights and Wrongs of Women.* Penguin, Harmondsworth.

MITCHELL, J. and OAKLEY, A. (eds) (1986) *What Is Feminism?.* Basil Blackwell, Oxford.

MITCHELL, J. and OAKLEY, A. (eds) (1997) *Who's Afraid of Feminism? Seeing Through the Backlash.* Penguin, Harmondsworth.

MITTERAUER, M. and SIEDER, R. (1982) *The European Family.* Basil Blackwell, Oxford.

MORGAN, P. (1996) *Who Needs Parents? The Effects of Childcare and Early Education on Children in Britain and the USA.* Institute of Economic Affairs, London.

MORGAN, R. (ed.) (1970) *Sisterhood is Powerful: An Anthology of Writings from the Women's Liberation Movement.* Vintage/Random House, NY.

MORGAN, R. (1980) 'Theory and Practice: Pornography and Rape', in Lederer, L. (ed.) *Take Back The Night.* Bantam Books, NY.

MORGAN, R. (1986) 'A Maddening Take On Our Movement', *Ms*, March.

MORRISON, D. E. and TRACEY, M. (1978) 'American Theory and British Practice: The Case of Mrs Mary Whitehouse and the NVALA', in Dhavan, R. and Davies, C. (eds), *Censorship and Obscenity*. Martin Robertson, London.

MORT, F. (1987) *Dangerous Sexualities: Medico-Moral Politics in England since 1830*. Routledge & Kegan Paul, London.

MOUNT, F. (1982) *The Subversive Family: An Alternative History of Love and Marriage*. Jonathan Cape, London.

MOYNIHAN, D. P. (1965) *The Moynihan Report: The Negro Family: The Case for National Action*. Reprinted in Rainwater, L. and Yancey, W. L. (1967).

MUELLER, C. M. (ed.) (1988) *The Politics of the Gender Gap: The Social Construction of Political Influence*. Sage, Newbury Park, California.

MURRAY, C. (1990) *The Emerging British Underclass*. Institute of Economic Affairs, London.

MURRAY, C. (1994) *Underclass: The Crisis Deepens*. Institute of Economic Affairs, London.

MYRDAL, A. and KLEIN, V. (1956) *Women's Two Roles*. Routledge & Kegan Paul, London.

National Economic Development Office/Training Agency (1989) *Defusing the Demographic Time Bomb*. NEDO/TA, London.

NAVA, M. (1983) 'From Utopian Feminism? Early Feminist Critiques of the Family', in Segal, L. (ed.), *What Is To Be Done About The Family?*. Penguin, Harmondsworth.

NORRIS, P. (1988) 'The Gender Gap: A Cross-National Trend?', in Mueller, C. M. (ed.), *The Politics of the Gender Gap: The Social Construction of Political Influence*. Sage, Newbury Park, California.

NOZICK, R. (1974) *Anarchy, State and Utopia*. Blackwell, London.

OAKLEY, A. (1980) *Becoming A Mother*. Schoken Books, NY.

OAKLEY, A. (1997) 'A Brief History of Gender', in Oakley, A. and Mitchell, J. (eds), *Who's Afraid of Feminism: Seeing Through the Backlash*. Penguin, Harmonsdworth.

O'CONNOR, J. (1998) 'US Social Welfare Policy: The Reagan Record and Legacy', *Journal of Social Policy*, vol. 27, part 1, pp. 37–61.

O'CONNOR, J. S., ORLOFF, A. S. and SHAVER, S. (1999) *States, Markets, Families: Gender, Liberalism and Social Policy in Australia, Canada, Great Britain and the United States*. Cambridge University Press, Cambridge.

Office of Population and Censuses and Surveys (OPCS) (1989) *Social Trends 19*. HMSO, London.

Office of Population and Censuses and Surveys (OPCS) (1990) *Social Trends 20*. HMSO, London.

Office of Population and Censuses and Surveys (OPCS) (1990) *General Household Survey 1988*. HMSO, London.

Ofsted/Equal Opportunities Commission (1996) *The Gender Divide: Performance between Boys and Girls at School*. HMSO, London.

OGBURN, W. F. and NIMKOFF, M. F. (1950) Sociology. Houghton Mifflin Boston Massachusetts.

O'HARE, W. P. (1993) 'America's Minorities: The Demographics of Diversity', *Population Bulletin*, vol. 47, no. 4, pp. 1–45.

ORTON, P. and FRY, J. (1995) *UK Health Care: The Facts*. Kluwer Academic Publishers, Lancaster.

PAGLIA, C. (1990) *Sexual Personae: Art and Decadence from Nefertiti to Emily Dickinson*. Yale University Press, Cambridge, Massachusetts.

PAGLIA, C. (1992) *Sex, Art and American Culture*. Viking Penguin, Harmondsworth.

PANKHURST, J. G. and HOUSEKNECHT, S. K. (1983) 'The Family, Politics and Religion in the 1990s: In Fear of the New Individualism', *Journal of Family Issues* vol. 4, no. 1 (March).

PARKS, R. Q. (1982) 'Interests and the Politics of Choice', *Political Theory*, vol. 10, no. 4.

PARSONS, T. (1942) 'Age and Sex in the Social Structure of the United States', in Parsons, T. (ed.), *Essays in Sociological Theory*. The Free Press of Glencoe, New York, 1954.

PARSONS, T. and BALES, R. F. (1956) *Family, Socialisation and Interaction Process*. Routledge & Kegan Paul, London.

PASCAL, G. (1997) 'Women and the Family in the British Welfare State: The Thatcher/Major Legacy', *Social Policy and Administration*, vol. 31, no. 3.

PATEMAN, C. (1988) *The Sexual Contract*. Polity Press/Basil Blackwell, Oxford.

PECK, E. and SENDEROWITZ, J. (1974) *Pronatalism: The Myth of Mom and Apple Pie*. Thomas Y. Crowell, NY.

PEELE, G. (1984) *Revival and Reaction: The Right in Contemporary America*. Oxford University Press, New York.

PERRIGO, S. (1996) 'Women and Change in the Labour Party 1979–1995', in Lovenduski, J. and Norris, P. (eds), *Women in Politics*. Oxford University Press, Oxford.

PETCHESKY, R. P. (1981) 'Anti-abortion, Anti-feminism and the Rise of the New Right', *Feminist Studies*, vol. 7, no. 2 (Summer).

PFEFFER, N. (1993) *The Stork and the Syringe*. Polity Press, London.

PHILLIPS, A. (1991) *Engendering Democracy*. Polity Press/Blackwell, Oxford.

PHILLIPS, M. (1978) 'Family Policy: The Long Years of Neglect', *New Society*, 8 June.

PHILLIPS, M. (1980) *The Divided House*. Sidgwick & Jackson, London.

PHILLIPS, M. (1999) *The Sex-Change Society: Feminised Britain and the Neutered Male*. The Social Market Foundation, London.

PIERSON, P. (1994) *Dismantling the Welfare State? Reagan, Thatcher and the Politics of Retrenchment*. Cambridge University Press, Cambridge.

POHLI, C. V. (1983) 'Church Closets and Back Doors: A Feminist View of Moral Majority Women', *Feminist Studies*, vol. 7, no. 2 (Summer).

POSNER, C. (ed.) (1970) *Reflections on the Revolution in France, 1968*. Penguin, Harmondsworth.

POWER, M. (1988) 'Women, the State and the Family in the US: Reaganomics and the Experience of Women', in Rubery, J. (ed.), *Women and Recession*. Routledge & Kegan Paul, London.

PRYOR, F. L. and SCHAFFER, D. L. (1999) *Who's Not Working and Why: Employment, Cognitive Skills, Wages and the Changing US Labor Market*. Cambridge University Press, Cambridge.

PUGH, M. (1992) *Women and the Women's Movement in Britain 1914–1959*. Macmillan, Basingstoke.

PURVIS, J. (ed.) (1995) *Women's History: Britain 1850–1945*. UCL Press, London.

PYM, B. A. (1972) 'Pressure Groups on Moral Issues', *Political Science Quarterly*, vol. 43.

QVORTRUP, J., BARDY, M., SGRITTA, G. and WINTERSBERGER, H. (eds) (1994) *Childhood Matters: Social Theory, Practice and Politics*. Avebury, Aldershot.

RABB, T. K. and ROTBERG, R. I. (eds) (1973) *The Family in History: Interdisciplinary Essays*. Harper & Row, NY.

RADICALESBIANS (1970) *Woman-Identified Woman*. Free Press, New England.

RAINWATER, L. and SMEEDING, T. M. (1995) *Doing Poorly: The Real Income of American Children in a Comparative Perspective*. Luxembourg Income Study Working Paper Series, Walferdange.

RAINWATER, L. and YANCEY, W. L. (1967) *The Moynihan Report and the Politics of Controversy*. MIT Press, Michigan.

RANDALL, V. (1987) *Women and Politics: An International Perspective*. Macmillan, London.

RANDALL, V. (1996) 'The Politics of Childcare Policy'. In Lovenduski, J. and Norris, P. (eds), *Women in Politics* Oxford University Press, Oxford.

REAGAN, R. with HUBLER, R. (1965) *My Early Life or Where's the Rest of Me?*. Sidgwick & Jackson, London, 1981.

REICH, W. (1932) 'The Imposition of Sexual Morality', in Bexandall, L. (ed.), *Reich: Sex-Pol Essays, 1929–34*. Vintage Books, New York, 1972.

RENDALL, J. (1985) *The Origins of Modern Feminism: Women in Britain, France and the United States, 1780–1860*. Macmillan, Basingstoke.

RICH, A. (1976) *Of Woman Born*. Norton, New York.

RICH, A. (1981) *Compulsory Heterosexuality and Lesbian Existence*. Only Women Press Ltd, London.

RICHARDS, M. P. M. and ELLIOTT, B.J. (1991) 'Sex and Marriage in the 1960s and 1970s', in Clark (1991).

RILEY, D. (1983) 'The Serious Burdens of Love? Some Questions on Child-Care, Feminism and Socialism', in Segal, L. (ed.), *What Is To Be Done About The Family?*. Penguin, Harmondsworth.

ROBERTS, Y. (1992) *Mad About Women: Can There Ever Be Fair Play Between the Sexes?*. Virago, London.

ROCHER, G. (1974) *Talcott Parsons and American Sociology*. Nelson, Exeter.

ROIPHE, A. (1996) *A Mother's Eye: Motherhood and Feminism*. Penguin, Harmondsworth.

ROSENFELT, D. and STACEY, J. (1987) 'Second Thoughts On The Second Wave: Review Essay', *Feminist Studies*, vol. 13, no. 2 (Summer).

ROSSI, A. (1977) 'A Biosocial Perspective on Parenting', *Daedalus* 106, Spring Special Issue on the Family.

ROSZAK, B. and ROSZAK, T. (eds) (1969) *Masculine/Feminine: Readings in Sexual Mythology and the Liberation of Women*. Harper & Row, NY.

ROUSSEAU, J-J. (1762) *The Social Contract.*

ROWBOTHAM, S. (1989) 'To Be Or Not To Be: The Dilemmas of Mothering', *Feminist Review*, no. 31 (Spring).

ROWBOTHAM, S. (1990) The Past Is Before Us. Penguin, Harmonds-worth.

ROWBOTHAM, S. (1997) *A Century of Women: The History of Women in Britain and the United States.* Viking Penguin, London.

ROWBOTHAM, S., Segal, L. and Wainwright, H. (1979) *Beyond The Fragments.* Merlin Press, London.

RUDDICK, S. (1980) 'Maternal Thinking', *Feminist Studies*, vol. 6, no. 2 (Summer).

SAPIRO, V. (1981) 'Research Frontier Essay: When Are Interests Interesting? The Problem of the Political Representation of Women', *American Political Science Review*, vol. 73, no. 3.

SAVAGE, S. (1981) *The Theories of Talcott Parsons: Social Relations of Action.* Macmillan, London.

SCHLAFLY, P. (1977) *The Power of Positive Woman.* Arlington House/ Crown, New York.

SCHOFIELD, M. (1973) *The Sexual Behaviour of Young Adults.* Allen Lane, London.

SCOTT, J. (1998) 'Changing attitudes to Sexual Morality: a Cross-National Comparison', *Sociology*, vol. 32, no. 4.

SCRUTON, R. (1980) *The Meaning of Conservatism.* Penguin, Harmondsworth.

SCRUTON, R. (1986) *Sexual Desire.* Weidenfeld & Nicolson, London.

SECCOMBE, W. (1974) 'The Housewife and her Labour under Capitalism', *New Left Review*, no. 83.

SEGAL, L. (ed.) (1983) *What Is To Be Done About The Family?* Penguin, Harmondsworth.

SEGAL, L. (1987) *Is The Future Female? Troubled Thoughts on Contemporary Feminism.* Virago, London.

SEGAL, L. (1999) *Why Feminism?* Polity Press, London.

SEVENHUIJSEN, S. (1998) *Citizenship and the Ethics of Care.* Routledge, NY.

SEVENHUIJSEN, S. and WITHUIS, J. (1984) 'The Policing of Families', in Meulenbelt, A. *et al.* (eds), *A Creative Tension: Explorations in Socialist Feminism.* Pluto Press, London.

SHORTER, E. (1975) *The Making of the Modern Family.* Basic Books, NY.

SIANN, G. and WILKINSON, H. (1995) *Gender, Feminism and the Future.* Demos, London.

SKOLD, K. (1988) 'The Interests of Feminists and Children in Child Care', in Dornbusch and Strober (1988).

SMART, C. (1984) *The Ties That Bind.* Routledge & Kegan Paul, London.

SMART, C. (ed.) (1992) *Regulating Womanhood: Historical Essays on Mariage, Motherhood and Sexuality.* Routledge, London.

SMITH, H. L. (ed.) (1990) *British Feminism in the 20th Century.* Edward Elgar, Aldershot.

SMITH, J. H. (1961) 'Managers and Married Women Workers', *British Journal of Sociology*, no. 12.

SMITH-ROSENBURG, C. (1985) *Disorderly Conduct: Visions of Gender in Victorian America.* Oxford University Press, NY.

SNITOW, A. (1992) 'Feminism and Motherhood: An American Reading', *Feminist Review*, no. 40 (Spring) pp. 32–51.

SOMERVILLE, J. (1992a) 'The New Right and Family Politics', *Economy and Society*, vol. 21, no. 2.

SOMERVILLE, J. (1992b) 'A Marriage Heading For Failure', The Times Higher Education Supplement, 16 October.

SPENDER, D. (1980) *Man-Made Language*. Routledge & Kegan Paul, London.

SPENDER, D. (1982) *Women of Ideas (and What Men have Done To Them)*. Routledge & Kegan Paul, London.

STACEY, J. (1983) 'The New Conservative Feminism', *Feminist Studies*, vol. 9 (Fall).

STACEY, J. (1986) 'Are Feminists Afraid to Leave Home? The Challenge of Conservative Pro-Family Feminism', in Mitchell, J. and Oakley, A. (eds), *What Is Feminism?*. Basil Blackwell, Oxford.

STACEY, J. (1990) *Brave New Families: Stories of Domestic Upheaval in Late 20th Century America*. Basic Books, NY.

STACEY, J. (1996) *In the Name of the Family: Rethinking Family Values in the Postmodern Age*. Beacon Press, Boston.

STAGGENBORG, S. (1998) *Gender, Family and Social Movements*. Pine Forge, Thousand Oaks, California.

STANWORTH, M. (1984) 'Women and Class Analysis: A Reply to Goldthorpe', *Sociology*, 18.

Statistical, Abstract of the United States (1990) US Government Printing Office, New York.

STEINEM, G. (1992) *Revolution From Within: A Book of Self-Esteem*. Bhomsbury, London.

STEINER, G. (1981) *The Futility of Family Policy*. Brookings Institution, Washington, DC.

STEINER, G. (1985) *Constitutional Inequality: The Political Fortunes of the Equal Rights Amendment*. The Brookings Institution, Washington, DC.

STONE, L. (1977) *The Family, Sex and Marriage in England 1500–1800*. Weidenfeld & Nicolson, London.

STRACHEY, R. (1928) *The Cause: A Short History of the Women's Movement in Great Britain*. Virago, London, 1978.

STROBER, M. H. (1977) 'Wives' Labor Force Behaviour and Family Consumption Patterns', *American Economic Review*, no. 67 (February).

STROBER, M. H. (1988) 'Two-Earner Families', in Dornbusch and Strober (1988).

SUTHERLAND, J. (1982) *Offensive Literature: Decensorship in Britain 1960–82*. Junction Books, London.

TAYLOR, B. (1983) *Eve and the New Jerusalem: Socialism and Feminism in the 19th Century*. Virago, London.

TEDIN, K. L., BRADY, D. W., BUXTON, M. E. GORMAN, B. M. and THOMPSON, J. L. (1977) 'Social Background and Political Differences Between Pro and Anti-ERA Activists', *American Political Quarterly*, vol. 5, no. 3.

THANE, P. (1982) *The Foundations of the Welfare State*. Longman, London.

THANE, P. (1990) 'The Women of the British Labour Party and Feminism 1906–45', in Smith, H. L. (ed), *British Feminism in the Twentieth Century*. Edward Elgar, Aldershot.

THATCHER, M. (1990) Speech to the 300 Group – the first Pankhurst lecture. Wednesday 18 July. See reports in *The Daily Telegraph* and *The Guardian*, 19 July 90.

THOMAS, G. (1948) *Women and Industry: An Inquiry into the Problem of Recruiting Women into Industry Carried Out for the Ministry of Labour and National Service, the Social Survey*. Central Office of Information, London.

THOMPSON, E. P. (1971) *The Making of the English Working Class*. Penguin, Harmondsworth.

THOMPSON, T. (ed.) (1987) *Dear Girl: The Diaries and Letters of Two Working Women (1897–1917)*. The Women's Press, London.

THORNE, B. and YALOM, M. (eds) (1982) *Rethinking the Family: Some Feminist Questions*. Longman, New York.

TILLYARD, S. (1999) 'Portrait: Germaine Greer', *Prospect*, April.

TITMUS, R.M. (1954) *The Family*. National Council of Social Service, London

TOBIAS, S. (1997) *Faces of Feminism: An Activist's Reflections on the Women's Movement*. Westview Press, Boulder, California

TOURAINE, A. (1971) *The Post-Industrial Society – Tomorrow's Social History: Classes, Conflicts and Culture in the Programmed Society*. Random House, New York.

TRACEY, M. and MORRISON, D. (1979) *Whitehouse*. Macmillan, London.

TRIBE, L. H. (1990) *Abortion: The Clash of Absolutes*. W. W. Norton, NY.

UNGERSON, C. (ed.) (1990) *Gender and Caring: Work and Welfare in Britain and Scandinavia*. Harvester Wheatsheaf, Hemel Hempstead.

VOGEL, U. (1992) 'Whose Property? The Double Standard of Adultery in 19th Century Law', in Smart, C. (ed.), *Regulating Womanhood: Historical Essays on Marriage, Motherhood and Sexuality*. Routledge, London.

VOGLER, C. and PAHL, J. (1994) 'Money, Power and Inequality Within Marriage', *The Sociological Review*, vol. 42, no 2 (May).

WALBY, S. (1997) *Gender Transformations*. Routledge, London.

WALKOWITZ, J. (1980) *Prostitution and Victorian Society*. Cambridge University Press, Cambridge.

WALKOWITZ, J. (1992) *City of Dreadful Delights: Narratives of Sexual Danger in Late Victorian London*. Virago, London.

WALLIS, R. (1976) 'Moral Indignation and the Media: An Analysis of the NVALA', *Sociology*, vol. 10, no. 2 (May).

WALTER, N. (1998) *The New Feminism*. Little, Browns Company, London.

WALTER, N. (1999) *On the Move: Feminism for a New Generation*. Virago Press, London.

WANDOR, M. (ed). (1972) *The Body Politic: Writings from the Women's Liberation Movement in Britain 1960–1972*. Stage 1, London.

WANDOR, M. (1990) *Once a Feminist: Stories of a Generation*. Virago Press, London.

WEAVER, R. KENT (1988) 'Social Policy in the Reagan Era', in Kymlicka, B. B. and Matthews, J. V. (eds), *The Reagan Revolution?*. The Dorsey Press, Chicago.

WEEKS, J. (1981) *Sex, Politics and Society: The Regulation of Sexuality since 1800*. Longman, Harlow.

WEEKS, J. (1985) *Sexuality and its Discontents: Meanings, Myths and Modern Sexualities*. Routledge & Kegan Paul, London.

WEITZMAN, L. J. (1985) *The Divorce Revolution: The Unexpected Social and Economic Consequences for Women and Children in America*. Free Press, New York.

WEYRICH, P. (1979) 'Building the Moral Majority', *Conservative Digest*, August.

WHEELOCK, J. (1990) *Husbands at Home: The Domestic Economy in a Post-Industrial Society*. Routledge, London.

WHITEHOUSE, M. (1967) *Cleaning up TV: From Protest to Participation*. Blendford Press, London.

WHITEHOUSE, M. (1977) *Whatever Happened To Sex?*. Wayland Publishers, London.

WHITFIELD, R. (1987) *Families Matter*. Marshall Pickering, Basington, Hants.

WILCOX, C. (1989) 'Feminism and Anti-Feminism Among Evangelical Women', *Western Quarterly*, vol. 4, no. 2 (March).

WILKINSON, H. (1994) *No Turning Back: Generations and the Genderquake*. Demos, London.

WILKINSON, H. (1999) 'The Thatcher Legacy: Power Feminism and the Birth of Girl Power', in Walter, N. (ed.), *On the Move: Feminism for a New Generation*. Virago, London.

WILKINSON, H. and HOWARD, M. (1997) *Tomorrow's Women*. Demos, London.

WILKINSON, H. and MULGAN, G. (1995) *Freedom's Children: Work, Relationships and Politics for 18–34 year olds in Britain Today*. Demos, London.

WILLIAMS, J., TWORT H. and BACHELLI, A. (1972) 'Women and the Family', in Wandor, M. (ed.), *The Body Politic: Writings from the Women's Liberation Movement in Britain 1960–1972*. Stage 1, London, 1972.

WILLMOTT, P. and YOUNG, M. (1960) *Family and Class in a London Susurb*. Routledge & Kegan Pane London.

WILSON, E. (1977) *Women and the Welfare State*. Tavistock, London.

WILSON, E. (1980a) 'Beyond The Ghetto', *Feminist Review*, no. 4.

WILSON, E. (1980b) *Only Halfway to Paradise: Women in Postwar Britain, 1945–68*. Tavistock, London.

WILSON, E. (1987) 'Thatcherism and Women: After Seven Years', in Miliband, R. *et al.* (eds), *Socialist Register*. Merlin Press, London.

WINNICOTT, D. W. (1957) *The Child and the Family: First Relationships*. Tavistock, London.

WINNICOTT, D. W. (1965) *The Family and Individual Development*. Tavistock, London.

WOLF, N. (1990) *The Beauty Myth*. Vintage, London.

WOLF, N. (1993) *Fire With Fire: The New Female Power and How It Will Change the 21st Century*. Chatto & Windus, London.

WOLLSTONECRAFT, M. (1792) *Vindication of the Rights of Women*. Penguin, Harmondsworth, 1985.

WOOD, M. and HUGHES, M. (1984) 'The Moral Basis of Moral Reform: Status Discontent vs Culture and Socialisation as Explanations of Anti-

Pornography Social Movement Adherence', *American Sociological Review*, vol. 49.

WYNN, M. (1972) *Family Policy*. Penguin, Harmondsworth.

YOUNG, H. (1989) *One of Us: A Biography of Margaret Thatcher*. Pan Books, London.

YOUNG, M. and WILLMOTT, P. (1957) *Family and Kinship in East London*. Routledge & Kegan Paul, London.

ZALD, M. N. and McCARTHY, J. D. (eds) (1987) *Social Movements in an Organisational Society: Collected Essays*. Transaction Books, New Brunswick, New Jersey.

ZARETSKY, E. (1976) *Capitalism, the Family, and Personal Life*. Pluto Press, London.

ZURCHER, L. A., KIRKPATRICK, R. G., CUSING, R. G. and BOWMAN, C. K. (1971) 'The Anti-Pornography Campaign: A Symbolic Crusade', *Social Problems*, vol. 19.

ZWEIG, F. (1952) *Women's Life and Labour*. Victor Gollancz, London.

ZWEIG, F. (1961) *The Worker in an Affluent Society*. Heinemann, London.

Index